The American Economy to 1975

The American Economy to 1975

AN INTERINDUSTRY FORECAST

by Clopper Almon, Jr.

Harper & Row, Publishers

NEW YORK, EVANSTON, AND LONDON

To
Wassily W. Leontief

CONTENTS

PREFACE

This book develops the first long-range forecasts of the American economy to make full use of what we now know about the supply connections among the industries of the economy. Within a framework which divides the whole economy into ninety industries, it presents mutually consistent forecasts of what consumers will buy, how much each industry will invest, what exports, imports, and government purchases will be, how technology will change, how much each industry will sell to each other industry, how labor productivity will increase, and how many people will be employed. The concept of this sort of consistent forecasting, its uses, and the proof-by-example that it can be done form the core of the work. Although many pages must be devoted to describing particular parts of the system used for this example, the main contribution of this work has been to integrate these parts into a unified, comprehensive, usable forecast of the whole economy.

The book stresses the usefulness of this sort of forecast in making business decisions; the public value of such forecasts has not been discussed because it is more difficult to demonstrate. Yet it is my own belief that they do have a public value which has kept me working on them. Briefly, I believe that these forecasts can help the private economy increase its efficiency and help the public sector to improve its decision making. We must make decisions which posterity will judge in the light of future events. Though we cannot know those events with certainty, we need not make our decisions blindfolded. The balanced look at the future which these forecasts offer should help business avoid wasteful over-investment in some fields and the retarding effects of insufficient investment in others. It should help us to build plants, to develop products, to plan regions and cities, to construct transportation and public utility systems, and to prepare our labor force for the needs of the future.

It therefore seemed to me that this kind of economics is too important to leave to economists alone. It had to be put in language which anyone concerned with our economy could understand. The book has been read, understood, and discussed by businessmen who had no formal training in economics. The first and most important chapter has no prerequisites; later chapters demand a bit more patience on the part of the reader but require no special knowledge beyond an acquaintance with the structure of the gross national product and with how equations are fitted to economic data. The whole book, therefore, should be easy and, I hope, pleasant reading for anyone accustomed to making and using business forecasts. Although the forecasting system is basically a mathematical model, it has been possible to describe it well enough verbally to dispense with most of the mathematical equations. Those equations which do appear are thoroughly described in words. It would have been easy, of course, to have embedded the whole discussion in a fearful array of formulas designed to make it look "sophisticated." But the subject is too serious for such play.

This same desire for directness has pervaded the econometric investigations which went into the system. Simplicity, which is somewhat out of style in econometrics these days, is still a virtue for me. Where I must make a simplifying assumption, I prefer to make it in a manner which makes its economic meaning obvious rather than to hide it away in a formula where the unsuspecting may not notice or understand. Consequently, readers accustomed to econometric writing will be disappointed by the lack of clever tricks or ingenious subtleties. These have been weeded out.

The development of this work owes much to the opportunity to apply it to a particular business decision problem for a client of Arthur D. Little, Inc. John R. White and other members of the staffs of Arthur D. Little and of the client went over the forecasts and made important substantive contributions. The exposition has also benefited greatly from their demands for clarity and thoroughness. I have borrowed heavily from the work of my colleague Anne P. Carter in the projection of technological change; she was also a constant source of good advice on exposition and on all matters relating to input-output analysis. My father made particularly helpful suggestions on the exposition of Chapter I. Jack Alterman of the Bureau of Labor Statistics assisted enormously by making available a preliminary version of his work on capital flows in 1958 and by keeping me generally abreast of government statistics. The only excuse for omitting the name of James C. Burrows from the title page is to exempt him from responsibility for the contents. In his service as a quarter-time research assistant, he made important contributions to most parts of the system and particularly to the consumption study in Chapter II, for which he did all the computing. To Wassily W. Leontief I am indebted, of course, not only for the encouragement and advice he has given over the past six years but also for many of the basic ideas from which this work springs. The Social Science Research Council partially supported this work during the academic year of 1964–1965.

Though all the words in this book were written by one author, my feeling of dependence on the others working with me made it difficult to use the first person singular. Consequently, I have fallen back on what might be called the "scientific we," except that where expressing my own opinions rather than describing work done, I try to own up to the personal nature of the assertions.

C.A., Jr.

Research Project on the Structure
  of the American Economy
Harvard University
Cambridge, Massachusetts

March 1966

The American Economy to 1975

I

Consistent Interindustry Forecasting for Long-Range Business Planning

Many fundamental business decisions which reach beyond the exigencies of the hour demand long-range, five- or ten-year forecasts to get at basic growth trends. This book describes a new system for making such forecasts, a system which incorporates many detailed forecasts into a consistent picture of the whole economy five or ten years hence. These forecasts provide background for a variety of business decisions:

Capital investment decisions. Not only do the heavy capital industries such as steel and electricity require forecasts to start building capacity years before it can be used, but any business deciding between putting in a new facility and modernizing an old one must study the size of the future market. Chances are, a rapid expansion will make the new facility pleasantly profitable, while slow growth will make it a costly operation indeed.

Product development decisions. To steer his product line toward fast growth, a paper maker needs to compare future trends in demand for newsprint, book paper, stationery, paper cartons, bags, towels, and so on. A machinery manufacturer will want to see which industries will be the big spenders on capital equipment and to consider whether the spending will be primarily for replacement of present units or for entire new systems.

Diversification decisions. A firm desiring a wider range of products needs a comprehensive but detailed frame of reference for comparing one opportunity with another.

Portfolio decisions. Back of a thoroughly analyzed stock purchase stands a comparison of one industry's opportunity with those of other industries. Again, a comprehensive set of forecasts gives a common background for systematic comparison.

Regional planning and manpower development decisions. A railroad or electric utility would like to encourage fast-growing industries to take root in its area. Public agencies responsible for worker training or guidance programs wish to tailor their efforts to the long-term needs of industry.

In all these examples, the decision maker has to consider and compare the growth of a number of industries in the economy. There are, however, many interconnections among these industries. The increase in the use of electricity depends on the growth of almost all industries, as does the demand for paper. The demand for machinery depends on the expansion of all parts of manufacturing, including those, such as steel, where growth depends, in turn, on the growth of machinery output. What consumers spend on clothes they cannot spend on food, and what they spend in total depends upon employment and earnings in all the branches of the economy. Forecasts for comparing one industry with another can ignore these interconnections only at the peril of self-contradiction.

The forecasting system described here was developed precisely to take all these relations into account, to put them together into a coherent picture, and to make clear their implications for long-range planning. The whole of the economy has been divided into ninety industries, and the sales of each of these industries to each of the other industries, to consumers, to government, export, and investment are forecast. Because the industry forecasts together cover the entire economy, we can be certain that each of them is an integral part of a total forecast which the economy can achieve. We can never have this certainty with isolated product forecasts, for there is always the suspicion that the sum of all such parts may exceed any reasonable gross national product. Moreover, since each dollar of sales in this system is identified by both the seller and by the purchaser, the system imposes a sort of double-entry check on the forecasts. Indeed, as the title of this chapter suggests, the keynote of the system is that it builds checks and balances into the forecasts, assuring a fivefold *consistency* between:

1. The sales projected for an industry and the purchases of its products by all its customers;

2. The output of an industry and the materials it purchases and the labor it employs;

3. The growth of each industry's sales and its capital investment;

4. Consumers' after-tax income and their spending on the products of each industry;

5. Total employment and the expected future labor force.

All this consistency, to be sure, does not guarantee that the forecasts will be right, but it is not without value. In the first place, it imposes on the forecaster the healthy discipline of being specific about where sales come from and of "balancing his books." Secondly, it automatically connects the forecast of sales of one industry, say farm machinery, to relevant developments in other rather remote parts of the economy, such as the demand for frozen food. Conversely, one can trace the forecast of farm machinery back to its sources, through agricultural production, food processing, and back finally to consumer spending. Each of the links on the way back can and should be critically examined. Thirdly, our consistency brings all the detailed forecasts into line with the one firm independent projection we have, namely, that of the future labor force. This consideration is particularly important now, for the effects of the accelerated growth of the labor force in the next decade will ramify through the economy in many ways. Finally, because a computer automatically produces this consistency, the forecaster is free to concentrate on the many problems which require special attention. How will consumers divide their income among the many goods and services they are offered? How much will each industry invest to achieve a given growth in sales? How fast will output per man-hour rise in the various industries? How many new electrical generating stations will be nuclear? These are questions on which the forecasts stand or fall. But they are also questions that people with expert knowledge of particular areas can help answer. The system can incorporate this expert knowledge into a consistent view of the whole economy, and bring out the implications of developments in one sector on other sectors. Unlike forecasts of the sort that tie, say, the sales of paint directly to gross national product, these have derivations which are sufficiently detailed and explicit to be scrutinized by people with special knowledge of an industry; and a forecast that can be scrutinized—and perhaps found wanting—deserves, I should think, more trust than an inscrutable one.

Such close study has already corrected some parts of the forecasts presented here, but there are many areas which I have not had the opportunity to discuss with people who know the business and *to whom these forecasts matter*. Plenty of room remains, therefore, for further improvements, and I hope readers will not fail to suggest them. Indeed, I wished to publish the system in its present state as much to free myself to undertake an extensive reworking of it and to elicit the comments of a wide circle of critics, as to present forecasts for general use. The forecasts do, however, represent my best judgment of what 1975 will look like; and I hope that, wherever a comprehensive set of forecasts is needed, these will form a useful starting point.

Economic forecasts all rest on some broad assumptions about government and world conditions.[1] Those in this chapter all assume that

> Defense and space spending and government employment in these programs will remain at about its 1964 level while other government spending and employment continue to rise with their recent trends. Defense procurement will decline about 1 percent per year.[2]
>
> Exports and imports continue their rapid expansion.
>
> Unemployment will be about 4 percent of the labor force in 1970 and 1975.

The last point really amounts to assuming that government policy, particularly tax policy, will successfully aim at high levels of employment. For long-range forecasting, this assumption seems safer than assuming any fixed tax law. Together with the projections of the labor force and labor productivity, which are developed in Chapter VII, this high-employment assumption determines the over-all size of the economy in 1975. If we wanted only a rough forecast of GNP, we need look no further. But for us, not only the size but also the structure of the future economy is of critical interest.

Even at the level of rather broad aggregates, the above assumptions spell a break in well-established trends in the American economy. The break originates in the labor force, where the postwar baby boom is at last showing up, as Figure I–1 shows. With the working population becoming an increasing proportion of the total population and the defense drain on the economy diminishing, consumption can rise much more rapidly than in the past decade. Expanding

---

[1] Some economists prefer to call their "conditional" forecasts "projections," which, however, are quickly unmasked as just Latinized forecasts. Such a convention would serve only to eliminate a fine Anglo-Saxon word from this book; I have therefore rejoiced in the riches of our language and used the two words almost synonymously. "Projection" is apt to be used when a fairly mechanical process is in mind.

[2] In the months between the time the graphs were drawn for this book and the time it went to press, any immediate decline has come to seem unlikely. Yet it may remain a goal for 1975.

Fɪɢ. I–1. Labor Force and Employment: History and Forecasts
(number of thousands)

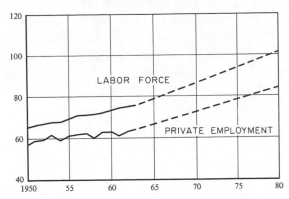

consumption, in turn, will stimulate investment, and, particularly, construction. Figure I–2, showing the history of forecasts of these aggregates, displays the differences between our forecasts (solid lines) and straight-line projections of the historical trend of the last four-

Fɪɢ. I–2. History and Forecasts of Major Aggregate
(billions of 1958 dollars)

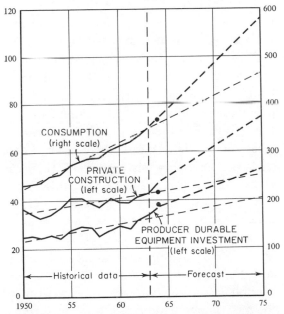

Sᴏᴜʀᴄᴇ: Historical data from *Survey of Current Business,*
August 1965.

teen years (dotted lines). Although these and subsequent graphs show forecasts for 1964 and 1965, it must always be borne in mind that the forecasts are of long-range trends and take no account of cyclical influences in any year after 1963. They cannot, therefore, be vitiated or vindicated by their failure or success in predicting any *one* year but only by their performance in forecasting a ten-year trend. Certainly they must not be compared with cyclical forecasts of the first two or three years.

These aggregates and generalities, however, are but trimmings on the real fabric of detail behind them. In the rest of this chapter, we first describe exactly what is forecast and present the forecasts to 1975; we then summarize how the system generates these forecasts; and lastly we examine the projection for one industry to show how the built-in consistency allows one to trace a forecast back to its origins and look hard at each step of the way. The following chapters explain the structure of the individual parts of the system. Here we concentrate on the workings of the organic whole.

WHAT DO THE FORECASTS FORECAST?

For each year from 1963 to 1975, the forecasts contain all the market information of a complete table of interindustry accounts. A schematic set of accounts is shown in Table I–1 (pp. 8–9) in abbreviated form which better conveys the concepts of these accounts than would one of the bulky, full-sized tables. Down the left side of one of the full-sized tables are listed the ninety industries as sellers, and across the top, starting from the left, the same ninety industries are listed again, but this time as buyers. (The complete list of the ninety industries appears on the left side of the Master Table, pages 155–172 at the back of the book; only four of them are named in Table I–1, where dotted lines indicate the omission of the others.) The number in any square of the "chessboard" of Table I–1 shows the sales *from* the industry on the left *to* the industry named at the top. The sales shown are totals for one year. We see, for example, that sales from livestock raising to meatpacking were $14,000 million, while steel purchases by engine and turbine makers came to $230 million. Though, in the complete ninety-by-ninety table, many of the cells are zero, about half of the total of 8,100 of them show some sale.

The sales shown in these ninety vertical columns are purchases of materials or services that are transformed into some further product. Capital investment and consumption appear in the remaining columns on the right-hand side of the table. First come a number of columns showing capital investment in equipment by the various industries. Because there is less information on the details of capital spending than on those of current expense, we have, in these columns, grouped the ninety sectors into a third that many as buyers of capital equipment.[3] Machinery industries find most of their sales in these columns. In Table I–1, we can see a capital purchase of $250 million worth of engines and turbines by public utilities. To the right of the equipment investment columns come the bills of materials for nineteen types of construction: residential, industrial, office, store, church, hospital, school, highway, water and sewer, and more, each type having its own column and its own particular materials requirements. A working capital item, net additions to inventories, is shown in the last column in the capital section.

Beyond the last of the capital columns come the ultimate-use columns, the last in order being the largest of them all, personal consumption. Reading down this column, we see people buying $1,500 million of produce, mostly eggs, directly from the livestock industry, $15,000 million of meat from the meatpacking industry, $20 million of steel industry products, and $160 million of engines, these being mostly boat motors. The preceding two columns show federal and state and local government acquisitions. The export column shows shipments abroad and the import column shows offsetting imports that compete with American-made goods. (Items which do not compete, such as manganese ore or coffee beans, are assigned directly to the industry which uses them, where they appear as purchases from the import industry, one of the ninety.)

In all we have a rectangular table with 90 sellers listed down the side and 144 markets listed across the top. Reading across an industry's row, we see a profile of its markets, who buys how much of its products. Reading down a column, we find, depending on where the column is in the table, an industry's bill of materials, or its spending on capital investment, or a consumer's shopping list, or a government budget, or the nation's export invoice.

The forecasts contain a table such as this for each year from the present to the target year, from 1963 to 1975. (The tables are in

---

[3] The forecasts actually use a total of 77 different investment columns. These 77 have been aggregated to 29 only for presentation in the Master Table.

constant dollars. Although the work on these forecasts was not completed until mid-1965, not enough data for 1964 had appeared to use
it as a base year.) From this series of tables emerge changes in market
profiles, changes in consumer spending patterns, changes in bills of
materials. Rather than show even two such tables and leave the
reader to struggle with a comparison of their four- and five-digit

TABLE I–1. INTERINDUSTRY ACCOUNTS
(millions of dollars)

| | | Intermediate Demands | | | Equipment Investment | | | |
	SELLER	Live-stock	Meat-packing	Steel	En-gines & Tur-bines	Agri-cul-ture	Pub-lic Utili-ties	Steel	Auto-mo-biles
1	Livestock	–	14,000	–	–	–	–	–	–
14	Meatpacking	–	–	–	–	–	–	–	–
43	Steel	–	–	–	230	–	–	–	–
49	Engines & turbines	–	–	–	–	22	250	–	–
	Employment (thousands)	5,000	1,640	1,300	85				

numbers, we present a digest of such a comparison in what we may
call a growth-volume table, the Master Table. The row and column
arrangement is the same as in Table I-1; the sellers are listed down
the side and the buyers across the top. Just below the buyer's name
at the top of the table appears the average rate of growth of that
industry or expenditure category between 1963 and 1970. Each
seller's row shows the percentage distribution of industry's 1975
sales.[4] These figures are printed in *tenths* of a percent with no decimal point shown. An "o" indicates a flow of less than .05 percent of
the sales of the industry; a "." marks a cell with no recorded flow.

[4] Actually, the percentages are of net supply, that is, domestic output plus imports
less sales within the same industry, e.g., the sales of automobile parts to automobile
manufacturers. The table does, however, show these intra-industry sales as a percent of
net supply. The Master Table omits the inventory accumulation column because the
uncertain nature of the base-year figures led to erratic and unrepresentative growth
rates in this column.

Some cells have only one number; others have a second number printed a line lower. The flows in the one-number cells grow at the same rate as does the using industry, and most cells are of this type. In over five hundred cells, however, trends have been projected in productive techniques, and markets grow at rates different from that of the using industry. These markets are readily spotted in the

TABLE I–1   (*continued*)

					BUYER				
						Ultimate Use			
	Construction						State-Local Go-vern-ment	Fede-ral Go-vern-ment	Con-sump-tion
SELLER	Resi-dential	Indus-trial	Of-fices	Inven-tories	Com-peting Im-ports	Ex-ports			
1 Livestock	–	–	–	100	–260	40	10	2	1,500
14 Meatpacking	–	–	–	300	–100	200	27	25	15,000
43 Steel	60	90	80	200	–700	100		120	20
49 Engines & turbines	–	–	–	20	–30	300	5	230	160

Master Table, for they are the two-number cells. The lower number is the average growth rate of that particular market, again printed in tenths of a percent with no decimal point shown. For example, the input of hardware (Sector 48) into household furniture (Sector 28) has no entry below it and therefore grows at the same rate as does the using industry, household furniture, namely, 3.8 percent per year. The sales of rubber and plastic products (Sector 38), however, to household furniture—2.5 percent of all rubber and plastic product sales in 1975—grow not at this rate of 3.8, but at the higher rate of 5.6 percent per year, as shown by the bottom number in the cell. In the consumption, export, import, and government columns, each cell has its own growth rate, so all the rates are shown, cell by cell. Across the bottom of the Master Table, the employment row shows the percentage distribution of employment in 1975 (again in tenths of a percent) and its rate of growth in each industry. The height of the shaded area in each industry is proportional to its growth rate.

So many growth rates are a bit difficult to digest all at once. To facilitate their comprehension, Figure I–3 puts the industry forecasts in historical perspective by showing, for selected industries, the course of output[5] from 1950 to 1963, followed by the forecast to

FIG. I–3. History and Forecast of Industry Outputs

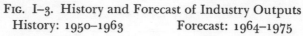
History: 1950–1963   Forecast: 1964–1975

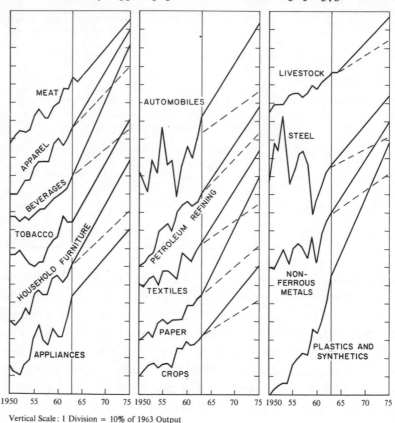

Vertical Scale: 1 Division = 10% of 1963 Output

1975. A dotted line projects the historical trend out to 1975 in the graphs where it is noticeably different from the forecasts. These graphs set the stage for describing how the forecasts were made and for studying some rows of the Master Table more closely in the following section.

[5] For manufacturing industries, the historical series is shipments of establishments in the industry deflated by appropriate portions of the wholesale price index.

Meatpacking continues its trend growth; the effects of accelerated income growth are offset by an expected firming of meat prices. Apparel sales display a definite acceleration in response to this faster growth of income. Beverages, especially alcoholic ones, and tobacco products can both look forward to a quickening expansion as the postwar babies leave behind the age of innocence. Spending on

Fig. I–3 (*Continued*)

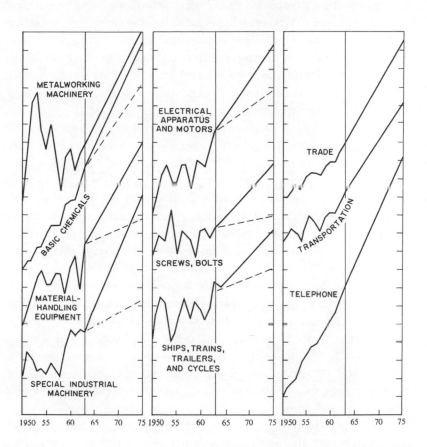

alcohol rises faster than on tobacco because alcohol purchases respond more to income increases, perhaps because there is a wider range of quality in it than in tobacco. The more rapid rise in income will pull the household furniture business up well above its historical trend. Household appliances will just maintain their growth trend; most of the major appliances, with the exception of dishwashers, have come to be thought of as necessities and their sales respond relatively frigidly to income changes. The automobile trend turns up sharply, but the industry will undoubtedly remain one of the most volatile in the economy; 1964 sales were about on forecast, but 1965 purchases are running slightly above the forecast. Petroleum refining and electric utilities continue their steady growth at only slightly quickened paces.

Moving from the consumer goods industries to basic materials industries, we see that textiles reflects the improvement in apparel and home furnishings prospects and pulls out of its long stagnation. Paper, a ubiquitous material whose growth sums up many influences, rolls up a substantially faster expansion. Crop raising also grows faster, though livestock raising, influenced almost exclusively by the demand for meat and dairy products, ambles along at its present leisurely gait. The steel industry is expected to weather the onslaught of plastics and aluminum well enough to stay out of the doldrums in which it spent much of the 1950s; it should tap the good growth of its automobile, machinery, and construction customers for a moderate increase in its own sales. Non-ferrous metals do better than ferrous, and plastics and synthetics, better than either. Most of the growth of plastics has come from its substitution for other materials; a slackening of this substitution offsets the acceleration in the growth of the using industries to produce a continuation of the historical trend. Basic chemicals also continue approximately their recent steady expansion.

The spurt of the 1965–1975 decade is nowhere more apparent than in the machinery sectors. Material-handling equipment, metal-working machinery, special industrial machinery (food-processing, paper-making, printing, textile and other such specialized machinery), and electrical apparatus and motors all spent a slow decade in the fifties, and all can expect their good growth since then to continue. Optimistic export projections impart the special luster to these forecasts, but solid domestic investment supports them also.

The defense industries, primarily ordnance, aircraft, and communication equipment, all slow down sharply under the *détente* defense assumption which we are using here. The growth rates for these industries under alternative defense assumptions appear in Chapter IV.

Because of the difficulty in obtaining historical series comparable in definition to the projections, only three of the service sectors are graphed here. Telephone service will continue to expand rapidly but with only a slight acceleration. Wholesale and retail trade increases its rate of growth 50 percent. The graph for transportation shows a very sharp break with the past, but definitional problems are serious here, and the comparison of history and forecast should be used with caution.[6]

These forecasts are not, it must be emphasized, unrelated speculations about different industries, but organic parts of a whole system; we now turn to how that system works to generate the forecasts and the whole growth-volume table.

HOW ARE THE FORECASTS MADE?

The work of forecasting falls into two parts. First we make what we call structural forecasts, and then we calculate the absolute, dollar-volume forecasts, which we have been discussing. The structural forecasts, which are all of a "per-dollar" sort, describe the technology and functioning of the economy but not its size. They are of four kinds:

1. Changes in consumer spending per dollar of additional income. If consumer income goes up 1 percent, how much will spending rise for meat, milk, clothes, appliances, automobiles, and so on? An analysis of the spending of families of different incomes has been combined with a study of the postwar changes in spending, income, and prices to produce the answer used here. Chapter II describes this work.

2. Capital spending required per dollar of sales expansion. By using annual capital investment data since 1947 and the Treasury Department's depreciation guidelines, stocks of capital equipment have been estimated for agricultural, manufacturing, mining, and utility industries. Comparing the growth of these stocks with the expansion of capacity or output in these industries produces estimates of the capital equipment required per dollar of expanded sales for each industry. Equipment replacements are implied by the investment history and the equipment lives, which, incidentally, have replacement of obsolete as well as worn-out machinery built into them.

6 One problem is that the historical series is for common carriers and reflects their loss of business to proprietary fleets. Such losses have not been considered in the forecasts, which therefore pertain more to the volume of transportation than to the transportation industry.

Construction requirements must also be related to the growth of output. Chapter III covers these topics.

3. Material requirements per dollar of sales. How much steel, aluminum, plastics, textiles, and electronic components will it take to build a car in 1975? The bills of materials per dollar of sales for each of the ninety industries in 1958 have been prepared by the Department of Commerce and recently published in a table known as an input-output matrix.[7] Each of these bills has been reviewed, and trends in them have been projected where they can be foreseen. The projected changes directly affect over three hundred interindustry flows. Likewise, the material composition of a dollar spent on each type of construction and capital investment by each industry has been determined and trends projected where possible. About ninety of these cells have trends in them. These projections, for which the author is wholly indebted to others,[8] are illustrated in Chapter VI.

4. Labor required per dollar of sales. Labor productivity in each industry has been projected by extending the trends of the last ten years. Chapter VII gives the details of this work.

Judgment, technical knowledge, and econometric research should combine in making the structural forecasts. The methods needed are as various as the problems, and few fields of economics escape untouched by the problems. The quality of the work at this stage determines the quality of the final forecasts, and there can be no doubt that more and better work on all areas can give us significantly more reliable forecasts than those shown here. Transplanting the findings of many qualitative studies of special parts of the American economy might improve many parts of the system, and some apology seems in order for the limited use we have been able to make of the results of others. But transplanting econometric results seems as ticklish as surgical transplanting; the host rejects the newcomer because its statistical definitions don't match, or it needs some element the system doesn't have, or it doesn't do all the system requires of it. Rather than trying to put together a new man out of pieces of adults, we have yielded to the more natural method of having a baby

7 "The Transactions Table of the 1958 Input-Output Study and Revised Direct and Total Requirements Data," *Survey of Current Business,* September 1965. In the published table there is only one food and one utility industry; we have separated these into the six food and three utility industries shown in the Master Table. In all other respects, the reader may consult this source for the precise definition of industries and for accounting practices.

8 Specifically, to Anne Carter and to Arthur D. Little, Inc.

ab ovo. It is to be hoped that the child will learn from his elders as he grows up.

With the structural forecasts in hand, we go on to calculate the dollar-volume forecasts. We proceed, essentially, backward, that is, starting with final demand on the right of Table I–1 and working our way back to the output of the industries, on the left. We shall go through this process step by step, but it may ease the way to note at the outset that there are some counter-currents, some important circular effects of outputs back on final demands. In particular,

1. Investment enters final demand, which determines output, but output in turn determines investment.

2. After-tax income determines consumer demands, which lead to outputs, which determine employment. To make employment match the labor force, we may have to come back and revise the forecast of after-tax income.

We handle this circularity by the time-honored method of trial and error, by taking a trial value and revising it as necessary. Hence, when the following outline says, "Take a trial value of income" or of output, rest assured that we will come back and revise it as necessary. The final answer is not at all affected by the initial choice.

After having made the structural forecasts, we develop the sales forecasts in six steps.

Step 1. We project government expenditures, exports, and competitive imports, which all stand on the right-hand side of Table I–1 on pp. 8–9. Historical trends, developments in trade negotiations, the military situation, and the domestic policy of the government all go into these projections. At present, they rest on judgment, not formal analysis. Chapter IV describes the various government projections; Chapter V deals with exports and imports.

Step 2. We pick a trial projection of after-tax income per capita, and calculate from it consumer expenditures per person on the products of each industry in each year of the forecast; multiplying these by the expected population gives the personal consumption column of Table I–1.

Step 3. We pick a trial projection of industry sales for each year of the forecast period, and deduce from it investment and construction spending and inventory accumulation by the industries in each year of the forecast. The total equipment investment of each industry is divided among the various types of equipment it uses in constant proportions which are based on 1958 experience.[9] The results go into the equipment-investment section of Table I–1. Construction spending is likewise decomposed into material requirements according to the type of construction, though all the manufacturing industries are assumed to use the same sort of construction. (The government construction columns, appearing in this part of the table, are actually forecast back in Step 1, and residential construction in Step 2 with the other consumer items.)

Step 4. We add across the rows of all the final demands to get a total final demand column for each year of the forecast. Now, using the structural forecasts of material requirements of each industry in each year, we work back from a year's final demands to its industry outputs. Ten dollars spent on a car requires one dollar's worth of steel; one dollar of steel requires 1.5 cents of electricity; 1.5 cents of electricity requires 0.1 cents of coal, and so on back. Industry outputs are built up in this way to equal what it takes, directly or indirectly, to satisfy the final demands. Circularity in production is also accounted for: It takes coal to make steel and steel props to mine coal. These calculations are, of course, performed by a computer; the IBM 7094 averages $3\frac{1}{2}$ seconds per year to complete all the calculations in Steps 1 through 4. Of this $3\frac{1}{2}$ seconds, about $2\frac{1}{2}$ are consumed by Step 4 in solving for the outputs of all industries.

Step 5. When industry sales have been calculated for each year of the forecast, we compare them with the sales assumed in making the investment forecast in Step 3. If they do not agree closely, we go back to Step 3, use the newly calculated outputs to deduce investment,[10] repeat Step 4, and again compare assumed sales with implied sales. Mathematical analysis (in the appendix) assures us that it will not be necessary to repeat this process often and that the final

---

[9] A table showing these shares of each supplying industry in each purchasing industry's capital equipment spending in 1958 has been prepared by the Office of Growth Studies of the Bureau of Labor Statistics. We were generously allowed to use this material before its publication, which, however, is expected shortly. A few trends are projected in these factors; but, for the most part, the 1958 shares are used without change.

[10] Actually, we fit a cubic polynomial to the time paths of outputs as they are calculated. This fitted curve is then used to deduce investment on the next pass through Step 3. The curve fit on one forecast is saved on computer tape to serve as the initial guess the next time a forecast is desired. On the very first forecast, all future outputs were initially assumed to be zero; even with this outlandish assumption, only two repetitions (i.e., three executions) of Step 3 were necessary. Each successive forecast—and there have been some forty of them in the course of revising and correcting the system—started from the course of outputs found by its immediate predecessor.

answer is independent of the initial trial projection of outputs. In practice, one repetition has usually been sufficient when we started from a reasonable initial guess. When close agreement has been reached, we proceed to Step 6.

Step 6. From the output and labor productivity forecasts, we calculate employment in the various industries. If total employment matches the specified percentage of the expected labor force, we are through. Otherwise, back we go to Step 2 to change the assumed course of income. If we find too little employment, we increase the assumed after-tax income, and vice versa.

We then repeat all of Steps 2–6 until we find the desired employment in Step 6. (In practice, it is seldom necessary to go back from Step 6 to Step 2 more than once.)

When we have finished, we have found the after-tax income which allows consumers to give industry the business it takes to employ, say, all but 4 percent of the labor force. With a projection of wage and profit rates, we could calculate from our sales and employment projections the tax base of future years. The difference between these two amounts would be the full-employment tax bill. The present or proposed tax laws could then be examined to see if they would produce this amount of revenue. Likewise, corporate after-tax income could be compared with capital spending requirements. These important tax calculations, however, present a number of technical problems and have not yet been tackled. At present, therefore, the concept of the full-employment tax rate is something of a *deus ex machina* who appears at the end to hold the piece together.

We have now calculated a table like Table I–1 for each year of the forecast. Moreover, we have built into this series of tables all the fivefold consistency announced in the introduction. To show how this consistency enables us to scrutinize the forecasts, let us take an example.

FORECASTING THE METALWORKING MACHINERY MARKET

Mr. G. S. Ledlow, president and chairman of the New Answer Electronics Company, a well-established maker of micro-electronic components, has not viewed his company's present heavy dependence on defense and space business with total equanimity. Long-range prospects for disarmament have led him, therefore, to look for other markets less dependent upon government programs. Several possible ways of diversification occurred to him. Medical electronics was one possibility, or he could try lighting and wiring devices, or components for consumer electronic items. One possibility which rather appealed to him was expanding into the field of numerical control devices for metalworking machines—rolling mills, automotive transfer machines, and machine tools of all sorts. He felt certain that, in the short run, this market would grow rapidly as control devices were added to an increasing variety of machines. But what of the long pull? If the metalworking machinery business grows as slowly in the future as it has in the past, he reasoned, the entry of many firms into this market in the next few years could lead to a painful shakedown, perhaps before New Answer could get on its feet in the business. If, on the other hand, metalworking machinery itself has good growth potential, then New Answer would have time to convert its technical competence into a profitable position in the field.

Unfortunately, Mr. Ledlow has never sold a machine tool in his life and has little more than hunches about the industry's future. Moreover, if he gets into the business, he will have to concentrate on some type of machine—rolling mills, automotive equipment, or general purpose machine tools. Which of these markets will grow fastest? It begins to seem to Mr. Ledlow that he will have to investigate not just metalworking machinery, but steel, automobiles, and all the machine-making industry as well. Moreover, he must compare this opportunity with the others, and to evaluate each of them requires forecasts. The task of decision grows bigger the more he thinks about it, until he realizes that perhaps, he is, after all, a man for whom this book was written. How can he use it?

He begins by looking across the "Office and Computing Machines" row of the growth-volume table (Master Table), since numerical controls are made by the "computing" part of this industry. At the intersection of this row with the "metalworking machinery" column he finds the sales of numerical control equipment to this industry forecast to account for 10.2 percent of the total sales of computing and office machinery by 1975. He notes with satisfaction its rapid growth rate, 13.7 percent per year, which is considerably above the 4.1 percent growth for metalworking machinery itself. It is this latter growth rate, however, which is Mr. Ledlow's real concern at the moment; he can and should examine more closely than we have done the amount of controls that will be needed per dollar of machine tools. Looking back to Figure I–3, he sees that metalworking machinery sales are, indeed, forecast to grow much more rapidly than they did in the last decade. "Why?" he will want to know. "Who will be buying them, and why will they buy them?" The metalworking machinery row of the Master Table gives the answer, and Figure I–4 shows the growth-volume profile of this row in graphic form.

Fɪɢ. I–4. Growth-Volume Profile of Metalworking Machinery

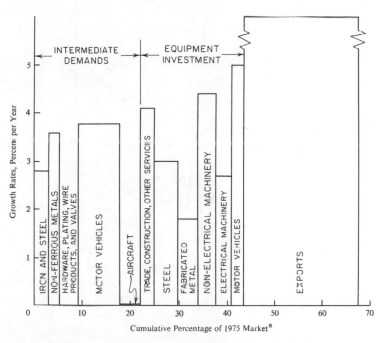

a Only markets using 2 percent or more of 1975 output are shown.

Growth rates are measured vertically, and the 1975 volume is measured horizontally. The width of a bar of the profile shows the volume of that market; the height of the bar indicates the rate of growth of the market. The chart shows at a glance, therefore, the relative size and growth rates of the principal markets for metalworking machinery. A few clearly dominate: exports, the style-dependent part of automobile tooling which appears as a current rather than a capital input, and capital investment by all the machine-making industries and by the steel industry. Mr. Ledlow may turn to Chapter V for a discussion of the large and fast-growing export market. Among the other markets, we shall trace back to its sources only equipment investment by steel, for no new principles would be required to trace back any of the others in the same manner.

Fig. I–5. Equipment Investment by the Steel Industry

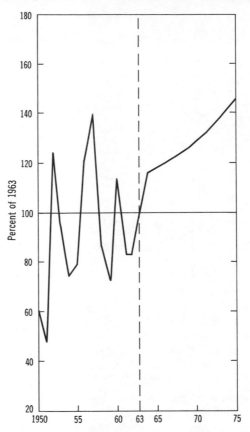

Figure I–5 shows the history and forecast for investment by the steel industry. Again a considerable improvement over the recent past appears. Mr. Ledlow will no doubt regard this forecast suspiciously, and we shall have to refer him to Chapter III on capital formation for a full explanation of how it is made. Suffice it to say here that the determining factor is the accelerated growth of steel output, which was shown in Figure I–3. But why is steel growing? Who is buying it?

Figure I–6, which is drawn similarly to Figure I–4, answers this question with a growth-volume profile of the steel row of the Master Table. Because important reductions in the amount of steel used per dollar of output are expected in many industries, it is interesting to see what the growth rates of the various markets would have been without these technological changes. In Figure I–6, a dotted line

FIG. I–6. Growth-Volume Profile of Steel Markets

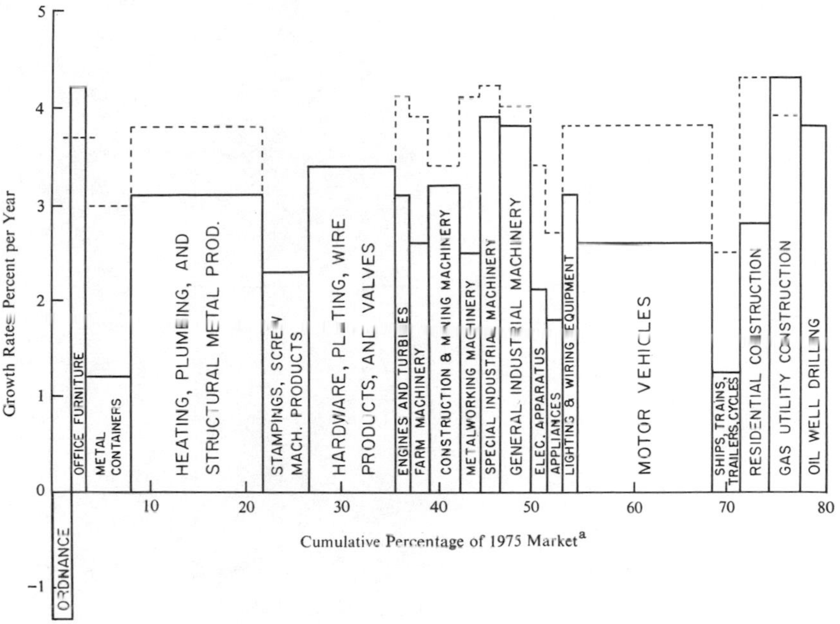

a Only markets using 2 percent or more of 1975 output are shown.

over the industry's rectangle marks the rate of growth of the industry's output wherever it differs from the rate of growth of steel use. The chart demonstrates that, in spite of these reductions, the outlook for steel remains good in several markets, notably in the automobile market.

In automobile purchases, we have finally reached the end of this root of the metalworking machinery forecast, for we have come home to the consumer. As Figure I–7 indicates, automobile purchases *per capita* will respond to the faster growth of consumer income in the next decade. The exact relations between *per capita* income and *per capita* expenditure on the various items in a consumer's budget are developed in Chapter II on consumption. From that work, we will

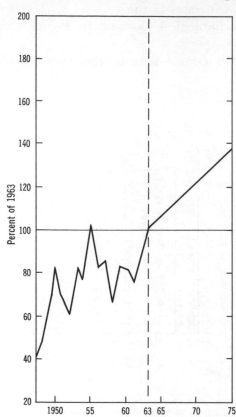

FIG. I–7. Automobile Purchases Per Capita

conclude that a 10 percent increase in income causes an 11.5 percent increase in an average consumer's spending on automobiles. The forecast growth in consumer income, as we have said, is determined so that the employment resulting from it will match the future labor force, that is, so that the jobs making numerical control devices to make the machines to make the steel to make the cars that consumers buy, plus all the other jobs directly or indirectly satisfying the final demands of the economy will, all together, employ the 1975 labor force.

All the forecasts can be traced back in this fashion because they are derived just exactly the other way around, from the cars to the steel, to the machines, to the control devices. In some cases the chain is longer; in some, shorter; but it is always there, tying each forecast to the ultimate demands of the economy and tying these, through the output and employment they generate, to the future labor force.

Similarly the forecasts relevant for each of Mr. Ledlow's other diversification possibilities can be pulled out and analyzed. They will all be mutually consistent parts of a unified frame of reference for his evaluation of his opportunities. Mr. Ledlow will soon observe, if he has not done so already, that there are some important developments which these forecasts do not even touch, notably prices, competitive structure of the industry, and the labor situation. On such matters, he will simply have to look elsewhere.

Mr. Ledlow did not get where he is by blindly trusting academic economists, and he will not take these forecasts at face value. He must examine closely the premises and methods on which they rest. In the following chapters, we shall set forth these foundations for his examination. He will not find them all satisfactory, and, indeed, the last chapter is entirely devoted to enumerating further developments which should make this sort of forecasting more useful. I hope, however, that Mr. Ledlow will agree that these forecasts are not just so many isolated fancies, but are members incorporate of a total structure. Each member rests on others and is rested upon by others. They all evolve consistently and organically from our vision of the working of the economy. Though they are by no means necessarily right, I hope that, because of their consistency, they will prove a useful starting point for business forecasting. They are easily recalculated under different assumptions; and, should one wish to see such variants, it should be possible to produce them. If these forecasts find uses, they can be kept current and become a regular part of the information system serving the American economy.

II

Personal Consumption

Whither the consumer's dollar leads, the American economy follows; and where our consumption projections go, the rest of the model trails along. Should consumers choose to spend more on cars and less on television, a whole chain of reactions runs through the economy as industries bring their production, purchasing, investment, and employment into line with the new demands. Steel and rubber industries would increase output, create new jobs, and expand their capital while the electronic components and the wooden cabinet industries decreased output, laid off workers, and contracted their capital.

Though similar changes follow upon a change in government purchases or exports, consumers dominate economic growth by their sheer bulk. According to standard national accounting definitions, consumption absorbs 65 percent of GNP; but if we exclude from GNP the production of government employees and count residential construction as a consumer purchase, the consumer's share rises to over 80 percent of privately produced GNP. Since much capital spending is for equipment to make consumer goods or to make materials or equipment for making them, the consumer's influence is even greater than these figures suggest. In the end, only government spending and exports escape his direction.

This primacy of the consumer is reproduced in the structure of our model. From consumption, we work back to industry outputs, investment, and employment. Since it is through consumption that the tax rate regulates the economy, the desired level of employment in the model is obtained by choosing the proper level of consumption. Because of this guiding and dominant role in building up the complete forecasts, consumption is the natural place to begin the detailed exposition of the forecasting model.

THE PROBLEM

Which way will the consumer take the economy? That is the question for this chapter in its simplest form. More specifically, how will the pattern of consumer spending be affected by:

A permanent increase in income?
Changes in relative prices?
A change in the rate of growth of income?
Shifts in the age structure of the population?
Trends in tastes, habits, social customs, or the availability of new products, or other influences we may lump together under the title "passage of time"?

In quantitative terms, the questions become what values shall be assigned to the parameters a, b_1, ..., b_4 in the following equation:

$$(1) \qquad c_t = a + b_1 y_t + b_2 p_t + b_3 t + b_4 \Delta y_t,$$

where c_t is the annual consumption per person of a particular item in year t, p_t is its price index divided by the over-all price index, y_t is disposable income per capita, $\Delta y_t = y_t - y_{t-1}$, and t is time in years. (In some cases, p is replaced by the fraction of the population in certain age groups; e.g., the fraction over 18 is useful in explaining alcohol consumption.) Estimating the parameters of this equation is the burden of this chapter; but before taking it up, let us make certain of its weight and contents.

In predicting the period 1950 to 1963, long-range forecasters could, by and large, have ignored the distinction between the effects of higher income and those of passing time. Disposable income per capita rose about $27 per year and only during the 1954 recession was it ever more than one average year's increment away from the straight-line trend. For long-range purposes, there was no *need* to distinguish between the effects of time and income on the pattern of consumer spending. Conversely, looking back at the period, there is no *possibility* of distinguishing between them from the history of spending alone. In the decade ahead, however, the yearly growth of income will run more than double that of the last. Will the yearly expansion of all commodities also double? Is all of their past growth to be attributed to rising income? Or does some of it come from changing tastes, or from new products, or from other changes which continue at about the same rate or even taper off? For example, are we to attribute all of the decline in spending on laundry and cleaning to the increase in washing-machine ownership and therefore, indirectly, to income, or does much of the credit go to orlon, dacron, and drip-dry? If we attribute to the change in income all the changes of the last fifteen years in the consumption of various items, we will find all the rates of change greatly accelerated in our forecasts. We must take care, therefore, to ascribe to income only what strictly belongs to it. "How much," we must ask, "will consumption of item X eventually increase if income increases 1 percent and remains at that level, provided tastes, prices, and the products available remain unchanged?"

The word "eventually" in this question deserves note. Spending on some items, such as rent, is unlikely to rise immediately upon a raise in salary, while on other items, such as automobiles, spending may shoot up during the following year and then return to a level only moderately above its former one. (This latter effect often shows up particularly strongly for items generally bought on credit.) In either case, we wish to find this *long-run equilibrium level;* the transient effect must not be forgotten, but we attribute it to the rate-of-change-of-income variable, Δy, which allows for a one-year delay in adjusting to a new income level, or, conversely, for a one-year boom in spending following a rise in income. Figure II–1 illustrates the two possibilities with the actual equations for natural gas and automobiles. In each case, income is assumed to have been at its initial level for several years; at time zero it rises 1 percent and continues at this new level indefinitely. As the graph shows, natural gas consumption rises gradually to its new equilibrium; automobile spending overshoots the mark as people buy on the credit their new income makes available.

Finally, in interpreting the income coefficient, we must know whose income is increasing, or more properly, how the distribution of income changes as its average increases. We shall make the simple and neutral assumption that everyone's income increases in the same proportion. More elaborate assumptions could easily have been substituted, but this one is readily understood and does not run strongly counter to recent experience.

There are no particular conceptual problems about the relative price variables.

As we shall see in the section on The Forecasts on p. 47, strong trends from "passage-of-time" variables show up in the spending on a number of items during the last fourteen years. Some of these influences appear to be definitely continuing; others seem to have run their course and to be slackening now. We shall examine them item by item in due course.

FIG. II–1. Responses of Spending on Automobile and Natural Gas to a 1 Percent Permanent Income Increase

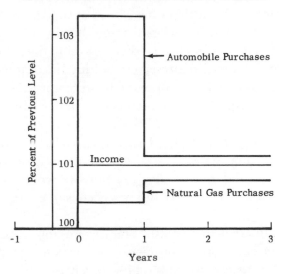

SOURCES OF INFORMATION

Two bodies of data can be used to estimate the constants in consumption equations such as equation (1). One, from the national income accounts (published in each July issue of the *Survey of Current Business*), gives a historical series on the annual total consumption of some eighty categories of commodities and services. The other, the outcome of a consumer survey conducted in 1960 and 1961, shows, for households of different incomes, the spending on a quite detailed list of goods (see note 3, below). This second source can serve only in estimating the income coefficient, b_1, in equation (1). The time-series data must be used for all the other coefficients. In this section, we shall explain those features of these two sources which affect our use of them.

The time-series data are printed in current dollars and, after aggregation into eleven categories, in constant dollars. The full detail of the constant-dollar series was kindly made available by the Department of Commerce, and a comparison of the two series produced the implicit price index for each category. The "item" column of Table II-2 (pp. 32–38) lists these categories with a few modifications to split down the food group and aggregate some of the financial and service items. One quickly sees that the resulting sixty-nine categories are not the same as the industries of our model. Some categories, such as automobiles, gasoline, apparel, and electricity, contain items from a single producing industry. Many, however, contain items from a variety of industries, for items have been grouped, not by how they are made as in the industrial classification, but by how they are used or by how a family might classify them in its budget. For example, boats, outboard motors, life preservers, fishing line, minnow buckets, cane poles, and fish hooks are all made by different industries; but in the consumer categories, they come together under "durable sporting equipment."

We will conduct our study of consumer behavior in these categories. Even if time series on the consumption of each industry's products were available—and they are not—we would prefer such a grouping which matches better the way a consumer thinks about his budget.[1]

Use of two different classifications requires us, of course, to convert forecasts of consumer spending from the consumer to the industry categories. Fortunately, we know how much each industry sold to each consumption category in 1958. Indeed, the "benchmarks" of the consumer series, which are established in years in which there is a Census of Manufactures, are made by a commodity-flow method which begins with the output of an item as reported by the Census, subtracts estimated use by industry, investment, or export, adds

[1] It must be admitted that the match is not perfect; there are a number of unfortunate peculiarities in the national accounts data. For example, tuition paid to a private college is an expenditure on education but tuition paid to a state college is not even an expenditure at all, but a "personal non-tax." Consumers, by definition, do not buy furnaces, hot water heaters, plumbing fixtures, linoleum, storm windows, or window shades; instead, home-owners rent their houses from the largely fictitious "rental" industry, and this industry buys all these items. The item "services rendered without payment by financial intermediaries" is unlikely to appear in a family's budget. At these and several other points, it should be possible to revise the national income concepts to yield categories better suited for economic analysis.

transportation and trade markups, and assigns the result to the appropriate consumption category. We forecast the amount in each consumption category and then just work through the process backwards. Specifically, since no other course is open, we assume that each industry will maintain its 1958 share in each consumer category.

The classification conversion also includes a price conversion. Industry outputs are in producer prices, while consumption is in retail prices. The difference—the markup for trade and transportation—the classification conversion strips off and places as a consumer demand for the services of these two industries. At the same time, it puts down the *producers'* value of the category as consumer demands on the appropriate industries. The output of the trade industry is not its sales, as in most other industries, but consists entirely of these markups.

Eight of the series listed in Table II–2 do not appear explicitly in the series published with the national accounts, namely, the food items—meat; poultry; dairy products; processed fruits and vegetables; fresh fruits and vegetables; flours, mixes, and cereals; bakery products; and other foods. In the accounts, food is grouped not by type, but by where it is eaten—at home, in restaurants, or in the armed services. There are several reasons for preferring the breakdown by type of food. First, food sales, especially of meat and poultry, are much affected by price. In the aggregate, the effects of these price changes could not be isolated, and reliable forecasting equations, consequently, could not be found. Secondly, the income elasticity for some foods is much higher than for others. Finally, the relative shares of manufacturing and agriculture in the value of foods vary considerably from food to food. The farmer gets a larger slice of a dollar spent on milk than of a dollar spent on cookies. To make useful forecasts of agriculture and its divisions between livestock and crops, we must make explicit what kind of food will be eaten. For the eight food items listed above, time series on consumption were constructed from the Department of Agriculture and the Census of Manufactures data. Because we were unable to eliminate a 10 percent excess in the sum of our 1958 estimates over the estimate of the Department of Commerce, the absolute numbers in these series cannot be accurate, but they should show the correct growth relative to one another.

The second basic source of information on consumer behavior is the Survey of Consumer Expenditures, conducted by the Bureau of

Labor Statistics (BLS) in 1960 and 1961. A sample of some 12,000 urban households was selected by stratified sampling techniques.[2] In interviews, the households were asked to report their income before and after taxes, their total consumption, and their spending on a long and detailed list of commodities and services. Usable replies totaled 9,476.

From a published summary[3] of this survey, we can construct tables showing the average expenditure by households of a given size and income on each of a large number of commodities. Table II–1 is such

TABLE II-1. EXPENDITURES OF URBAN HOUSEHOLDS ON FURNITURE
CLASSIFIED BY SIZE AND INCOME OF HOUSEHOLD

Number of Persons in Household	After-Tax Income (dollars per year)					
	$3,000 to $3,999	$4,000 to $4,999	$5,000 to $5,999	$6,000 to $7,499	$7,500 to $9,999	$10,000 and Over
2	66	71	85	134	153	177
3	54	65	86	95	147	177
4	73	82	86	88	125	164
5 and over	64	52	94	81	97	175

SOURCE: Bureau of Labor Statistics, *Survey of Consumer Expenditures 1960–61*, Report 237–38, Supplement 3-Part A, July 1964.

a table for furniture. Looking across a row, we see how spending on furniture rises with income for families of the same size; looking down a column, we see how the size of households affects the spending of families in the same income group. Such a table enables us to separate the effects of family size and income and invites us to ask, "How much would total spending on furniture rise if every family's income rose 10 percent while family sizes remain unaltered?" We shall try to answer this question in the next section.

Table II–1 is actually a condensation and truncation of the published tables. Spending data on families in the $2,000–$3,000, $1,000–$2,000, and the under $1,000 after-tax income brackets are also published; five-person families are distinguished from those of six persons and over; data on single-person households is available;

[2] Rural households were also sampled, but, since using both groups would have doubled the work and yielded a minimal increase in accuracy, the present study was confined to the preponderant urban sample alone.

[3] Bureau of Labor Statistics, *Survey of Consumer Expenditures 1960–61*, Report 237–38, Supplement 3-Part A, July 1964.

and the $10,000 and over income category is divided between $10,000 to $15,000 and the $15,000 and over categories. The sample, however, wears thin in these fringes;[4] for determining the effect of increasing income on spending, we preferred the firmer figures left after trimming off these edges, or folding them under by combining categories.

Many consumer categories in the time-series data can be matched quite closely by survey data; others, such as the "durable sporting equipment" mentioned before, can only be approximated; still others, such as "flowers, seeds, and potted plants" or "funerals" could not be matched at all.

ESTIMATION OF EQUATIONS

We shall use the consumer survey to determine the effect of income increases on consumption; with this effect known, the influence of prices, the rate of growth of income, demographic variables, and other trends will be determined from the time series. We must explain:

1. How we estimated the influence of income from the survey.

2. How this estimate was transferred to the time-series data, and how the other coefficients were then determined.

3. Why this combination of time-series and survey data, against which one is often warned, is, in fact, necessary and justified.

The results of the estimation are shown in Table II–2. The meaning of its columns will emerge step by step through the rest of this section.

INCOME ELASTICITIES FROM THE CONSUMER SURVEY

By the "income elasticity of demand" for some item, we mean simply "the percent by which spending on that item increases when income increases 1 percent." That is,

$$(2) \qquad n = \frac{\frac{\Delta c}{c}}{\frac{\Delta y}{y}} = \frac{\Delta c}{\Delta y} \cdot \frac{y}{c}$$

[4] For example, the sample shows that households with income under $1,000 spend more on major appliances ($39) and on concerts and plays ($2) than do any of the next three higher income groups (which reach up to $4,000), and more on hospitalized illness than does any group below $15,000. This last fact reminds us of an additional reason for excluding the very low income families: Many of them are accustomed to higher incomes and spend accordingly.

TABLE II-2. PER CAPITA CONSUMPTION FORECASTING EQUATIONS

Item	Constant a	Income Coefficient b1	Price or Demographic Coefficient b2	Time Coefficient b3	Change of Income Coefficient b4	R²	Time Fraction and Price Elasticity	1963 Spending Per Capita	Income Elasticities Consumer Survey	Income Elasticities Time Series	Forecast Growth Rate (percent per year)
1 Alcoholic beverages	-325.55 (77.43)	.04031	475.47a (121.82)	0.66 (0.52)	-.0037 (.0087)	0.98	1.15 / 5.21	58.06	1.37	-0.44	2.8
Revised	-81.40	.04031	91.26	-0.52		0.74	-0.90			0.95	
2 Meat	102.87 (8.25)	.02593	-0.0576 (0.0091)	-0.39 (0.14)	-.0013 (.0146)	0.83 / 0.93	-0.38 / -0.49	105.02	(0.50)	0.51 / 1.97	0.9
3 Poultry	12.15 (0.80)	.00430	-0.0057 (0.0007)		-.0065 (.0055)	0.86 / 0.92	-0.27	16.40	(0.50)	2.01 / -0.59	1.5
4 Dairy products	70.01 (0.56)	.01022		-0.84 (0.08)		0.90 / 0.80	-0.95	89.07	(0.22)		0.0
5 Fruits & vegetables	41.40 (0.99)	.02241		0.16 (0.14)		0.09 / 0.72	0.18	87.59	(0.50)	0.40 / -0.22	0.5
Fresh fruits & vegetables	Decrease of 1.3% per year										
6 Grain mill products	34.54 (10.73)	.00171	-0.0169 (0.0084)	0.37 (0.06)	-.0028 (.0023)	0.95 / 0.96	2.27 / -1.32	16.40	(0.20)	1.15 / -0.76	2.1
7 Bakery products	89.76 (39.32)	.01000	-0.0476 (0.0309)	0.96 (0.24)	-.0014 (.0085)	0.89 / 0.95	1.88 / -1.18	51.39	(0.40)	1.14 / 0.23	1.9
8 Other food	0.44 (0.53)	.03764		1.15 (0.07)		0.95 / 0.99	1.50	77.14	(1.00)	1.78 / -0.21	3.6
9 Farm home consumption	Decrease of 10% per year										
10 Tobacco	-192.46 (94.11)	.00717	341.24a (148.05)	1.46 (0.63)	-.0067 (.0106)	0.35 / 0.54	3.69 / 5.48	39.66	0.35	0.21 / -0.92	1.5
Revised	14.80	.00717	62.24	-0.19	-.0067		-0.48				

11 Footwear	4.02 (0.43)	.00901		−0.42 (0.05)	.0172 (.0070)	0.86	0.62	−1.90		22.30	0.78	−0.79	−0.76
													0.7
12 Clothes	89.77 (24.14)	.07937	−1.1727 (0.2458)	−2.05 (0.24)	−.0044 (.0107)	0.94	0.96	−1.57	−0.89	130.94	1.19	0.52 / 0.07	
													2.2
13 Jewelry & watches	2.14 (3.87)	.00893	−0.0782 (0.0426)	−0.14 (0.12)	.0004 (.0024)	0.68	0.97	−1.09	−0.54	12.86	1.41	1.49 / 0.54	3.2
14 Cleaning & repair of clothing	−13.61 (0.24)	.01686		−0.74 (0.03)		0.97	0.82	−3.69	−2.65	20.19	1.61	−1.15 / −0.02	2.2
Revised	−13.21			−0.53									
15 Toilet articles	18.25 (10.40)	.00433	−0.0998 (0.1062)	0.47 (0.05)	.0041 (.0052)	0.94	0.96	2.60	−0.54	18.11	0.49	2.19 / −1.69	3.5
16 Barber & beauty shops	−0.91 (0.25)	.00741		0.19 (0.03)		0.71	0.91	1.37		14.13	1.02	1.57 / −1.59	3.7
17 Housing	102.27 (31.08)	.11473	−0.9921 (0.3043)	2.36 (0.23)	−.0490 (.0170)	0.95	0.99	1.02	−0.43	231.45	(1.00)	1.55 / −0.10	3.3
18 Farm housing	10.62												0.0
19 Furniture	20.87 (6.74)	.01313	−0.2011 (0.0684)	−0.11 (0.07)	.0114 (.0080)	0.58	0.84	−0.43	−0.70	27.89	0.98	0.87 / 1.99	2.7
20 Appliances	44.69 (12.14)	.00730	−0.3521 (0.1369)	−0.89 (0.49)	.0235 (.0084)	0.81	0.90	−3.06	−1.04	29.33	0.51	1.24 / 3.58	1.0
21 Tableware & cooking utensils	7.51 (4.99)	.00715	−0.0986 (0.0495)	−0.24 (0.07)	.0023 (.0034)	0.96	0.87	−1.95	−0.79	12.42		−1.18 / −0.44	1.4
China & glassware	0.39	.00223		−0.05	.0005						1.64		
Eating utensils	−0.29	.00236	−0.0217 (0.0197)	−0.04	.0004						1.91		
Cooking utensils	7.42	.00255	−0.0572	−0.14	.0013						0.71		

[a] Coefficient of fraction of population 18 and over.

(Table continued)

TABLE II-2. PER CAPITA CONSUMPTION FORECASTING EQUATIONS (continued)

Item	Constant a	Income Coefficient b_1	Price or Demographic Coefficient b_2	Time Coefficient b_3	Change of Income Coefficient b_4	R^2	Time Fraction and Price Elasticity	1963 Spending Per Capita	Income Elasticities Consumer Survey	Income Elasticities Time Series	Forecast Growth Rate (percent per year)
22 Rugs & miscellaneous household durables	−9.18 (0.61)	.01433		−0.41 (0.08)	.0142 (.0100)	0.74	−2.02	20.80		−0.32	1.7
Rugs	−6.52	.00693		−0.15	.0052	0.29			1.85	0.29	
Miscellaneous household durables	−2.66	.00740		−0.26	.0090				1.16		
23 Semidurable house furniture	−3.18 (0.37)	.00998		−0.17 (0.04)	.0084 (.0060)	0.60	−0.95	18.26	1.16	0.62	2.9
Revised	−2.08	.00998			.0084	0.45				0.21	
24 Household cleaning & paper supplies	14.23 (0.15)	.00241		0.45 (0.02)	.0086 (.0025)	0.98	2.27	20.03		1.72	2.2
Laundry & cleaning supplies	11.40	.00103		0.32	.0061	0.98			0.15	0.51	
Household paper supplies	2.83	.00138		0.13	.0025				0.49		
25 Writing supplies	5.55 (2.07)	.00322	−0.0561 (0.0205)	0.10 (0.01)	−.0004 (.0014)	0.80 / 0.95	1.59 / −0.85	6.53	1.06	1.38 / −1.35	4.0
26 Electricity	1.43 (0.14)	.01642		1.29 (0.01)	−.0054 (.0023)	1.00 / 1.00	3.68	35.27	(1.00)	3.79 / 0.22	4.9
27 Gas	4.92 (0.15)	.00673		0.57 (0.01)	−.0039 (.0025)	0.99 / 0.99	3.13	18.32	(0.75)	3.10 / 0.75	4.3
28 Water	5.89 (1.24)	.00237	−0.0387 (0.0115)	0.13 (0.03)	.0003 (.0009)	0.81 / 0.96	2.10 / −0.63	6.57	0.72	0.72 / 0.52	2.8
29 Other fuel	17.95 (12.29)	.00644	−0.1189 (0.1234)	−0.66 (0.04)	.0056 (.0054)	0.96 / 0.94	−3.43 / −0.61	19.47	0.65	−1.79 / 1.33	−1.9

						R^2				
30	Telegraph & telephone	14.02 (5.99)	.01041	−0.0888 (0.0604)	.62 (0.02)	.0001 (.0025)	0.99 / 1.00	2.28 / −0.32	27.26 0.81	2.51 / 0.64	3.7
31	Domestic service	−32.75 (0.48)	.02589		−.97 (0.07)		0.94 / 0.53	−5.58	17.46 2.69	−0.82 / 1.80	3.3
32	Other household operations	10.64 (4.49)	.00692	−0.1184 (0.0423)	.17 (0.05)	.0003 (.0019)	0.53 / 0.96	1.47 / −1.07	12.06 1.16	1.02 / 0.19	3.2
33	Drugs & sundries	10.42 (0.24)	.00612		.61 (0.03)		0.96 / 0.98	2.66	23.28 0.54	2.39 / 1.13	3.5
34	Glasses & orthopedic supplies	0.80 (0.14)	.00305		.20 (0.02)		0.89 / 0.94	2.93	6.95 0.92	2.44 / −0.21	4.5
35	Physicians	36.04 (17.04)	.00775	−0.2369 (0.1594)	.66 (0.32)	.0039 (.0076)	0.59 / 0.86	2.46 / −0.94	27.25 (0.59)	0.82 / −1.44	2.3
36	Dentists	4.75 (0.13)	.00334		.15 (0.0)		0.84 / 0.93	1.32	11.45 (0.59)	1.42 / 0.62	2.7
37	Other professional services	1.94 (0.03)	.00142		0.0 (0.0)		0.32 / 0.93	0.20	4.92 (0.59)	0.68 / 0.07	1.6
38	Hospitals	11.75 (0.14)	.00859		.7 (0.2)		0.99 / 0.99	2.40	29.60 (0.59)	2.30 / −0.23	3.4
39	Medical insurance	3.56 (0.40)	.00318	−0.0078 (0.0042)	.35 (0.1)	−.0003 (.0013)	0.99 / 1.00	3.84 / −0.09	9.30 0.70	3.87 / 0.79	4.6
40	Funerals	3.25 (0.05)	.00253		−.07 (0.1)		0.91 / 0.40	−0.92	8.29 (0.60)	−0.14 / 1.15	0.9
41	Personal finance	18.77 (6.38)	.02336	−0.2600 (0.0574)	.4 (0.5)	.0096 (.0086)	0.73 / 0.94	2.14 / −0.70	39.46 1.25	1.25 / −0.22	4.1
42	Life insurance handling	−9.28 (0.38)	.01721		.5 (0.4)	−.0135 (.0062)	0.61 / 0.94	0.65	24.57 1.41	1.72 / 0.63	4.0
43	Legal services	25.51 (5.59)	.00504	−0.2346 (0.0499)	.4 (0.7)	.0054 (.0029)	0.81 / 0.71	7.36 / −2.79	9.66 (1.00)	−0.02 / −2.65	2.9
44	Personal debt	−25.72 (0.37)	.03200		.87 (0.5)		0.96 / 0.99	2.23	39.10 (1.75)	3.70 / 1.75	5.3
45	Other personal business	−0.08 (0.07)	.00288		−.02 (0.1)		0.30 / 0.76	−0.38	5.69 (1.00)	0.39 / 0.00	2.3

(*Table continued*)

35

Table II-2. Per Capita Consumption Forecasting Equations (continued)

Item	Constant a	Income Coefficient b₁	Price or Demographic Coefficient b₂	Time Coefficient b₃	Change of Income Coefficient b₄	R²	Time Fraction and Price Elasticity	1963 Spending Per Capita	Income Elasticities Consumer Survey	Income Elasticities Time Series	Forecast Growth Rate (percent per year)
46 Automobiles	62.91 (79.60)	.04447	−0.6690 (0.7781)	0.21 (0.67)	.1670 (.0840)	0.44 / 0.56	0.22 / −0.66	99.32	1.13	1.36 / 3.31	2.5
47 Tires, batteries, parts & accessories	31.89 (8.13)	.00504	−0.2798 (0.0896)	−0.33 (0.18)	.0176 (.0069)	0.80 / 0.88	−1.77 / −1.28	19.15		1.07 / 0.72	1.3
Tires	20.64	.00376	−0.1874	−0.22	.0118				0.65		
Batteries, parts & accessories	11.26	.00128	−0.0923	−0.11	.0058				0.45		
48 Auto repair	14.31 (11.48)	.01381	−0.1423 (0.1100)	0.10 (0.13)	−.0051 (.0052)	0.33 / 0.87	0.39 / −0.54	27.04	1.04	0.88 / −0.13	2.2
49 Gasoline & oil	22.02 (0.98)	.02253		0.99 (0.12)	−.0193 (.0160)	0.85 / 0.94	1.51	65.55	0.69	1.94 / 1.25	3.2
50 Tolls	0.57 (0.03)	.00059		0.07 (0.01)	−.0005 (.0005)	0.96 / 0.98	4.27	1.74	0.70	3.53 / −1.00	5.0
51 Insurance less claims	5.26 (1.63)	.00351	−0.0258 (0.0136)	0.15 (0.03)	−.0064 (.0042)	0.77 / 0.89	1.82 / −0.38	8.64	0.83	2.91 / 4.66	3.7
52 Local transportation	0.73 (0.45)	.00390		−0.96 (0.05)	.0081 (.0073)	0.96 / 0.95	−10.62	9.06	0.77	−6.32 / −2.58	−4.0
Revised	1.64	.00390		−0.60	.0081						
53 Intercity transportation	−10.12 (0.14)	.00926		−0.23 (0.01)	−.0036 (.0023)	0.94 / 0.39	−2.78	8.48	2.28	−0.22 / 2.51	3.8
Revised	−10.12	.00926		−0.13	−.0036						
54 Books & maps	−3.44 (0.29)	.00586		0.02 (0.03)	.0001 (.0047)	0.06 / 0.71	0.37	8.03	1.30	1.40 / −1.36	4.2

	(1)	(2)	(3)	(4)	(5)	(6)	(7)	(8)	(9)	(10)	(11)
55 Magazines & newspapers	3.78 (2.85)	.00709	−0.0448 (0.0272)	−0.17 (0.04)	−.0020 (.0014)	0.98 / 0.67	−1.35 / −0.38	12.78	1.04	−0.20 / 0.68	1.5
56 Nondurable toys	11.81 (0.25)	.00728		0.31 (0.03)	.0051 (.0042)	0.89 / 0.91	2.06	15.27	0.17	1.86 / 0.82	2.1
57 Durable sporting equipment	−9.65 (0.15)	.01144		0.24 (0.02)		0.91 / 0.98	1.86	13.17	1.80	2.59 / 1.18	5.4
58 TV, radio, phonograph, musical instruments	9.61 (2.81)	.00834	−0.0492 (0.0317)	0.36 (0.11)	.0126 (.0067)	0.91 / 0.96	1.53 / −0.18	24.03		2.73 / 2.40	2.9
Radio, TV, & phonographs	10.50	.00694	−0.0458	0.34	.0117				0.70		
Musical instruments	−0.88	.00140	−0.0034	0.05	.0008				1.87		
59 TV & radio repair	4.77 (0.46)	.00148	−0.0263 (0.0044)	0.17 (0.01)	−.0015 (.0004)	0.99 / 1.00	3.38 / −0.56	5.08	(0.60)	2.83 / −1.39	3.7
60 Flowers & seeds	0.55 (0.64)	.00395	−0.0264 (0.0069)	0.03 (0.01)	−.0004 (.0014)	0.92 / 0.98	0.61 / −0.45	5.85	1.30	2.43 / 1.60	3.9
61 Amusements	−5.61 (0.39)	.01138		−0.64 (0.05)		0.91	−3.70	17.40	1.24	−1.71 / −0.96	0.8
Revised	−5.10	.01138		−0.54		0.72					
62 Clubs	−8.07 (0.06)	.00620		−0.15 (0.01)	−.0022 (.0011)	0.97	−4.07	3.99	2.93	0.07 / −0.51	3.4
Revised	−8.07	.00620		−0.22	−.0022	0.02					
63 Other recreation	−4.95 (0.08)	.00605		−0.01 (0.01)		0.13	−0.20	7.20	(1.70)	1.14 / −0.13	4.0
Revised						0.95					
64 Private education	−133.40 (33.54)	.03161	310.30[a] (109.97)	−1.59 (0.16)	−.0816 (.0066)	0.84	−6.71	23.77	2.72	1.47 / −0.77	4.3
Revised	−62.60	.03161	76.02	−0.67		0.95	4.08 / −2.84				
65 Religious & welfare activities	19.26 (19.37)	.02455	−0.4084 (0.1907)	0.14 (0.11)	−.0068 (.0062)	0.43 / 0.94	0.55 / −1.52	26.95	1.85	1.30 / −1.10	4.4

(*Table continued*)

TABLE II-2. PER CAPITA CONSUMPTION FORECASTING EQUATIONS (continued)

Item	Constant a	Income Coefficient b_1	Price or Demographic Coefficient b_2	Time Coefficient b_3	Change of Income Coefficient b_4	R^2	Time Fraction and Price Elasticity	1963 Spending Per Capita	Income Elasticities		Forecast Growth Rate (percent per year)
									Consumer Survey	Time Series	
66 Foreign travel by U.S. residents	−15.99 (0.12)	.01491		0.17 (0.01)		0.88 0.99	1.20	14.22	2.30	3.06 −0.12	5.5
67 Govt. personnel foreign spending	7.97										0.0
68 Cash remittances	0.75										0.0
69 Foreign spending in U.S.	−5.54										0.0

a Coefficient of fraction of population age 5–21.

where n is the elasticity, y is initial income, c is initial consumption of some item, Δy is change in income, and Δc is the resulting change in consumption. Elasticities have several advantages over the linear coefficient $b = \Delta c / \Delta y$ in equation (1). Most important perhaps is that elasticities are readily understood subjectively and can be easily compared. For example, one is apt to have an income elasticity for food less than 1.0, possibly about 0.5, while for books it may run about 1.8. The reader can make judgments of his own elasticities for food, books and other items. Asked directly what his b_1 is for food or books, one would probably have to figure first how much was spent on them, c, his income, y, and then apply his elasticity estimate to calculate $b_1 = n(c/y)$. It is natural to call items with elasticities less than 1.0 necessities, while those with elasticities over 1.0 rank as luxuries. Such a classification cannot be made on the basis of b_1. Elasticities have the further advantage that they are dimensionless; that is, they are independent of the units of measurement. An elasticity for food is the same whether consumption is measured per year and income per month or consumption is measured per week and income per year. Such changes of units *do* change b_1. The elasticity of a family for food is the same whether one is speaking of its total consumption and per capita income or its total income and per capita consumption. Finally, commodity groups with slightly different definitions may be safely assumed to have the same elasticities; the elasticity for "major appliances, including hot water heaters," is surely very close to that for "major appliances, excluding hot water heaters." We shall have to rely on this property when it is impossible to match survey and time-series categories exactly.

To calculate an income elasticity from data such as Table II-1 contains, we have posed the following question: If the total consumption expenditure of all households increased 1 percent and if they all used this additional income to move as far as possible toward the consumption pattern of households of the same size in the next higher income group, by what percent would the spending on each item increase? The question, it must be admitted, can be made completely clear only by working through the answer. Two points must be noted now, however. First, because income is correlated with family size and expenditure patterns are very much affected by the latter, we have been careful to strain out the influences of size to find out what happens when every household's income goes up, while its size remains constant. Secondly, we ask how the *pattern* of consumption changes when *total consumption,* not income, rises 1 percent. The reasons for choosing total consumption follow our answer to the question.

We present this answer in a formula which will then be explained step by step. The following notation is necessary:

C_{si} = average consumption of the item by households of s persons in income category i. (The six income categories are shown in Table II–1; the value of 5 for s indicates households of five or more persons.)

N_{si} = number of households in the si (size-income) group in the population.

Y_{si} = average total expenditures of households in the si (size-income) group.

$S_{si} = (C_{s,i+1} - C_{s,i}) / (Y_{s,i+1} - Y_{s,i})$, for i = 1 , . . . , 5.

$S_{s6} = S_{s5}$.

$$A = \sum_{s=2}^{5} \sum_{i=1}^{6} N_{si} S_{si} Y_{si}$$

$$B = \sum_{s=2}^{5} \sum_{i=1}^{6} C_{si} N_{si}$$

The formula we propose for the elasticity, n, is then,

$$(3) \qquad n = \frac{A}{B} = \frac{\sum_{s=2}^{5} \sum_{i=1}^{6} N_{si} S_{si} Y_{si}}{\sum_{s=1}^{5} \sum_{i=1}^{6} N_{si} C_{si}}$$

Its source is a set of graphs such as Figure II–2. On the vertical axis of Figure II–2 is measured the expenditure of two-person households for furniture; on the horizontal axis, total consumption expenditure of the households. At the points $P_1, \ldots, P_6$, the average furniture expenditure of two-person households in an income group is plotted against the average total consumption for the group. The length of the horizontal line, $P_i Q_i$, extending to the right of each point P_i is equal to 10 percent of total consumption at P_i. Our basic assumption is that if households formerly at P_i are allowed to increase their total consumption by $P_i Q_i$, they will increase their expenditures on furniture by $Q_i R_i$, R_i being on the line between P_i and P_{i+1} and directly above Q_i. Multiplying $Q_i R_i$ by N_{2i}, the number of (two-person) families originally at P_i, and summing over all income groups, we find how much the furniture purchases of all two-person families will increase when the total consumption of each increases 10 percent. Note that the highest income group, number 6, moves further to the right along the line determined by P_5 and P_6. Performing similar calculations for the larger-sized households and summing the total increases for households of all sizes gives the increase in furniture spending when everyone's total consumption rises 10 percent. This quantity is exactly 10 percent of A in equation (3), for S_{si} is the slope of the line from P_i to P_{i+1} on the graph for s-person families; $0.10Y_{si} = P_iQ_i$, and therefore $0.10Y_{si}S_{si} = Q_iR_i$, the increase in spend-

FIG. II-2. Expenditures of Two-Person Urban Households on Furniture

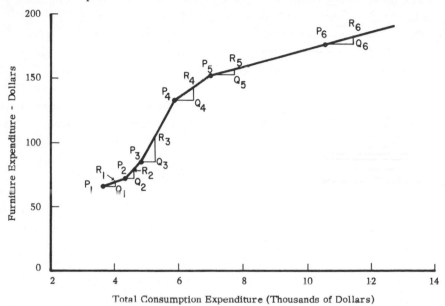

Total Consumption Expenditure (Thousands of Dollars)

SOURCE: Table II-1.

ing per family in group si. We then just multiply this amount by N_{si} and sum over all income and size groups. One percent of A would be the amount furniture purchases increase when total consumption increases 1 percent. Therefore, by equation (2),

(4)
$$n = \frac{\dfrac{.01A}{B}}{\dfrac{.01y}{y}} = \frac{A}{B},$$

and equation (3) is thereby justified.

As we remarked, "total consumption expenditure" has been substituted for "after-tax income" in the calculation of n. For families in the $3,000 to $4,000 income bracket, the two are almost identical;

but across households, income rises faster than consumption so that, in the highest income group, consumption is only about two-thirds of after-tax income, the other third going into savings. Historically, however, as everyone's income goes up, total consumption rises proportionally. Households with $8,000 incomes will definitely spend more of it in 1975 than did families with that income in 1961. The several reasons which have been advanced for this phenomenon need not detain us; its existence, however, warns us to ask of our survey data only how the *pattern* of spending shifts, not how total spending changes as income increases. In the time-series study, however, we shall use these elasticities with disposable income on the (correct) assumption that, over time, spending rises proportionally with disposable income. True "income" elasticities from the survey are decidedly smaller than the "total expenditure" ones, and their use therefore would contradict the historically valid proposition that consumption and income increase in the same proportion. The expression "total consumption expenditure elasticity" is, however, cumbersome, and we shall henceforth say in its place simply "income elasticity."

The elasticities calculated by formula (3) are shown without parentheses in the "income elasticities, consumer survey" column of Table II–2. Those in parentheses were assigned on the basis of judgment without specific calculation. The published survey data contain no detail on food, but this cut of consumer spending, fortunately, has already been thoroughly studied. An analysis of the Department of Agriculture's 1955 food use survey[5] and a summary of other work in the field[6] were consulted in assigning elasticities to the food items.

The elasticities paint an unmistakable portrait of the American consumer. For him, it seems, television (n = .39) and tobacco (n = .35) are more necessary than meat (n = .50), and, indeed, more than a radio (n = .85). A phonograph (n = 1.32) is a luxury, but not so great a one as a musical instrument (n = 1.87). The greatest luxuries are domestic service (n = 2.69), education (n = 2.72), clubs (n = 2.93), and intercity travel (n = 2.28). It would seem that the ancient Roman was well supplied in luxuries but lacked most necessities. Automobiles (n = 1.13) just barely rank as luxuries, but the oil and

5 G. R. Rockwell, *Income and Household Size: Their Effects on Food Consumption,* USPA Marketing Research Report, No. 340, 1959.

6 G. E. Brandow, *Interrelations among Demands for Farm Products,* Bulletin 680, Pennsylvania Agricultural Experiment Station, 1961.

gasoline elasticity ($n = .69$) reveals that the necessity of driving them is no luxury. Shoes are more necessary for men ($n = .64$) than for women ($n = .90$); watches and jewelry are quite luxurious for women ($n = 1.58$), but not for men ($n = .90$). A pleasant way to get acquainted with these elasticities and with the consumer categories is to cover the elasticity column in Table II–2 and try to guess its entries.[7]

For "housing," the survey data gave $n = .75$; we have increased this value to 1.00 because, in the time-series data, most of this item is space-rental value of owner-occupied houses, whereas the survey shows only out-of-pocket charges, e.g., mortgage payments. The value of n was increased on the notion that value would probably prove more elastic than out-of-pocket charges.

ANALYSIS OF TIME SERIES

From the income elasticity, n, which we have found for a category of the time-series data, we calculate the income coefficient, b_1, for equation (1) by

$$b_1 = \Delta c / \Delta y = n \, c \, (1961) / y \, (1961).$$

The 1961 values of income (y) and the consumption of the category (c) are used because the survey data relate to this year. (It would have been correct to use the average of 1961 and 1960, but the differences would be slight.) These values of b_1 appear in the "income coefficient" column of Table II–2.

Using this value of b_1, we define

$$z_t - c_t - b_1 y_t$$

and then regress z_t on t, p_t, Δy_t, thus

(5) $$z_t = a + b_2 p_t + b_3 t + b_4 \Delta y_t.$$

This equation was fitted to data for the years 1950 to 1963; the period 1947 to 1949 was initially included, but postwar adjustments in many categories made these years more nuisance than help. The constant and the price, time, and income change coefficients of Table II–2 are the coefficients from this regression; their standard errors are beneath them in parentheses. The price variable was retained only if its coefficient was negative and at least as large as its standard error. If the price variable was dropped, the Δy variable was retained only

---

[7] Elasticities for television, radio, phonograph, shoes for men and women, and watches and jewelry for men and women are not shown separately in Table II–2.

if its coefficient was greater than its standard error. Inclusion or exclusion of this variable generally had little effect on the time and price coefficients; it therefore seemed permissible to leave it in all equations using the price variable and thus save the trouble of estimating an equation without it.

To make the price and time coefficients easier to assess, the "time fraction and price elasticity" column of Table II–2 shows the time coefficient, b_3, as a percent of 1963 spending on the category and, beneath it, the price elasticity of demand. The time fraction is the percentage (of the 1963 level) by which spending on the category would change each year if income and price remained constant; the price elasticity, of course, is the percentage by which spending would increase if price increased 1 percent (again calculated at 1963 levels of price and spending).

In the R^2 column of Table II–2, two numbers are found for each category. The first is the usual R^2 for the regression actually performed; it indicates the fraction of the variance of z explained by p, t, and Δy. The second R^2 is the fraction of the variance of c which p, t, y and Δy explain when the values of a, $b_1, \ldots, b_4$ shown are used as their coefficients. It indicates how much better the entire equation predicts consumption than would the assumption that consumption remained constant. Sometimes one R^2 is higher, sometimes the other. If the time trend and the income effect offset one another, so that z_t has more trend than c_t, the first is usually larger. If the trend is up or is small relative to the income effect, the second is apt to be higher.

Some of the consumer categories group together products for which the survey data showed decidedly different elasticities, e.g., television (n = .39), radio (n = .85), and musical instruments (n = 1.87) make up a single category. If, as in this case, the items are made by different industries (communications equipment and miscellaneous manufacturing respectively), we used the additional information to make up equations for the parts having the same time fraction and price elasticity as the aggregate, but with appropriate income elasticities. First, we split the aggregate into its parts by using the 1958 proportions—the only ones we have. Then, using the income elasticities, we calculated income coefficients for each part by equation (4), summed them, used the total as b_1 to calculate z, and then performed the regression (5). The coefficients of the equations for the components were obtained by splitting up the aggregate equation in the 1958 proportions, replacing the resulting "proportional" income coefficients by using the income coefficients already calculated, and adjusting the constant term so that the "predicted" values of the components in 1961 are in the 1958 proportions but sum to the 1961 predicted value.[8] These component equations appear below the standard errors of the category equation.

For several categories, the estimated time trend caused the predicted values to diverge steadily from observed ones during the last five or six years. For forecasting, these time coefficients were altered to eliminate this divergence, and the constant terms were then adjusted to bring the modified equation through the 1963 observation. In Table II–2, the revised equation is shown below the estimated one. The revisions will be discussed in The Forecasts section, below.

It proved unnecessary to force the sum of the forecasts of all of the categories to equal a constant proportion of the disposable income forecast; for quite without any scheme to *insure* such equality, the forecasts gave it. More precisely, the ratio of the sum of components to disposable income rose four-tenths of 1 percent over twelve years, a trivial discrepancy. The forecasts are therefore mutually consistent with respect to the consumer's budget restraint. Considerable room remains for tightening the consistency of one category with closely related ones: e.g., automobiles with debt and gasoline, furniture with housing, appliances with electricity, and so on. There is no shortage of problems for further work.

[8] In symbols, let c be the spending on the category; r, the number of components in the category; w^i, the 1958 weight of the ith component; and n^i, its elasticity.

Then

$$\sum_{i=1}^{r} w^i = 1,$$

and we define

$$b_i^i = n^i w^i c (1961) / y (1961), \quad i = 1, 2 \ldots, r$$

$$b_1 = \sum_{i=1}^{r} b_1^i$$

and

$$z = c - b_1 y.$$

Let a, b_2, b_3, b_4 be the coefficients of regression equation (5); then the coefficients of equations for the components are:

$$b_j^i = w^i b_j, i = 1, \ldots, r; j = 2, 3, 4.$$

and

$$a^i = w^i a + (w^i b_1 - b_1^i) y (1961).$$

MIXING TIME SERIES AND SURVEYS

Applying consumer survey elasticities *alone* to predict the time series of spending on particular items almost never forecasts satisfactorily. This fact has naturally raised doubts about any crossing of the two sources of data. At their simplest level, such doubts are allayed by our explicit inclusion of a trend term; we do not expect purchases to expand as income alone would make them but explicitly recognize other factors which we want to separate from income. Although the survey income elasticities, as we have calculated them, correspond rather closely to the concept of the "pure" income coefficient described in the first section, The Problem, a subtler objection to their use remains. Families in a particular income group have not necessarily grown accustomed to that income nor do they necessarily expect it to continue. The expenditure patterns of families with higher- or lower-than-usual incomes may differ systematically from those of families accustomed to their incomes. A truly "pure" income elasticity should relate to families at their accustomed income and expenditure; but since the lower-than-usual families will tend to fall in the lower income groups and the higher-than-usual families in the upper groups, our elasticities may possibly be distorted by families which are out of their usual places. The use of elasticities with respect to total consumption rather than income reduces but does not eliminate this problem. For example, the automobile share of spending by a family with an unusually high income and spending \$7,000 a year may differ from that for families spending \$7,000 at their accustomed income. Not much is known about how important this problem may be. It was comforting to see that one recent study of the durable purchases by households for which budgets are available in three consecutive years found that "The coefficient of past income change $[y_t - y_{t-1}]$ does not appear statistically significant in any of the regressions."[9] It was, to be more specific, positive in all eight regressions and larger than its standard error in half of them, but it was much smaller than the income coefficient itself.

Nevertheless, because of this problem, we did not resort to mixing time-series and survey data until convinced of the impossibility of segregating income effects from trends using only the time-series data. Such a separation was attempted by regressing consumption on in-

[9] Lewis Schipper, *Consumer Discretionary Behavior*, Amsterdam, North-Holland, 1964, p. 33.

come and time without any prior specification of the income coefficient. The income elasticities found appear in the next-to-last column of Table II–2 where there are two entries for each category. The first is the elasticity using only income; the second is the income elasticity using both income and time. Though the coefficients were frequently "significant" by the usual statistical test, the results are certainly largely nonsense. The "income-alone" elasticity is usually the more sensible of the two, but it is the second erratic elasticity which supposedly represents the "pure" income effect. Any relation between these elasticities and those in the neighboring "consumer survey" column can hardly be said to be striking. Indeed, because we have here an independent estimate of the income elasticity, comparing the numbers in these two columns beautifully illustrates the danger of relying on time-series regression to separate the effects of variables so closely collinear.[10]

THE FORECASTS

The *per capita* forecasts for all of the consumer categories appear in the last column of Table II–2, where they are shown as growth rates in percent per year. The rates shown are averages over the period 1963–1975. When surveying these forecasts, a good standard of comparison to remember is that disposable income, and therefore the average of these forecasts, is projected to grow 2.7 percent per year instead of the 1.7 percent per year which it grew between 1950 and 1963, or the 0.7 percent per year it averaged during the 1956–1963 period.

The history and forecasts of some of the large or noteworthy categories are shown in Figure II–3. The following discussion of each of these twenty-two items, with which we conclude our study of consumption, should impart some feeling for how the consumption

10 Lester Taylor and Hendrick Houthakker greatly facilitated the entire development of this model and particularly influenced the work on consumption by graciously making available their then-unpublished consumption equations. (H. S. Houthakker and Lester D. Taylor, *Consumer Demand in the United States 1929–1970*. Analyses and Projections, Cambridge, Mass., Harvard University Press, 1966.) They were used in many trial runs of the forecasting model and were replaced only after the consumer survey data became available. Many of their equations used, in addition to income, a lagged value of the dependent variable, c_{t-1}, to predict c_t. For forecasting one or two years ahead, these equations appear excellent, for the lagged value is just about the perfect trend variable. On the other hand, including it as an explanatory variable, like including time, leaves shaky income coefficients; and in long-run forecasting, the income coefficients dominate the projection. When the survey data appeared, therefore, we decided to develop a new equation using it.

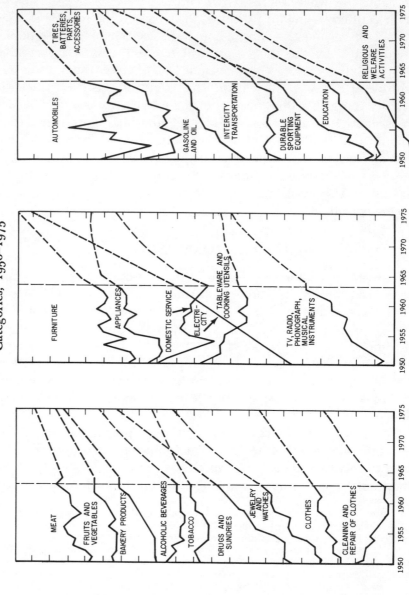

FIG. II-3. History and Forecasts of Per Capita Consumption—Selected Categories, 1950–1975

Vertical Scale: 1 Division = 10% of 1963 Value. For each series, 1963 Value = 100%

48

equations work as well as for the nature of the growth they forecast.

The equation for meat yielded one of the most decided price coefficients; although the elasticity comes out at only —0.49, the price variable explains almost singlehandedly the bump in the meat consumption curve between 1951 and 1958. In spite of a rather liberal allowance for income effects, the trend to frozen fruits and vegetables has led to a slight upward time trend in spending on all fruits and vegetables. The equation in Table II–2 relates to all fruits and vegetables—frozen, canned, dried, and fresh; but because the farm and manufacturing shares of fresh and processed produce are quite different, the fresh component was also forecast separately to continue its decline at the recent rate of 1.3 percent per year. The demand for processed produce is then found as the difference between the total and the fresh component. Most of the growth in bakery product consumption is probably also traceable to new frozen or brown-and-serve products; its low income elasticity, 0.4, is therefore offset by a strong upward trend of 1.88 percent per year. Most of the growth of bakery products, therefore, comes from trend; so it does not accelerate in the future.

In the equations for alcoholic beverages and tobacco, we used, in place of the relative price variable, the percentage of the population over 18. Similarly, for private education, we used the percentage of the population of school age, 5–21, which proved more significant than the percentage in the college ages, 17–21. These variables proved to be very significant; in fact, they took on such large coefficients that as the adult proportion of the population increases and the school-aged proportion stabilizes, these equations would forecast us to become a nation of ignorant, smoky topers. Fortunately, we do not stand helpless before the least-squares oracle but can make an independent judgment of the values of these coefficients, for it seems reasonable to assume that alcohol consumption *per adult* is a function of *per capita* income and time. Consumption *per capita* is then found by multiplying this function by the ratio of adults to total population. A 1 percent increase in this ratio will therefore lead, other things being equal, to a 1 percent increase in spending *per capita*. We have fixed the coefficient of the ratio so that this relation will hold exactly for 1963; we then re-estimated the coefficient of t. These revised equations for alcoholic beverages (item 1), tobacco (item 10), and private education (item 64) appear in Table II–2. Although there is a slight trend to sobriety among adults (0.9 percent per year less spending on alcohol), the accelerated growth in income, the relatively high income elasticity of drink (1.37), and the rise in the drinking age population will combine to uncork a liberal flow of spending on beverages. Because of its low income elasticity (0.35), tobacco sales will rise much more moderately, while private education, with a high income elasticity (2.72), will rise sharply. The negative time trend in the private education equation reflects, no doubt, the rising share of state schools in higher education. It may also be to some extent the product of the deflation procedure; a rise in *average* faculty salaries may mean that more "teaching" is being bought, but the deflation procedure interprets it to mean merely that the cost of schooling has gone up.

Expenditures on drugs and sundries, which are quite income inelastic ($n = 0.54$), continue steadily upward on the strength of a trend, stemming no doubt from new products, which amounts to nearly 3 percent per year. The jewelry and watch industry has owed much of its sales expansion in the last fifteen years to a relative decline in its prices. This decline appears to have slackened since 1960 and is projected to continue at this new, reduced rate. If it resumes the rapid price decline of the 1950s, this industry will convert its high income elasticity into a real boom instead of the steady growth shown in Figure II–3. The rise in clothing prices, on the other hand, is expected to continue at no more than its historical rate; the accelerated growth of income should counteract the influence of changes in style of living and customs and pick up the growth of the garment industry. Cleaning and laundry expenditures are expected to turn up after a long decline. Our suspicion that the new fibers may have caused much of this decline but that their full effect should be manifest by now seems to be confirmed by the rise in these expenditures after 1960. The regression line fitted to the 1950–1963 data continued to plunge downward during this period; so we reduced the negative time coefficient from 3.7 to 2.7 percent per year in order to make the equation fit these recent years. With this reduced trend and its high income elasticity, 1.61, the laundry and cleaning business should have a bright future compared to its past.

For furniture, which has an income elasticity almost exactly 1.0, the effects of declining prices offset the "passage-of-time" decline and leave the rise in income free to reproduce here exactly its own growth rate, 2.7 percent per year. The high price elasticity of appliances, -1.04, made sales rise in response to the drastic price cuts of the 1950s. Since 1960, the price decline has been only moderate and is projected at this new rate. The influence of the Δy term will quickly move appliance sales several percent points above the 1963 level; but in the long run, the low income elasticity (0.51) and the heavy hand of increasingly saturated markets will hold their growth to about 1 percent per year. Because saturation effects for refrigerators are certainly different from those for dishwashers, a disaggregation of this category would improve the reliability of the forecast.

Perhaps the conjugate of the low appliance forecast is the high domestic service forecast. In spite of the downward pull of social change, which is expected to continue at over 5.5 percent per year, the upward push of income, with an elasticity of 2.69, is overpowering. This forecast and a similar one for clubs seem, frankly, implausible. Because the amounts concerned are not large and do not directly affect the principal industries of the model, they have been left as they are so that, looking back several years hence, we can perhaps see how the method worked in an extreme case.

Electricity, another purchasable source of household energy, continues its upward sweep. The consumer survey elasticities for electricity and gas came out at 0.57 and 0.44 respectively. Because it may take a household years to acquire the house, appliances, and habits necessary to bring its utility bill up to the equilibrium level, it was felt that these elasticities were probably on the low side, and they were revised upward to the 1.00 and 0.75 shown in Table II–2. Both of these utilities still owe most of their growth—some 3 percent per year—to trend factors, partly, perhaps, to the spread of air conditioning, partly to the substitution of gas and electricity for oil and coal in home heating.

Postwar increases in income have been too weak to drive spending on china, glassware, and utensils against the tide of informality rising about our style of living. The future's more rapid growth of income should succeed slightly better, especially on the high-elasticity items, china and silverware, which should grow at a rate of about 2 percent per year. The low income elasticities of television and radio hold the total of the "TV, radio, phonograph, and musical instruments" category to its historical trend, but the musical instrument part marches forward with an allegro vivace tempo of 5 percent per year.

Automobile purchases grow at about the same rate as income from the 1963 level. The 1964 purchases fell about on trend, while 1965 may be running a little ahead of forecast; but this series will no doubt remain volatile, with purchases in good years 10 percent or more above the trend and for bad years equally far below it. Tires and batteries have little income elasticity and have depended for their growth on price cuts. The rate of decline in prices has slackened since 1960 and is projected at this lower rate. Battery purchases, incidentally, decline between the $10,000–$15,000 income families and the over $15,000 families; the original equipment on a new car lasts, after all, from one to three years. As the automobile stock accumulates, gasoline and oil expenditures mount up. In contrast to the rather sedate projection of the automobile categories, the forecast for public intercity transportation takes off sharply. The drag of declining bus and train travel is about spent, and the luxury of airplane travel begins to dominate the sector. A desire for travel seems common to people of all income levels; and it seems safe to expect them to indulge it as prosperity permits.

Lest the moderate automobile forecast lead one to suppose that Americans are losing their taste for the fast and flashy, the "durable sporting equipment" forecast shows them filling the country with motorcycles, scooters, bicycles, boats, outboard motors, guns, airplanes, tents, and baseball gloves. This category roars off at such a rate, 5.4 percent per year, because it has not only a high income elasticity, 1.80, but also a shift-of-taste trend of nearly 2 percent per year.

We can anticipate a worthy growth of 4.4 percent a year for religious and welfare activities, for not only do the rich contribute proportionally more than the poor—the elasticity is 1.85—but changes in our outlook or ideals have contributed over 0.5 percent per year to the growth of this category. The decided price elasticity for this item probably only indicates that it is the dollar volume of contributions rather than the quantity of services which matters to the contributor; were it not for the expanding economy, the quantity of services would decrease as the cost of services goes up. The cost went up about 6 percent between 1950 and 1956; it has since remained constant, and is projected as constant in the future.

Do these forecasts paint a harsh or cynical portrait of the American consumer? They do, to be sure, reveal a few foibles, such as his absolute dependence on television and tobacco and his proclivity for going into debt. They show a bit of weakness in his propensity to spend more money on alcoholic beverages—better wines, perhaps —and in his increasing reliance on drugs—or is he just keeping healthier? But in the main, the forecasts show that he will use prosperity to eat and dress a little better, furnish a larger house better, educate his children better, and buy more, perhaps even better, books to read. He will travel more in this country and, particularly, abroad, but he will not encumber the nation with an exorbitant number of automobiles. Rather, he will increasingly use sporting goods to enhance his enjoyment of his leisure. Finally, in his affluence, he will not forget his neighbor.

III

Capital Investment

American business spent $31 billion on producers' durable equipment in 1963. Seven years earlier, spending ran at almost the same level in constant dollars. Our forecasts for 1975 show this spending should reach about $48 billion, averaging 3.6 percent per year growth. This swing from stagnation to growth in capital investment should put new life into a number of slow-growing equipment sectors. Indeed, perhaps the most striking result of the forecast is the accelerated growth of such sectors as engines and turbines, construction machinery, material-handling equipment, machine tools, pumps and compressors, and other machinery sectors. Before basing decisions on the forecasts for these industries, it is, therefore, particularly important to understand what has, and what has not, gone into the analysis of future capital requirements.

The growth of construction is also expected to accelerate. Between 1956 and 1963, construction averaged 2 percent per year growth; the forecast to 1975 calls for a growth of 4 percent annually from 1963. This acceleration can be seen in the demand for the major building materials.

The first section of this chapter explains the theory behind the equation used to calculate equipment spending by each industry. The second section describes the data and gives the results of fitting the equations. The third section presents the forecasts of equipment spending under several alternative assumptions. The fourth section describes the equations used in forecasting construction spending and presents the construction forecasts. A brief note on inventory requirements concludes the chapter.

To hold this material in proper perspective, it must be remembered that most consumer goods sectors are little affected by capital investment. Should equipment investment rise between 1963 and

1975 by only $9 billion (half as much as forecast), consumption in 1975 would have to be increased by less than 2 percent to maintain the same level of employment. To permit this rise in consumption, personal taxes would have to be approximately $9 billion less than they should be in the case of the capital-spending forecast. Such a reduction in the consumer tax bill would require a reduction of 10 or 12 percent in the tax rate, or about twice the 1964 cut. Therefore, we may fairly say that the full-employment tax rate is quite sensitive to capital requirements.[1]

Fortunately, we do not have to decide on the 1975 tax rate in 1965, and we can assume that by the time this tax rate does have to be set, we shall have accumulated enough knowledge to set it to give a high level of employment. Our forecasts of consumption sectors can then be thought of as fairly independent of the investment sectors. The sensitivity of full-employment tax policy to capital requirements does, however, point up the need for better data on capital investment for the planning of government tax policy. As we shall see, our present knowledge is spotty and tenuous.

THE THEORY OF THE EQUIPMENT INVESTMENT GENERATION EQUATIONS

We calculate each industry's spending for each type of capital goods in two steps. First, we determine the industry's total expenditure for producers' durable equipment (exclusive of construction); then, as the second step, we divide this total among the various types of equipment. In this section and the next, we are concerned with the first step; the third section deals with the second step.

For industries for which sufficiently long time series on investment spending were available, we tried to disentangle the effects on investment of replacement requirements, expansion requirements, and changes in the productivity of capital.[2] It soon became apparent that this separation could not be done by applying the usual sort of regression equation to this historical data alone. It was necessary to supplement the historical data by an assumed length of life for the equipment. The capital stock in a given year could then be com-

[1] Of course, this sensitivity is reduced by any tendency of corporations to adjust dividends to investment requirements; but such a tendency is not easily detected.

[2] The valuable new work by Bert Hickman, *Investment Demand and U.S. Economic Growth*, Washington, D.C., Brookings Institution, 1965, describes an alternative method of using this sort of data.

puted by converting the investments of previous years to their value in constant dollars and then accumulating the amounts which, according to the life-span estimate, would still be in use in that year. Dividing this stock by output or, better, by capacity output should give the capital-output ratio to be used for determining investment required for expansion. Replacement demands should follow from the rate at which old machines were being retired.

Two refinements were introduced into this scheme: One provided for trends in the output-capital ratios, and the other allowed for gradual rather than precipitant retirement of the capital purchased in a year. An exponential trend was allowed in the expansion output-capital ratio, the output made possible by one dollar of *new* investment. In symbols, the yearly output which can be produced by one (constant) dollar's worth of new capital installed in year t is assumed to be

$$(1) \qquad\qquad k\,(t) = k_0\,(1 + r)^t,$$

where k_0 is the ratio in year o, some arbitrary initial year, and r is the annual rate of change of the ratio. The capital is assumed to provide the same amount of output as long as it remains in service. That is, the productivity of *new* capital may increase—1965 investments may yield more output per dollar than did 1964 investment—but once the investment has been made, it does not become more productive. Technical change of this sort is often said to be "embodied" in the capital equipment.

Lest the reader feel letdown at the end of our discussion, we must admit at the outset that we were unable to produce reliable estimates of r. Consequently, no trends in output-capital ratios have been extended into the future. The effort to estimate r and the nature of the problems encountered, however, are not without interest.

To understand the economic meaning of r, we must consider how improved design of equipment affects the effective price of capital relative to output, how this price affects the amount of capital desired per unit of output, and the extent to which r is affected by the deflator used for converting capital expenditures from current to constant dollars. We may safely assume that, as new-model machines with improved designs make older ones obsolete, the effective price of capital is declining, or to say the same thing differently, the marginal product of a dollar's worth of machinery is increasing. This decline in the effective price will certainly lead to increased mechanization, but whether it brings increased capital expenditure is another question. The answer depends, of course, upon whether the increase in use is proportionally greater or proportionally less than the decrease in the price of a unit of productive capacity. If we could measure the productive value of capital, counting machines of different years according to their marginal products, we could conceive of a demand curve for "productive capital per unit of output" as a function of its price. If this demand curve has elasticity, n, and the price of constant productivity capital falls at an exponential rate, p, then r can be shown to be equal to $-(1 + n)p$.[3] Since p is negative, r is negative when the demand curve is elastic; that is, $n < -1$. Conversely, r is positive for an inelastic curve. Both positive and negative values of r have been found in a range between approximately $+.04$ and $-.04$. As mentioned above, the estimates for r were felt to be unreliable, and the 1963 values of the expansion output-capital ratios were used in the forecasts. This assumption may be interpreted as postulating unitary elastic demand curves for capital in the future. The estimates of the 1963 capital-output ratio might have been different if we had assumed these elasticities to have been zero in the past.

Deflation of expenditures alone does not account for the changing costs of a unit of capital, although the choice of the deflator directly affects the value of r found. If we substituted a deflator which grew 1 percent per year faster than the one actually employed, the resultant value of r would be exactly .01 less than the one found. The choice of deflator, however, was not made to make constant the marginal product of a dollar's worth of investment. Since the ultimate purpose of the investment equations is to generate the sales of these industries, it was hoped that the deflator would put the investments of different years into units requiring approximately the same material inputs on the part of the capital producing industries. The price indexes

---

[3] Letting P be the price of a unit of capital of constant productivity, we assume $P = P_o e^{pt}$. Let C be the quantity of capital used per unit of output, so that $n = P \, (dC) \, / \, C \, (dP)$. Going over to the exponential version of (1), we have $PC = (1/k_0) \, e^{-rt}$, from which it follows that

(a) $$[d \, (PC) \, / \, dt] \, / \, PC = -r$$

But also,

(b) $[d \, (PC) \, / \, dt] \, / \, PC = (CdP + PdC) \, / \, PCdt = (1 + n) \, / \, (Pdt \, / \, dP) = -(1 + n) \, p$

where the second equality is proved by dividing the numerator and denominator of the expression on its left by CdP. Since the left sides of (a) and (b) are identical, their right sides are equal, proving that $r = -(1 + n) \, p$.

used are all based upon the wholesale price index. In it, new, improved models of machines selling for the same price as the old models are apt to be considered identical to their predecessors. No decline in the effective price of capital will be shown. What these indexes do reflect are price changes resulting from increased material or labor costs or from market conditions which allow firms to increase, or force them to cut, their profits. These are precisely the price changes we wish to offset by deflation. The full effect of changes in the productivity of machinery, however, should be found in r.

FIG. III–1. Alternative Replacement Schedules

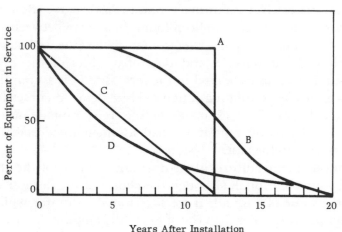

Years After Installation

The second refinement in the scheme for computing the output-capital ratios was that, rather than assuming that all capital invested in a given year would wear out at the same time, we smoothed its retirement over a number of years. Figure III–1 shows various possible assumptions about the percentage of equipment bought in a given year which will remain in service t years later. Curve A shows the simple assumption that the whole stock remains intact for twelve years, whereupon it suddenly falls apart. In Curve B, all of the capital remains in use for five years or so; replacement then begins, and after twelve years, the average life, only half of the equipment remains in service, but some equipment continues to operate for another six or seven years. Curve C shows the accountant's straight-line depreciation, and Curve D shows double-declining balance depreciation, both for assets with an average life of twelve years. Curves of type B were used in this study. This type was chosen over the more conventional

C and D because we needed to know the quantity of capital in use rather than the value of the capital. To illustrate this difference, consider a factory consisting of twelve machines each with the life pattern shown by Curve A (twelve-year life and collapse). The value of this installation will decline approximately according to Curve C. On its eleventh birthday, it will be worth about one-twelfth as much as when new. But if we ask, not how much is it worth—how much one would pay for it—but how many new machines it would take to produce what it is producing, the answer is clearly twelve, not one.[4] It is the second sort of question which we must answer when we ask how much investment will be required to increase output 10 percent. While agreeing, then, that curves C or D are appropriate in approximating the value of an industry's capital, and therefore for accounting purposes, we must choose a curve more like A. Since it seems unlikely that all equipment in an industry would have exactly the same life, curves of the general shape of B were used. The exact form employed was

$$R(\tau) = 1 - \Phi(\tau - 1)$$

where $R(\tau)$ is the fraction of original capacity still in use as its τth year of service begins, and Φ is the cumulative distribution function of a normal distribution with mean equal to the average life of equipment in the industry and having a standard deviation equal to the square root of this mean.[5] Curve B is such a curve. No special significance is attached to this particular form; it was merely a convenient way to find a curve with the general shape shown by B.

The two features of our capital model, the changing output-capital ratio and the smooth retirement pattern, can now be combined to show the capacity resulting from a given investment series, namely:

$$(2) \qquad Q(t) = k_0 \sum_{\tau = 0}^{L} (1 + r)^{(t - \tau)} E(t - \tau)R(\tau),$$

where $E(t)$ is the deflated investment in year t and L is the maximum life of any part of the equipment, i.e., $R(\tau) = 0$, for $\tau > L$. In calculating, $R(\tau)$ was considered zero for values of τ two standard deviations beyond the average life.

Values of k_0 and r were determined by fitting equation (2) to his-

4 This point is made particularly forcefully by Zvi Griliches in "The Demand for a Durable Input: Farm Tractors in the United States, 1921–1957," in A. Harberger (ed.), *The Demand for Durable Goods*, University of Chicago Press, 1960.

5 This, in effect, assumes that the lives of the machines have a Poisson distribution.

torical data on Q and E which will be described in the next section.[6] From these constants and the future growth of output, we can now calculate future investment by the following formula, derived in the footnote.[7]

$$(3) \quad E(t) = \frac{Q(t) - Q(t-1)}{k_0(1+r)^t} + \sum_{\tau=1}^{L+1}(1+r)^{-\tau}E(t-\tau)[R(\tau) - R(\tau-1)].$$

The first term on the right is the expansion investment, the increase in output divided by the output-capital ratio prevailing in year t. The second term is replacement investment. Of what was invested τ years before, $E(t) - \tau$, that fraction which has to be replaced now is $R(\tau) - R(\tau-1)$. But at the present capital-output ratio, the same amount of capacity requires $(1+r)^{-\tau}$ times as much capital investment as it did then. Thus, we may call the second term "replacement at the current capital-output ratio."

To find what investment would be in year t if the capital-output ratio of a year T years earlier prevailed, we multiply the right side of (4) by $(1+r)^T$. As remarked before, the capital-output ratios in the forecasts were set at their 1963 values. We now see that from such investment forecasts, the forecasts with changing capital-output ratios can be calculated immediately. If F(T) is the fixed-ratio investment forecast for the year $1963 + T$, then

$$(4) \quad F_c(T) = (1+r)^{-T} F(T)$$

is the changing-ratio forecast. This calculation, of course, neglects secondary effects from changes in Q(t) caused by the change in r; they are likely to be quite small.

[6] Since (2) is not linear in r, it had to be estimated by approximation. This was done by taking the first two terms of the Taylor series of (2) in r.

$$Q(t) = k_0 \sum_{\tau=0}^{L}(1+r_0)^{(t-\tau)}E(t-\tau)R(\tau) + \Delta r k_0 \sum_{\tau=0}^{L}(t-\tau)(1+r_0)^{(t-\tau-1)}E(t-\tau)R(\tau)$$

Choosing $r_0 = 0$, the values under the summations were calculated; k_0 and $(\Delta r) k_0$ were then estimated as regression coefficients; and from their ratio, r was found. A second iteration, using as r the value of Δr just found, did not change r noticeably.

[7] To derive (3), we begin by taking the first difference of equation (2), and writing

$$(2') \quad Q(t-1) = k_0 \sum_{\tau=0}^{L}(1+r)^{(t-1-\tau)}E(t-1-\tau)R(\tau)$$
$$= k_0 \sum_{\tau=1}^{L+1}(1+r)^{(t-\tau)}E(t-\tau)R(\tau-1).$$

Then, subtracting (2') from (2), we find

$$Q(t) - Q(t-1) = k_0(1+r)^t E(t)R(0) + k_0 \sum_{\tau=1}^{L+1} (1+r)^{(t-\tau)}E(t-\tau)[R(\tau) - R(\tau-1)].$$

Since $R(0) = 1$, solving this equation for E(t), the investment requirements, yields equation (3).

DATA AND ESTIMATES OF CAPITAL-OUTPUT RATIOS

Three types of data are needed to estimate k_0 and r in equation (2): $E(t)$, a series on equipment expenditure by each industry in constant dollars; an estimate of the average life of equipment in the industry; and $Q(t)$, a series on the capacity output of the industry.

Most of the data needed for $E(t)$ comes from the Censuses and Annual Surveys of Manufacturers. For 1939, 1947, and 1949 to 1962, they report equipment spending by each of the twenty major ("two-digit") industries. It is not difficult to fill in the 1948 gap and to extend the series to 1963 by the indexes of total investment, including construction, in these industries. For eleven of the largest spenders, it is possible to extrapolate the 1939 value back to 1921 and up to 1941 by such total-spending series.[8] For the remaining industries, the period from 1925 to 1938 was extrapolated back from 1939 by the estimates for equipment investment in all manufacturing which are published in the national accounts; 1940 and 1941 were estimated by the method used in the World War II years for all industries. For these years, series were prepared on the investment implied for each industry by tax information published by the Internal Revenue Service in *Statistics of Income*. For example, the investment implied for 1945 was found by subtracting the depreciated value of corporate fixed assets in 1944 from the same item in 1945 and adding to the difference the depreciation during the year. The result is correct provided (1) that companies do not move from one industry classification to another during the year and provided further (2) that the assets brought into the industry by proprietors or partners incorporating and the assets lost to the industry through failures are negligible or offsetting. Unfortunately, the first proviso was not met during the war; the results clearly showed that some firms switched into a defense industry during the war and back out again after it. Precise yearly figures, therefore, often could not be obtained, but a general average for the period could be found and distributed over the years in a reasonable pattern. The second proviso, about incorporations and failures, made it impossible to use this method of estimating capital spending for the construction and trade industries

---

[8] These indexes, prepared by Lowell J. Chawner, are in the *Survey of Current Business*, March 1941, December 1941, and May 1942. They cover primary metals, motor vehicles, stone, clay, and glass, food, textiles, paper, lumber, printing, petroleum refining, rubber products, and leather.

on which there are no other spending series. In good years, corporate capital in these industries shoots up as proprietors and partners incorporate; in bad years, it disappears just as rapidly.

Equation (2) could not be estimated separately for each of the 57 manufacturing sectors of the model; these sectors had to be lumped into 22 groups corresponding to the major industries, with primary metals divided between ferrous and non-ferrous, and transport equipment divided between automotive and other. This grouping was necessitated by the change in the industrial classification in 1958. Putting the postwar investment data for years prior to 1958 into the model categories was judged, frankly, more work than it was worth. Besides, the 22 groups match fairly well with the McGraw-Hill capacity indexes, one of the major sources of Q(t). Within each group, we assumed that all the industries required the same capital per dollar of value added.

For the nonmanufacturing industries, investment series came from a variety of sources. Farmers' purchases of equipment are reported by the U.S. Department of Agriculture in *Farm Income Situation*. New Rural Electrification Administration loans were added to investment by investor-owned utilities reported in the Edison Electric Institute's *Bulletin,* and from their total, electric utility construction (from Census Bureau, *Construction Reports*) was subtracted. Communication investment was likewise found by subtracting construction (*Construction Reports*) from the total spending published with the national accounts. Railroad equipment purchases were found in exactly the same way. For nonrail transport, the entire amount shown in the national accounts table was considered equipment. The 1958 and 1954 Censuses of Mineral Industries report equipment bought for petroleum extraction. These amounts were extrapolated up to 1963 and back to 1946 with the index of shipments of oil field machinery.

All these series are in current dollars. They were converted to constant 1958 dollars by a variety of deflators. In manufacturing, the implicit deflator for equipment in the Capital in Manufacturing table of the national accounts was used. Wholesale price indexes for motor vehicles and agricultural equipment were used to deflate farm investment; electrical equipment price indexes deflated electric utility and communication investment. The oil field machinery index was used on petroleum extraction; and the motor vehicle index, on transportation other than rail.

To calculate replacements to 1975, it was necessary to extend the investment series into the future. Initially, investment was assumed to rise 3 percent per year from its 1963 level. After one set of forecasts was made, they replaced this assumption for all the manufacturing industries.

Railroad investment presented special problems for the capital-output-ratio approach to investment. In the end, it was merely projected at a constant $800 million per year, about its present level.

The average length of life of equipment in each industry comes from the Treasury Department's *Depreciation Guidelines.* These lives explicitly take account of obsolescence: that is, of the fact that a machine may often be replaced, not because it is worn out, but only because new machines are so much more efficient that it is uneconomical to employ labor on the old one. The guideline lives were based on a survey of actual replacement practice; and while they are not the last word in accuracy, industry seems to have greeted them as generally realistic. They should give reasonable estimates of capital in use.

The third and last set of data required was the series on capacity output, $Q(t)$. In all cases, we assumed that 1963 output was capacity output. The high level of corporate capital appropriation in that year suggests that this assumption will not lead us astray in many industries. Two different capacity indexes were used to find the value of $Q(t)$ in earlier years, relative to 1963. The first was a "peak-output" series derived from output by connecting adjacent peaks with straight lines. When several model sectors had to be combined for determining their capital demand, value-added weights were used in combining their output indexes. These peak-output series were available for every sector for which we had a time series on capital spending. The second source of $Q(t)$ was available for only some of these. This source, the McGraw-Hill index of manufacturing capacity, is made from a questionnaire circulated once a year by the McGraw-Hill Department of Economics. It asks companies by what percentage their capacity has increased over the previous year. Chaining these percentages together year after year produces the published figures. The definition of capacity is left to the respondent, but companies in the same industry seem to follow the same convention. Since the companies in the sample tend to be large ones, the indexes are not always representative of the entire industry, especially not of the industries with many small firms. The McGraw-Hill indexes do, however, reflect a direct statement by business of how much capacity has increased. It, therefore, seemed desirable to try both indexes for the fourteen industries for which the McGraw-Hill indexes are available.

The capital stocks, replacements, and values of r resulting from fitting equation (2) to these data are displayed in Table III–1. The values of r from the two capacity series are found in the first two columns. The asterisk in column (1) or (2) indicates which value of r was used in calculating the values shown in columns (4)–(7) and in the forecasts. Column (3) shows the 1963 capital stock in 1958 dollars,

$$\sum_{\tau=0}^{L} E(1963 - \tau)R(\tau).$$

An asterisk in column (3) indicates that both estimates of r were rejected as unreliable and a value of zero used in place of either. Column (4) shows the cost, in 1958 dollars, of replacing this capacity at the 1963 capital-output ratio, that is

$$\sum_{\tau=0}^{L} (1 + r)^{-\tau} E(1963 - \tau) R(\tau).$$

The replacements in 1963, 1970, and 1975, at this same 1963 capital-output ratio, are shown in columns (5)–(7). The 1962 expenditures of these industries are shown in column (8) for comparison.

For each industry, we picked the capacity index yielding the value of r closest to zero. Several considerations prompted this conservative choice. In the first place, systematic errors in the fit of equation (2) usually accompanied large values of r. Large negative values of r caused the capacity calculated on the right side of the equation to rise much less rapidly than the capacity series, Q(t), in the last three or four years of the fitting period. This tendency indicated that, though these values of r were useful in adjusting the historical series, they were not to be trusted for forecasting the future. Small values of r were associated with uniform fits of equation (2), and therefore seemed preferable. Secondly, with demand elasticities for capital, n, in a reasonable range—say, −0.5 to −1.5—absolute values of r greater than 0.02 imply productivity increases of over 4 percent per year, which, in comparison with labor productivity, look implausibly high. Thirdly, for reasons set out below, constant capital-output ratios were used in the forecasts; it seems, therefore, desirable for these ratios to be such that slow change in them is sufficient to explain past history. Lastly—the real reason—equations with big values of r produced patently improbable projections. Of course, where the values of r are close together, the choice between them matters little.

[columns (3)–(7) in millions of 1958 dollars; column (8) in millions of current dollars of 1962]

Industry	Peak Output r (1)	McGraw-Hill r (2)	Capital Stock 1963 (3)	Replacement Cost at 1963 Ratio (4)	Replacements 1963 (5)	Replacements 1970 (6)	1975 (7)	Expenditure 1962 (8)
Agriculture	.025*		30,083	26,403	2,510	2,655	3,295	3,060
Petroleum mining	.026*		5,676	5,198	780	850	1,108	820
Other mining	Time-series data not available							600
Food products	—.006*	.011	8,671	9,067	644	785	1,040	890
Tobacco	—.062		44?		22	27	32	41
Textiles	.030*	.032	3,715	3,023	222	217	278	306
Apparel	.023*		674	608	56	71	88	70
Lumber	—.011*		2,165	2,296	214	226	249	214
Furniture	—.006*		53?	551	54	57	71	51
Paper	—.045	—.011*	7,285	7,832	382	525	607	672
Printing	—.01?*		2,945	3,121	237	294	360	321
Chemicals	.023	.021*	10,57?	9,490	645	916	1,262	1,100
Petroleum refining	.016	.006*	3,336	3,129	154	200	214	182
Rubber and plastic products	—.019	—.019*	2,720	2,383	125	172	218	299
Footwear and leather	—.004*		2,008	2,244	26	26	26	28
Stone, clay and glass	—.079	—.040	5,28?*		215	320	400	418
Iron and steel	—.053	—.008*	11,65?	12,460	529	662	776	663
Non-ferrous metals	—.067	—.021*	2,83?	3,231	168	246	272	22?
Fabricated metal products	—.063	—.005*	4,37?	4,499	314	381	443	38?
Machinery, except electrical	.025	.022*	6,76?	5,939	450	516	645	535
Electrical machinery	.001*	.006	4,37?	4,360	257	373	441	475
Automobiles	—.034	—.023*	5,42?	6,289	475	534	607	36?
Other transport equipment	—.111	—.007*	2,20?	2,289	133	200	207	229
Instruments	.002*		1,20?	1,190	71	103	134	129
Miscellaneous manufacturing	.003*		1,64?	1,566	114	132	173	146
Transportation, except railroad	.039*		12,67?	11,460	1,270	1,928	2,564	2,070
Railroad					800	800	800	620
Communication	—.008*		27,12?	28,797	1,004	1,512	1,997	2,575
Electric utility	.024*		31,29?	25,307	309	502	780	1,535
Trade, construction, other	Time-series data not available							10,000

* An asterisk in column (1) or (2) indicates that the peak output or the McGraw-Hill capacity series, respectively, was used to determine the capital-output ratio. An asterisk in column (3) indicates that the 1963 capital stock in 1958 dollars was used.

On the basis of the smallest-r criterion, the McGraw-Hill index wins ten of the fourteen contested industries; the other four come out close. This superior performance may, of course, only reveal how McGraw-Hill's respondents make up their answers. It does suggest, however, that, were McGraw-Hill indexes available for the remaining industries, most of them would also have lower values of r. For some important capital-using sectors, the McGraw-Hill indexes almost certainly do represent an independent and appropriate measure of capacity growth. We should beware, therefore, of large values of r found in industries lacking a McGraw-Hill index.

Even in some sectors with McGraw-Hill capacity indexes, large values of r may be caused by special historical circumstances which should not be projected into the future. Note that if the 1953 stock is overstated relative to the 1963 stock, r will be biased upwards, and vice versa. In textiles (r = .030) the machines standing idle in New England as a result of the industry's move to the South may have been included in the 1953 count, while by 1963, the stock was approximately correctly estimated. In chemicals (r = .021), we may have counted defense facilities in 1953 which had already been retired. On the other hand, in non-ferrous metals (r = .021) the beginning stock may be understated by omission of plants built by the government during the war and sold to the industry afterwards. In automobiles (r = −.023) we may have been counting in the 1963 stock machines which, though only a few years old, had already been replaced by the transfer machines. In nonrail transportation (r = .039) we used the *Guideline* life of aircraft, six years; casual observation suggests that it may be too short and may understate the 1963 stock.

Under the shadow of the doubts, the idea of projecting future changes in the capital-output ratio from these past trends appeared somewhat less than bright. Such trends might be found and projected with confidence from a deeper analysis of each industry, an analysis which compares the capital costs of new plants with old and studies the differences in the equipment needed for expansions and for modernizations. At present, it seems wiser to admit that our study has failed to demonstrate such trends than to claim that it has done so. Therefore, we use the 1963 ratio unchanged in the forecasts. In all but two industries, we used the capital stock adjusted to 1963 capital-output ratios, column (4) of Table III–1, as the basis of the forecasting ratio. In tobacco, and stone, clay, and glass, however, the extremely large negative values of r (−.063 and −.048, respectively), prompted us to discount the estimates and use the unadjusted stock, column (3) of Table III–1, as the basis of our forecasts. Lastly, the aircraft industry, which declines under some of our assumptions about government spending, was assumed to invest in proportion to its output. Using the capital-output-ratio approach, this industry's investment would immediately fall considerably below its 1963 level in the *détente* forecasts of military spending. It was felt that the nature of this industry's business, with its changing products, would require the industry to invest in new types of equipment even if total output were declining.

Thus far, we have dealt only with the investment of industries for which a time series of equipment expenditures could be constructed. But *these industries accounted for less than two-thirds of total equipment investment in 1962.* The other third came from forestry and fisheries, agricultural services, the construction industry, mining, trade, finance, real estate, personal services, business services, research and development, automobile repair, amusements, and medical and educational institutions. As-yet-unpublished Bureau of Labor Statistics estimates of 1958 and 1962 spending by these industries were constructed primarily by distributing the output of various types of equipment among user industries. Paper machines clearly go to the paper industry, just as looms go to textiles; but distributing conveyor belts, trucks, air conditioners, or adding machines among purchasing industries is a far less exact operation. For manufacturing, mining (1958 only), agriculture, and the utilities, checks exist on the total equipment industry purchases; for other sectors, the BLS had to rely almost exclusively upon assignment by type of equipment. The recession in 1958 makes that year unreliable as an indicator of normal investment behavior, leaving only the 1962 figure as a typical year's observation. In this case, about all one can do is to assume that industry investment grows at the same rate as does industry output.

This unsatisfactory situation cannot really be remedied without the collection of source information from these industries. Since the equipment demands of these industries represent such a significant share of the machinery market and of the investment requirements of the economy, improved coverage by the Bureau of the Census or other agencies would be highly valuable both for private market analysis and for the shaping of public policy. Without this information, a very high degree of uncertainty must be attached to this third of the investment forecasts.

FORECASTS OF EQUIPMENT INVESTMENTS

The history and forecasts of equipment investment by sixteen of the largest spenders are shown in Figure III–2. The solid-line forecasts, based on the guideline equipment lives and constant capital-output ratios after 1963, are the standard forecasts used in all other parts of this study. The dashed-line forecasts are based on equipment lives 20 percent shorter, while the dotted-line forecasts are based on the standard lives but project changes in the capital-output ratio to continue at the same rate in the future as in the past. They are derived from the standard forecasts by using, in equation (4) of the first section, the starred values of r from Table III–1.

Many of the industries show a considerable upward jump from 1963 to 1964; these jumps indicate that, although 1963 spending for equipment was high in comparison to previous years, it was generally below that required to support the new rate of growth of the next decade. The high level of spending in 1964 and 1965 seems to bear out this finding. For the few industries which decline between 1963 and 1964, the drop is small. Where the upward jump is large—as in paper, printing, steel, non-ferrous metals, autos, and petroleum refining—the regular-life and the short-life forecasts are in substantial agreement on its size. Preliminary 1964 data on the paper and automobile industries does, in fact, show such spurts. Because petroleum refining investment, the other one with a really big jump, is buried under petroleum extraction spending in current statistics, it is not possible to approximate it at the time this is written. The investment forecast for petroleum refining is not high relative to the investment of 1951–1954 or 1957, but it is enormous in comparison to investment since 1957. We therefore checked our capital-output ratio against that of one large, integrated refinery built in recent years. Had we found the statistically estimated ratio the higher of the two, we would have had grounds for reducing it and thereby bringing the forecast down into line with recent years. Instead, it turned out to be less than half that of the single refinery and gave us no grounds at all for decreasing the forecast. Standard measures of capacity utilization did not indicate excess capacity,[9] so we retained the forecast.

In any version of the forecasts, spending is sturdy indeed by his-

[9] See, for example, Bureau of the Census, *The Measurement of Performance Potential in Manufacturing Establishments*, Working Paper No. 18, Washington, D.C., 1965, p. 7.

Fɪɢ. III–2. History and Forecasts of Equipment Investment

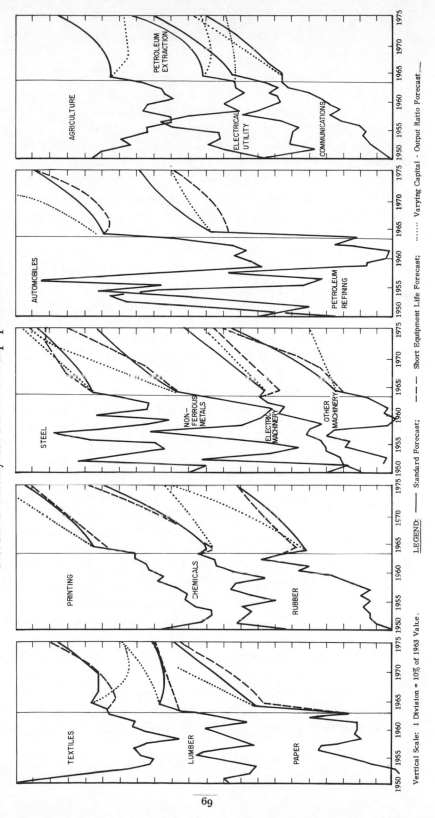

Vertical Scale: 1 Division = 10% of 1963 Value.

LEGEND: —— Standard Forecast; — — — Short Equipment Life Forecast; ······· Varying Capital - Output Ratio Forecast.——

AGRICULTURE

PETROLEUM
EXTRACTION

ELECTRICAL
UTILITY

COMMUNICATIONS

AUTOMOBILES

PETROLEUM
REFINING

STEEL

NON-
FERROUS
METALS

ELECTRIC
MACHINERY

OTHER
MACHINERY

PRINTING

CHEMICALS

RUBBER

TEXTILES

LUMBER

PAPER

69

torical standards. Taken individually or all together, they spell good business for the machinery industries and provide a firm domestic base for these important export industries. In spite of this general agreement among the three versions of the forecasts, however, the differences between them deserve notice.

Comparing the regular-life (solid line) and the 20-percent-shorter-life (dashed line) forecasts shows the forecasts to be surprisingly *insensitive to variations in the assumed length of life of equipment*. In the short-life forecasts, the expansion investment requirements are smaller than in the regular-life forecasts, because the capital stock and, therefore, the capital-output ratios are smaller. The upward trend in investment in most industries, however, makes the replacement forecasts generally higher in the short-life case. It was not clear a priori which of these counteracting influences would prevail, and the graphs of Figure III–2 show that sometimes one, sometimes the other, is stronger. Indeed, they usually almost exactly cancel out one another. This canceling seems to be a happy chance for which we should be duly grateful; it does not reduce our need for a more satisfactory knowledge of capital requirements.

This need for a better understanding of investment requirements becomes particularly clear in comparing the standard forecasts with the dotted-line, varying-capital-output-ratio forecasts. Here the differences are quite striking, though there seems little reason to repent of our decision to use the constant-ratio forecasts. Where the standard forecast looks suspiciously high—as in paper, printing, non-ferrous metals, and automobiles—the varying-ratio forecast is often higher. Nor does there appear to be any point in pulling down the electrical utility forecast while pushing up communications spending. But the dotted-line forecasts serve to remind us of the uncertainty which surrounds the standard projections, for the dotted lines cannot be rejected on the basis of the information we have studied. Though the differences between them and the standard forecasts are as often positive as negative and tend to cancel one another in the aggregate, they are also uncomfortably large in a model where detail matters. They heavily underline, as we have said, our need for firmer knowledge of the equipment needed for growth.

In spite of these shortcomings, the forecasts are sufficiently unanimous in their upward surge to suggest that the worries of the early 1960s over our not growing because we were not investing were misplaced. Perhaps we were not investing because we were not growing. The more rapid growth of the decade ahead should continue to bring out investment dollars by the billion just as has the growth from 1962 to 1965.

NEW CONSTRUCTION SPENDING

"Construction," the subject of this section, comes close to synonomy with "growth," although expansion of physical productive capacity is but one of many motives for building. War, worship, learning, housing, healing, even swimming, add to the list. Material requirements, moreover, vary as much as motives and may differ as widely as those for parks and pipelines or houses and railroads. No growth model, therefore, with aspirations of being specific should lump all types of construction together. We have divided the total construction field into the nineteen categories listed in Table III–2. For these, the Department of Commerce has prepared bills of materials[10] which, naturally, vary in reliability. The best, those of residential, hospital, highway, and educational construction, are based upon sample surveys. The current- and constant-dollar value of spending on each of these categories for every year since 1946 is reported by the Census Bureau in its *Construction Reports*.

Material requirements for each kind of construction are calculated by forecasting the amount spent on it and then distributing this quantity to the material-supplying industries according to the appropriate bill-of-materials column. Value added is distributed to the construction industry. This industry's output, therefore, is the sum of the value added by all the different construction categories; this output is used only to generate the employment and investment needs of the construction industry.

In the several categories where there is both public and private spending, we have forecast the two separately.[11] We project all government items and a few private ones by simple, straight-line trends. In Table III–2, these exogenous or outside-the-model forecasts have "time" in the "determining variable" column; the "equation" column shows the forecasting equation. Most of the private construction is endogenous, that is, it has been determined inside the

10 *Survey of Current Business*, May 1965. The columns not published are available upon request to the Office of Business Economics.
11 Education building is an exception; here we forecast only the total.

TABLE III-2. CONSTRUCTION FORECASTING EQUATIONS

Type of Construction	Determining Variable X	Equation	1963 Value (millions 1957–59 dollars)
1 Residential			
Private (including farm)	Consumption in billions of 1954 dollars	$153.8X_t - .0644S - 12409.0(.98)^t$ (t = 0 in 1946) $(115.0)\ (.07900)\ (11975.0)$	24,236
Public	Time	$723. + 25.3\,t$	723
2 Industrial			
Private	Construction-weighted index of manufacturing output	$2.429X_t - .06706S - 2245.0(.98)^t$ (t = 0 in 1948) $(1.016)\ (.0475)\ (1865.0)$	2,774
Public	Time	$421. + 0.\,t$	421
3 Offices & warehouses			
Private	Consumption in billions of 1954 dollars	$14.58X_t - .0288S - 2435.0(.98)^t$ (t = 0 in 1947) $(4.05)\ (.0402)\ (863.0)$	2,487
Modified Public	Time	$18.57X_t - .0690S - 3275.0(.98)^t$ $1377. + 48.006$	1,377
4 Stores, restaurants, garages			
Private	Output of trade in millions of 1958 dollars	$.04296X_t - .0492S - 2088.0(.98)^t$ (t = 0 in 1948) $(.01765)\ (.0493)\ (1359.0)$	1,981
Modified		$.0598 - .1000S - 3437.0(.98)^t$	
5 Hospitals, churches, social, recreational, miscellaneous			
Private	Consumption in billions of 1954 dollars	$-1371. + 12.47X_t$ $(279.)\ (1.08)$	2,636
Public (hospitals)	Time	$397.$	397

6	Farm (non-residential)	Time	$742. - 10.30t$	742
7	Railroad	Time	$201. + 7.00t$	201
8	Gas utility	Output of gas utility, in millions of 1958 dollars	$1.63\Delta X$	857
9	Electric utility	Output of electric utility in millions of 1958 dollars	$2.6e^{-.016t}\Delta X$	1,912
10	Telephone & telegraph	Output of telephone & telegraph utility in millions of 1958 dollars	$.362X_t - .237S - 1180.0(.98)^t$ (t = 0 in 1949) $(-.07)\ (.088)\ (543)$	1,041
11	Oil and gas wells	Output of oil and gas extraction in millions of 1958 dollars	$.54654 - .06519S - 2013.0(.98)^t$ (t = 0 in 1947) $(.05242)\ (.01046)\ (360.0)$	2,003
12	All other private	Time	$265 + 12.50t$	265
13	Military	Time	$1455. - 21.00t$	1,455
14	Water and sewage	Time	$1684. + 62.50t$	1,684
15	Highway	Time	$6560. + 241.0t$	6,560
16	Public service enterprises	Time	$455. + 18.0t$	455
17	Conservation & development	Time	$1330. + 50.0t$	1,330
18	Education (private & public)	Time	$3259. + 26.5t$	3,259
19	Parks & all other public	Time	$343. + 20.0t$	343

NOTE: Consumption is in billions of 1954 dollars, time is in years with 1953 = 0 unless otherwise noted; industry outputs in millions of 1958 dollars; $\Delta X = X_t - X_{t-1}$.

model and depends upon the outputs and consumption forecasts. We take up first the exogenous projections and then the equations for the endogenous categories.

Rapid expansion is expected for "conservation and development" and the "parks and other" categories, which should start off at 3.8 percent and 5.8 percent per year respectively. Both have spurted upward recently, and the poverty program should assure a continuing rise. Water supply and sewer construction also rush ahead at about 3.7 percent per year as the nation catches up with these needs. Railroad and local transit construction should pull out of its long decline as more cities turn to the problems of mass transit and railroads improve roadbeds for high-speed intercity trains. This turn-around in railroad construction may, of course, prove to be only wishful thinking, but it is at least a good possibility at present. Highway construction on the other hand, may slacken its pace in the future as the interstate program nears completion. We project 3.7 percent growth per year. School building, which shot up from 1946 to 1956, has since remained steady, and will continue at about its present rate with only a slight upward trend. The yearly increment in the number of children aged 5 to 17 is expected to remain approximately the same as in the past decade, so that continuing the same rate of school building will maintain the present standards of floor space per student. In fact, because there is probably some catching up in the present rate of spending, our forecast, which grows 1 percent a year, should allow standards to continue to improve. Military construction we anticipate to continue its decline; we foresee non-residential farm building going the same way. The "all other private" category we can only suppose to expand along its present trend line at about 4.5 percent per year.

The major types of private construction, accounting for 98 percent of all private, depend upon other variables forecasted by the model. In Table III–2, the "determining variable" column specifies the variable to which the item is tied; this variable is referred to as X in the "equation" column, which shows the relation used to forecast. For the equations derived from regression analysis, the standard errors of the parameters are shown in parentheses beneath them. The meaning of S in these equations will be explained in a moment.

The most common forecasting equation is a stock-adjustment relation which we may illustrate by the residential construction equation. The desired stock of housing in year t is assumed to be proportional to total consumption in that year, X_t. Letting C_t denote the construction in year t, and b the stock in year o, the actual stock at the beginning of year t is equal to b plus the construction since time o, $\sum_{\tau=1}^{t-1} C_{t-\tau}$, and less removals, which we assume to be a fixed proportion, d, of the initial stock. Thus,

$$\text{actual stock} = \sum_{\tau=1}^{t-1}(1-d)^\tau C_{t-\tau} + b(1-d)^t,$$

while

$$\text{desired stock} = aX_t.$$

Construction during year t we then assume to be proportional to the gap

$$(5) \qquad C_t = \lambda\left[aX_t - \left(\sum_{\tau=1}^{t-1}(1-d)^\tau C_{t-\tau} + b(1-d)^t\right)\right], \text{ for } t \geq 2.$$

In Table III–2, the summation on the right is denoted simply by S; its regression coefficient is, of course, $-\lambda$, while that of X_t is λa and that of $(1-d)^t$ is $-\lambda b$. Depreciation guideline lives for most structures lie in the neighborhood of fifty years; the corresponding value of d, .02, has been used for all types of construction. Because no constant terms were used in these regression equations, there is no convenient measure of goodness of fit, such as R^2; we have, therefore, plotted in Figure III–3 the actual and "predicted" values so that the reader may judge the fit for himself. In these graphs, the actual total spending, private plus public, is shown by a solid line for each type of construction. Equation (5) was fitted, of course, only to the private component; for comparison with the "actual" line, we have, therefore, added actual public spending to the predicted private spending. This sum is shown by the dotted lines in Figure III–3.

The residential construction equation shown in Table III–2 implies that the value of the desired stock of houses is about 2.2 times annual consumption.[12] The Survey of Consumer Finances shows a ratio of about 2 to 1 for house value and before-tax income.[13] The findings of time-series and cross-section analysis support one another very nicely in this instance. According to this equation, 6.4 percent of the gap between the desired and actual housing is closed in one

[12] In Table II–2, construction is in millions of 1958 dollars while consumption is in billions of 1954 dollars. Multiplying the X series, consumption, by 1,073 to put both series into the same units, millions of 1958 dollars, would divide the coefficient of X_t by 1,073, making it .143, and would leave the other coefficients in the equation unchanged. Then $a = -(\lambda a)/(-\lambda) = -(.143)/(-.0644) = 2.2$.

[13] See James N. Morgan, "Housing and Ability to Pay," *Econometrica*, April 1965.

Fig. III-3. The Fit and Forecasts of the Construction Equation

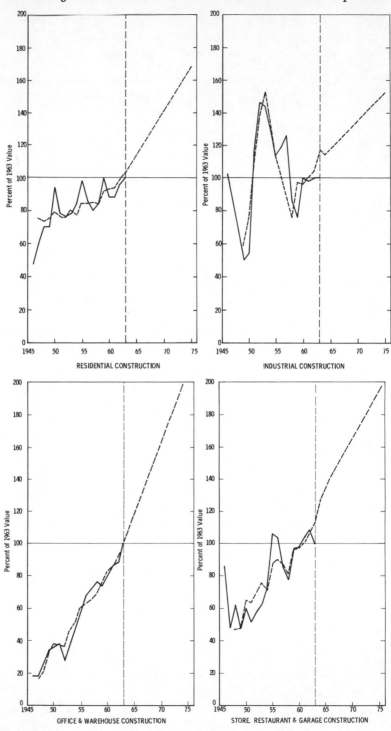

RESIDENTIAL CONSTRUCTION

INDUSTRIAL CONSTRUCTION

OFFICE & WAREHOUSE CONSTRUCTION

STORE, RESTAURANT & GARAGE CONSTRUCTION

76

FIG. III-3 (*Continued*)

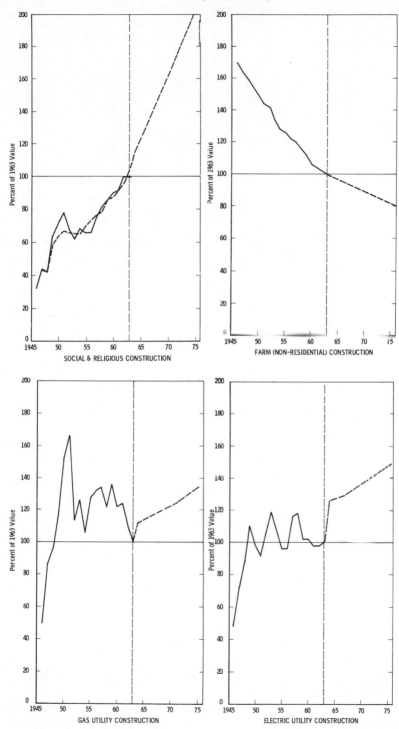

Fig. III–3 (*Continued*)

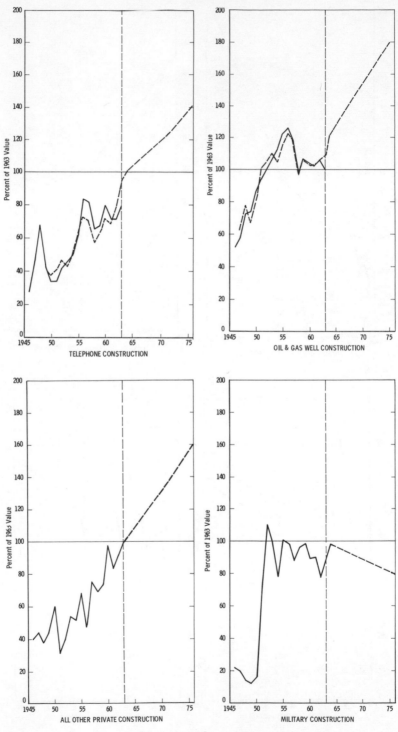

FIG. III-3 *(Continued)*

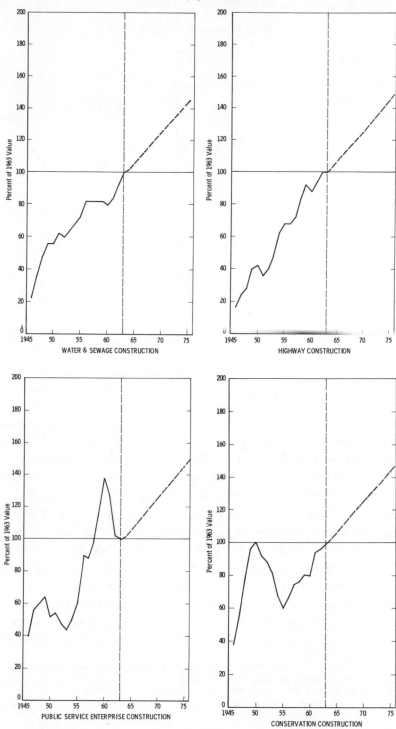

FIG. III–3 *(Continued)*

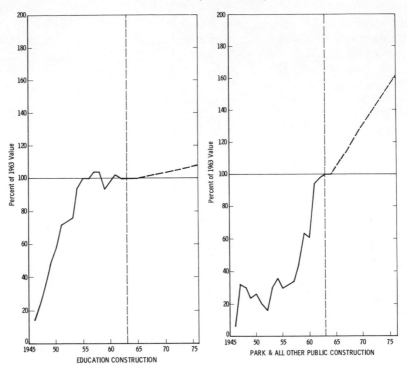

EDUCATION CONSTRUCTION   PARK & ALL OTHER PUBLIC CONSTRUCTION

year. The adjustment to a higher level of income is therefore only half complete after eleven years.[14] This slow adjustment of housing to income does not seem out of line with everyday experience. The graph of residential construction shows that though our equation portrays the trend well enough, it fails rather badly to predict the peaks of residential building in 1950, 1955, and 1959. These decided peaks reflect the impact of changing financing costs on speculative construction, the upswing in business cycles, and changes in the relative costs of renting and owning.[15] The effect of these factors is more spectacular in the short run than persistent in the long.

The forecast for residential construction grows so rapidly in comparison with past experience that it is perhaps not amiss to assure the reader that this part of the computer program was checked very

[14] The half-life, t, of a gap which is closed at the exponential rate λ is $t = \ln 2/\lambda = .693/\lambda$, for t must satisfy the equation $e^{-\lambda t} = \frac{1}{2}$.

[15] For an analysis of short-term, quarterly movements in housing starts, see Sherman Maisel, "Fluctuations in Housing Starts," *American Economic Review*, June 1963.

carefully. The effect of higher incomes will gradually build up a big expansion in house building. The arrival of the postwar babies on the housing market has not been explicitly considered, but it certainly does not diminish our confidence in the forecast. Credit conditions, no doubt, will continue to fluctuate, and the residential construction business will remain subject to cycles. Its growth in 1964 and 1965 has been disappointing relative to this forecast, but its long-term prospects look sound.

Industrial construction depends upon a variable especially prepared for the purpose, a construction-weighted index of output. The output indexes of all the manufacturing industries were combined using their 1962 construction expenditures as weights:

$$X_t = \Sigma_i \, C_i \, (1962) \, Q_i(t)/Q_i(1962)$$

where the summation on i extends over all manufacturing industries C_i (1962) = construction (in millions of dollars) of industry i in 1962, and $Q_i(t)$ = output of industry i in year t.

It would have been preferable, of course, to use the stocks of buildings in each industry as weights; use of a single year's construction was simply a short cut defensible only for its shortness. The resulting equation in Table III–2 indicates that the equilibrium stock of industrial buildings for the 1962 level of output was 36 times the 1962 construction of manufacturing establishments. This result falls fairly well in line with an average life of about fifty years for industrial plants. The adjustment is again slow, requiring ten years to close half of a gap. The graph shows, however, that on several occasions (1950, 1957, and 1959) the "predicted value" proved a leading indicator for the actual series. It seemed inappropriate, therefore, to speed up the reaction time. The forecasts show moderate but sustained growth. By the mid-1970s, the industry should again reach the levels of the early 1950s when it soared with Atomic Energy Commission construction.

For office and warehouse construction, we find a little twisting of the equation in order. Because people in the service professions which sell primarily to consumers occupy a large proportion of office space, we use total consumption to predict this sort of construction. The resulting equation, shown in Table III–2, implies that the desired stock of offices is nearly one-half the annual rate of consumption and, therefore, about *one-fifth* the size of the desired stock of houses. But for many years, office construction has run a *tenth* the size of residential construction, or less. Clearly the equation errs on the high side of the equilibrium office-consumption ratio. The rate of adjustment, moreover, is entirely too slow; closing half of a gap between desired and existing office space takes twenty-four years. A more reasonable and trustworthy equation can be had by putting $\lambda = .69$ and then choosing the remaining two constants to minimize the sum of squared errors. (This value of λ is exactly one standard error greater than the estimated value.) The resulting equation, shown below the estimated one in Table II–2, implies an office-to-residence ratio of one-tenth and a ten-year half-life for a gap between desired and existing offices. The graph in Figure III–3 shows the values predicted using the modified equation; the unmodified equation would show an even faster growing forecast. The forecast shown ticks off 6 percent per year—fast enough. By showing the "predicted" values of both the estimated and the "twisted" equation, I had hoped to emphasize the methodologically important fact that regression equations *forced* to be reasonable often give almost as good a fit as the unreasonable least-squares equation they replace. Unfortunately, we cannot see this point demonstrated graphically here; at this scale, the two "predicted" series cannot be distinguished in the historical period!

Construction of stores, restaurants, and garages is calculated from the output of the trade industry, that is, from value added by trade. Again, the delay between needing the stores and building them seemed excessive at $\lambda = .049$. The value of λ was again raised one standard deviation to .1, giving a half-adjustment time of seven years. The graph indicates a continuation of a long-run upward trend. It should be noted that this trend could not be seen in the data for 1955–1963, for after having lagged behind demand during the Korean War, building raced ahead of demand in 1955 and 1956, precipitating the slump of 1957 and 1958. Since 1959, growth has resumed, and we expect it even to accelerate in the future.

Private construction of churches, hospitals, and social and recreational buildings was made a linear function of consumption. For some of these buildings, notably churches, consumers probably regard their outlays as current rather than capital expense, so that the stock-adjustment equation is inappropriate. An attempt to fit it produced an equation in which all the coefficients had standard errors larger than themselves and the coefficient of S was of the wrong sign. We have relied, therefore, on the simple regression equation shown in Table III–2, which gives an R^2 of 0.90 and implies an income elasticity of 1.56 in 1963. This elasticity is corroborated by the elasticity of 1.85 for religious and welfare activities which we found in the consumption study.

Telephone construction is forecast by a stock-adjustment-type equation with the gross output of the telephone industry as the determining variable. The half-adjustment time of three years was the shortest of any found. The equation was used without modification. It indicates that 1963 spending was well below trend, but that after coming up to the trend line, this type of construction will grow only modestly.

For electric and gas utility construction, the stock-adjustment equation was also tried. Although the fits were satisfactory, all variables had the wrong signs in both equations. Apparently these industries anticipate demand by several years, and thereby make the stock-adjustment model inappropriate for them. The ratio of construction in year t to the output increment between year t and t + 2 was plotted for these two industries. The curve for electricity is fairly smooth, and the ratio prevailing since 1958 has been used to calculate the building needed for future expansions. The resulting forecast runs at about the level of the peak years of the 1950s; like the past history, the forecast shows little upward trend. The curve for gas is more erratic; in the end, we divided five years' investment, 1959–1963, by the five-year output increment over 1959–1964 and used this average for the forecasts. The forecast is for a continuation of the level of recent years.

Oil and gas well construction was forecast from the output of petroleum mining by the stock-adjustment method also. The same depreciation rate, 2 percent per year, was used for the wells. Because the depreciation guidelines do not apply to petroleum extraction, our usual source of equipment lives fails us; other sources could not be found. One may observe, however, that the 596,385 oil wells producing in 1962 were equal to the sum of all the oil wells completed since 1934.[16] Discounting the historical series at 2 percent would apparently give a total close to the reported number still in production. With secondary extraction lengthening service lives, the 2 percent discount did not seem unrealistically slow. The resulting stock-adjustment equation gave a surprisingly good fit to a rather erratic history, and its reasonable parameters did not call for

[16] Historical data in American Petroleum Institute, *Petroleum Facts and Figures,* 1959 Centennial Edition.

modification. The forecast shows growth slower than that of the gusher decade of 1946–1956, but faster than the stagnation of the subsequent years. It must be remembered that this rapid growth depends on domestic petroleum extraction which, in turn, may depend as much on import policy as on domestic use.

These soaring forecasts for most types of construction underline the importance of shaping the growth of our cities so that all this new construction does not interfere with the use of existing buildings but, instead, creates pleasing new urban spaces in which to live and work. If these forecasts are right, the urban sprawl of the future will make that of the past look minor beside it, unless we learn better ways to guide our own growth.

IV

Government Demands

Speculation's share of the cross between science and conjecture, which we have met before in this study, waxes doubly strong in projecting government demands. For not only do we have to contend with the uncertainties of the future international situation and domestic policy, but even the present pattern and level of government expenditures are difficult to determine. The government budget categories match the sectors of our model so poorly as to be of little use in identifying supplying industries. Census reports, which match our sectors, seldom show the fraction of goods bought by governments. There are few other sources.

The national accounts do, however, divide government spending into three basic parts: the compensation of employees, construction, and other purchases. We are concerned only with the "other purchases" part in this chapter. Government employment is projected in Chapter VII, on labor; government construction, by type of construction, was forecast in Chapter III. These remaining "other purchases" fall into three categories:

Federal purchases for defense, atomic, stockpiling, and space activities—defenselike purchases, for short
General federal purchases—all those which are not defenselike
State and local government purchases

These three will be taken up in the order listed. We shall estimate the 1963 expenditure and forecast the 1980 expenditure in each class (1980, rather than 1975, was used to facilitate comparison with other, unpublished forecasts).

The published input-output table shows, for the year 1958, the industry structure of all federal spending and state and local spending separately, but it does not divide the federal spending into the two components we need. We shall make this separation in the 1958 data, and for the defenselike category, we shall try to update this industry structure to 1963. We shall forecast a few changes in this structure for 1980. For the other two categories, no changes will be made in the structure of the spending; only the total will be forecast. Special treatment is, however, required for changes in the crop holdings of the Commodity Credit Corporation, which are included in government purchases.

FEDERAL GOVERNMENT SPENDING FOR DEFENSELIKE PURCHASES

In 1963, the Department of Defense, the National Aeronautics and Space Administration, and the Atomic Energy Commission together bought over $33 billion of goods and services, excluding construction, from the industries of this model. This sum not only surpasses by a ratio of more than ten-to-one the purchases of all other federal agencies for these items; it also exceeds all private spending on producers' durable equipment, $31 billion; private non-residential construction, $21 billion; and all exports, $31 billion. Though no official estimate for this spending is published, one can be constructed from the national income accounts (NIA) with minor adjustments from the U.S. Budget. Table IV–1 presents such an estimate for 1958 and 1963.

Between 1958 and 1963, the pattern of this spending changed noticeably. Serial production of bombers had ceased; missiles were the order of the day. NASA was appearing as a major customer, but the government had stopped acquiring new defense production facilities. To give a realistic basepoint to our projections, therefore, it is necessary to construct a new defenselike column for 1963. We can directly assign values to some dozen of the largest items, accounting for about 65 percent of the total. The unallocated balance will then be prorated over the remaining industries in proportion to their 1958 shares.

The major items of the defenselike bill of goods can be found in published sources more easily if we first undo some of the work of the makers of the input-output table. In the federal column of the published table, research and development expenditures are handled differently from all other purchases. For example, of the aircraft industry's sales of $8,450 million to the federal government, $2,150 million are considered sales of research and development services; only the balance of $6,300 million appears as a purchase of aircraft.

The $2,150 million is counted as a government purchase from the research and development industry, which, in turn, buys these same services from the aircraft industry. Thus, the services end up being provided by the aircraft industry just as if they had been purchased from it in the first place. The research and development portion of spending on missiles, communication equipment, and all other items is handled similarly. In the published table, about 88 percent of the

TABLE IV–1. TOTAL DEFENSELIKE PURCHASES[a]
(billions of dollars)

		1963	1958
1.	Military equipment	$17.6	$16.7
2.	Other Defense Department purchases	11.4	7.5
3.	NASA purchases	2.8	0.4
4.	AEC purchases	2.0	1.9
5.	Defense production facilities	0.0	0.4
	Total	$33.4	$26.9

SOURCE: Row 1: National Income Accounts (NIA) Table 26, line 7. *Survey of Current Business*, July 1964. 2: NIA Table 26, line 8, minus a fraction of line 2 (wages and salaries) to remove the wage supplements from this item. In 1963, 5 percent of line 2, in 1958, 8 percent of line 2 was subtracted. Comparison of NIA Tables 50 and 51 shows these averages for wage supplements in federal employment. 3: NIA Table 22, line 5, minus an estimate of $0.3 billion for NASA employment and construction expense, estimated from U.S. Budget for 1965. 4: NIA Table 22, line 4, minus $0.3 billion for AEC employment and construction expense, estimated from U.S. Budget for 1965. 5: NIA Table 26.

[a] Excluding employee compensation and construction.

business of the research and development industry consisted of these transfers into it of government contract work really done by other sectors.

We have undone all this careful transferring out and transferring back in, and have put spending for research and development on aircraft back with aircraft purchases, missile research and development back with missile purchases, and so on. The research and development industry which remains after returning these transfers to their native industry is composed of establishments whose primary business is research. This simplified version of the input-output table makes it easier to find the major items of the defenselike bill of goods in published information. The awkward lumping of medical and missile research is eliminated, as is the necessity to change coefficients in the research and development industry when trying various government forecasts. The necessity to change coefficients in, say, the aircraft sector as the research and development proportion of its output changes is exactly the same under either treatment.

The federal government spending column resulting from this treatment of research and development is shown as column 1 in Table IV–5. (This table is placed at the end of the chapter because it summarizes the whole of it.) The all-federal column for 1958 was obtained from the published table, which shows only the percentage structure of spending, by assuming a total expenditure of $52 billion in 1958, the figure shown in the old version of the national income accounts. The transfers into the R&D industry column were all assigned to the corresponding category of federal spending, and their total was subtracted from federal research and development purchases. The resulting column was then split between defenselike and general spending on the basis of judgment and conversations with persons in the Office of Business Economics. The resulting division is approximate to say the least. In the first place, the figures in the all-federal column are subject to rounding errors of up to $3 million. In the second place, the division of this sum into its two parts is always subject to at least a 5 percent error. The split does, however, give us two columns for which the purposes of the spending are more homogeneous than those of the total column.

The estimates for 1963 purchases of major defenselike items are shown (with their sources) in Table IV–2. Research and development expenditures for particular types of hardware are shown as a purchase from the hardware-producing industry. A few items require further explanation, principally the apparently arbitrary shift of $2 billion from ordnance to aircraft. The problem back of this shift lies in the Standard Industrial Classification (SIC), which puts complete missiles and space vehicles in ordnance (SIC 19), but classifies their engines and propulsion units with aircraft engines (SIC 3722) and their components and subassemblies, such as space capsules, with aircraft equipment (SIC 3724). The input-output table follows this classification, putting all of SIC 19 into its ordnance sector and all of SIC 3722 and 3724 into its aircraft sector. This classification evolved naturally enough historically; the rockets of World War II were definitely ordnance. They grew up into missiles and missiles turned into space vehicles before the SIC could catch up with them. Nonetheless, the custom of separating missiles from their components has today become awkward, and it is not observed in much current information on the aerospace industry. In particular, it is not followed in the Census Bureau's *Current Industrial Report on the Aerospace Industry* (CIRA), the only source available at the time of writing which divides the net sales of the aerospace industry into its principal products and also shows the portion of those sales going to the U.S. government. Consequently, when the first three "ordnance" categories of Table IV–2 are added to nonmissile ordnance and a further $167 million of sales to other customers is also added in, the total comes to $6,290 million, a round $22,000 million more than the total of shipments of SIC 19, $4,139 million. This difference must be accounted for by the components and subassemblies. SIC 3729, where they are classified, had shipments of $2,815 million, a figure which can accommodate the $2,200 million of missile components. The total shipments of SIC 372, $13,893 million, are still happily in excess of the total net sales implied for it by the transfer, $11,780 million, including $2,520 million of commercial or foreign sales. (The shipments include sales to other aerospace firms; the net sales do not.) Although we have managed to live with the outmoded SIC, it is certainly clear that a new classification which reunited missiles and space vehicles with their engines and subassemblies should be welcomed if historical data on the new classification could be provided.

Moving on down Table IV–2 to the subtotal of directly allocated items, we see that it increased 25 percent between 1958 and 1963, leaving the balance of unallocated items to rise by 29 percent. This growth falls between the 52 percent growth of the "other Defense Department purchases" of Table IV–1 and the 19 percent growth of "operations and maintenance procurement" as reported by the Comptroller of the Department of Defense (see source note 8 to Table IV–2). We may therefore assume that the 29 percent growth is roughly correct for these remaining items. The fourth column of Table II–5 shows the estimates of the complete 1963 defenselike column.

The projection of these defenselike purchases to 1980 is, of course, largely a matter of conjecture. We have tried two alternative hypotheses about their future trends. One, which we may call the *détente* assumption, envisages a reduction of these items by about a fourth; the other sees a continuation and slight intensification of the cold war, leading to a 5 percent increase in spending. Table IV–3 sets forth the particulars of the two views. In the *détente* prospect, conventional ordnance and missile expenditures are reduced 60 percent from their 1964 level; airplanes decline 50 percent, as do ships. Com-

TABLE IV–2. ESTIMATES OF FEDERAL PURCHASES OF MAJOR DEFENSELIKE ITEMS,
1958, 1963
(millions of dollars)

Sector Number	Industry Name		1963	1958
56	Communication equipment (1)		3,540	1,710
61	Ships, trains, trailers, & cycles (2)		900	630
13	Ordnance			
	Missile systems & parts (4)	3,150		
	Military space vehicles & parts (4)	1,060		
	Nonmilitary space vehicles & parts (4)	850		
	Nonmissile Ordnance (3)	1,060		
		6,120		
	Less: transfer to aircraft	−2,200	3,920	3,200
60	Aircraft and parts			
	Complete aircraft & parts	2,990		
	Aircraft engines & parts	1,170		
	Engines for military missiles	890		
	Engines for Nonmilitary space vehicles	400		
	Conversions, modifications, drones, and other	1,610		
		7,060		
	Transfer from ordnance	2,200	9,260	7,800
6	Non-ferrous ore mining (12)		248	193
27	Basic chemicals (8)		1,010	792
43	Engines and turbines (5)		17	216
45	Construction & mining machinery & equipment (6)		130	72
47	Metalworking machinery & equipment (6)		15	154
49	General industrial machinery & equipment (7)		20	187
51	Office, computing & accounting machines (6)		210	60
57	Electronic components (1)		230	345
59	Motor vehicles (9)		570	422
62	Instruments and clocks (6)		700	490
63	Optical & photographic equipment (6)		160	125
76	Research and development (10)		1,160	465
82	Noncompetitive imports		1,800	2,300
	Subtotal—major items		23,890	19,161
	Other (rounded)		9,900	7,700
	Total (rounded)		33,800	26,900

SOURCE: The principal documents used in estimating the major categories of defenselike purchases come from the Census Bureau. The documents and the abbreviations used for them are:

Document	Abbreviation
1963 Census of Manufactures Preliminary Reports on:	
General Statistics	MCGS
Industry Statistics	MCIS
Shipments of Defense Oriented Industries	MCDOI
Current Industrial Report Series M37D, "Backlog of Orders for Aerospace Companies, Summary for 1964."	CIRA

NOTES TO TABLE IV–2

The first two documents observe the same division between ordnance and aircraft that the table uses. The last two do not observe this classification, but do separate sales to the government from other sales. The second item, MCIS, may do both, but the reports on the most relevant industries had not been published when this report was written. The numbers in parentheses in the table refer to the sources below. (DoD is for Department of Defense.)

(1) MCDOI, Table 2, Sum DoD prime contract plus a fraction of the NASA and AEC columns. The fraction used was the ratio of DoD prime contract to DoD total purchases of the item.
(2) MCIS, Shipbuilding and repairing, military items.
(3) MCDOI, Table 2, item "shipbuilding and repairing and ordnance (except guided missiles and space vehicles)" minus the shipbuilding estimate of note (2).
(4) CIRA.
(5) MCDOI Table 3, Prime Contract.
(6) MCDOI Table 3, Prime Contract, less an allowance for purchases by other government agencies. Table 2, "other agencies" column provides an upper bound for these allowances. In the case of Sector 63, an additional $15 million has been allowed for photocopy paper and other supplies.
(7) Reduced from 1958 by the same proportion as machine tools.
(8) Increased from 1958 by the same percentage as missile procurement shown in "Order of Magnitude Data on Comparative Expenditures by Functional Title as of FY 1966 Budget Structure Had Been Adopted Circa 1948; FY 1954–1966," prepared by the Comptroller of the Department of Defense.
(9) "Ordnance and motor vehicle" figure from source in note (8) less non-missile ordnance estimate.
(10) Increased by the same percentage as RDT&E in source of note (8).
(11) "Military expenditures" in the balance of payments includes personal spending of military and civilian personnel abroad, which is not part of government spending. We estimated this personal spending item at $915 million for 1963 by moving up the last reported figure, that for 1961, by the index of armed forces abroad. The index of "military expenditures" less this item, plus AEC purchases of foreign uranium ore, was multiplied by the 1958 figure to obtain the 1963 number shown here.
(12) AEC purchases of domestic uranium ore, Bureau of the Census, *Statistical Abstract of the U.S.*, fiscal year figures.

munication equipment drops only 20 percent, and the remaining items drop only 10 percent. This pattern would seem to meet the needs of a nuclear stalemate in which limited war capabilities are maintained. In this alternative, the space exploration program is supposed to continue, rising to 50 percent more than its 1964 outlay by the end of the period. In the cold war prospect, the missile and airplane programs rise 10 percent above their 1964 levels, while ships, ordnance, and all other expenses hold their own. A slower growth in space exploration, 30 percent, fits this picture because its cost would be felt more keenly in this situation than in the *détente*.

Major differences between the industry growth rates under the two assumptions are narrowly confined to the defense industries. The principal differences are shown at the bottom of page 92.

TABLE IV–3. PROJECTIONS OF MILITARY PROCUREMENT FOR 1980
(dollars in millions)

SECTOR	1963	1964	Détente As Per cent of 1964 or 1963	Détente Value	Cold War As Per cent of 1964 or 1963	Cold War Value
Ordnance						
Nonmissile	$1,060	n.a.	40[a]	$420	100[a]	$1,060
Missile	3,151	$2,405	40	960	110	2,650
Military space vehicles	1,061	732	40	290	110	800
Nonmilitary space vehicles	850	1,490	150	2,230	130	1,940
Transfer to aircraft	−2,200			−1,500[b]		−2,300
Total	3,920		61[a]	2,400	106[a]	4,150
Aircraft						
Planes & parts	4,158	4,568	50	2,280	110	5,000
Military Missile engines	894	547	40	220	110	600
Nonmilitary missile & space vehicle engines	404	584	150	880	130	760
Conversions, etc.	1,611	1,418	50	710	110	1,560
Transfer from ordnance	2,200			1,500		2,300
Total	9,260		60[a]	5,590	110[a]	10,220
Communications equipment	3,540		80[a]	2,800	110[a]	3,900
Ships	900		50[a]	450	100[a]	900
All other	16,200		90[a]	14,600	100[a]	16,200
Total (rounded)	33,800		76[a]	25,800	105[a]	35,400

n.a. = not available.
SOURCE: See Table IV–2.
   [a] Percent of 1963.
   [b] Forty-five percent of preceding three items, as in 1963.

In the consumer-goods industries, the growth rates run about a tenth of a percent per year lower under the cold war assumption. Growth of basic material and machinery industries was even less affected. Far from being "shored up" by defense expenditures, most industries in the economy would grow slightly faster with smaller defense expenditures, provided taxes were adjusted to give full employment.

		Average Annual Growth Rates Détente	Cold War
13	Ordance	−1.3%	0.8%
66	Aircraft	−0.5	1.6
62	Communication equipment	1.8	2.6
63	Electronic components	3.5	3.7
67	Ships, trains, trailers, and cycles	2.5	2.8

GENERAL FEDERAL GOVERNMENT

Of the three categories of government spending, the general federal is by far the smallest, coming to about $3 billion in 1963. No official figures are published on it, and we have to make some rather uncertain calculations to approximate its magnitude and distribution

FIG. IV–1. General Federal Purchases Except Employment, Construction, and Farm Commodity

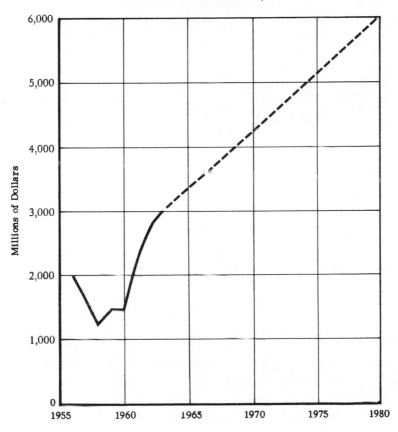

SOURCE: Table IV–1.

among industries. Figure IV–1 shows the estimated trend in total spending for recent years; Table III–4 presents the derivation of these estimates; and Table III–5 shows the distribution of spending among industries. The general federal column of the input-output table contains three items not included in the sum graphed in

Figure IV–1: net increases in inventories of the Commodity Credit Corporation, payments for research and development work done by nonprofit institutions, and interest paid to foreigners. The first item has been purposely removed—see line two of Table IV–4—because it is often large, always volatile, and little related to the other items in purpose. In line with present policies by which the government

TABLE IV–4. GENERAL FEDERAL PURCHASES EXCLUDING EMPLOYMENT AND
CONSTRUCTION, 1956–1963
(millions of dollars)

	1956	1957	1958	1959	1960	1961	1962	1963
Nondefense GNP[a]	5,706	5,727	8,281	7,879	8,024	8,944	10,152	10,296
Less: Farm price stabilization[b]	−403	−581	1,466	520	183	−140	130	−173
General government purchases of goods & services	6,109	6,308	6,815	7,359	7,841	9,084	10,022	10,469
Less: Wages & salaries[c]	2,999	3,137	3,686	3,717	4,132	4,443	4,732	5,229
Wage supplements[d]	126	188	247	256	302	333	345	397
Construction[e]	988	1,308	1,644	1,958	1,951	2,141	2,204	1,915
General government purchases of goods	1,996	1,675	1,238	1,428	1,456	2,167	2,741	2,928

[a] This sum does not include R&D work done by nonprofit institutions, interest paid abroad, or nonmilitary grants in kind to foreign countries. The general government column includes all of these and, therefore, has a considerably larger total than the sum shown in the bottom line of this table.

[b] *Survey of Current Business*, July 1964, and earlier years, national income accounts (NIA), government account.

[c] Total civilian wages and salaries (NIA) minus Defense Department wages and salaries (NIA), minus AEC and NASA wages and salaries, from U.S. Budget.

[d] Calculated as a percentage of wages and salaries, the percentage being based on the budgets of a sample of government agencies.

[e] Total federal construction, NIA, less Defense Department (from the NIA also), NASA, and AEC construction.

pays subsidies to farmers for not producing rather than buying up surplus commodities, no federal purchases of crops have been projected for the future. Research and development purchases from nonprofit institutions have been advanced from their 1958 level by the index of research in these institutions supported by federal funds, including AEC and NASA sources. Interest payments to foreigners are directly available in the foreign transactions section of the national accounts.

Figure IV–1 shows the balance of federal purchases of goods declining during the second Eisenhower administration, turning around, and rising rapidly in the first two years of the Kennedy administration. Analysis of the Budget by function shows that much of this rise was in the expenditures on the promotion and regulation of air and water transportation. Much of this additional expenditure must, therefore, have gone for communications equipment, electronic components, aircraft, and shipbuilding. Fortunately, a special supplement to the 1963 Census of Manufactures (see MCDOI in the sources of Table IV–2) enables us to identify these items with some precision. After accounting for these items, the remaining ones must then all be increased by 30 percent to bring the total up to the 1963 level shown in Table IV–4. Purchases of manufactured food were not included in this circulation, since many of them come under the farm program. Their 1963 values were chosen at what seemed a probable structure for future years rather than reproducing 1963 specifically. All of the resulting estimates are exposed in the seventh column of Table IV–5. It may be doubted that they are accurate enough to print; but if weak data must be used, isn't it better to let the reader see it than to cover it up?

The recent past history of this spending, as shown in Figure IV–1, hardly forces a future trend projection upon us. Surely the rate of growth from 1960 to 1963 cannot hold up. A 4 percent per year growth has been projected, approximately the rate from 1956 or 1957 to 1963, and roughly the same as the growth of the GNP forecast. All elements of the column grow at the same rate from their 1963 levels. The model, of course, could make use of different rates for different elements if we had the knowledge on which to base these differences.

STATE AND LOCAL GOVERNMENT SPENDING

In 1963, state and local governments spent $10,202 million on purchases of goods and services other than construction and employment. Figure IV–2 shows the history of these expenditures and the projection used in the forecasts. The input-output table gives the percentage structure of these purchases in 1958. The ten largest items and their percentage share were:

Maintenance construction	35.1%
Business services	5.8
Electricity, gas, & water	5.1
Motor vehicles	4.6
Transportation, warehousing	4.2
Petroleum refining	4.0
Medical & educational services	3.3
Food products	2.8
Chemicals	2.5
Rental and real estate	2.4
Other, smaller items	30.2
Total	100.0%

Fig. IV-2. State and Local Government Expenditures[a]

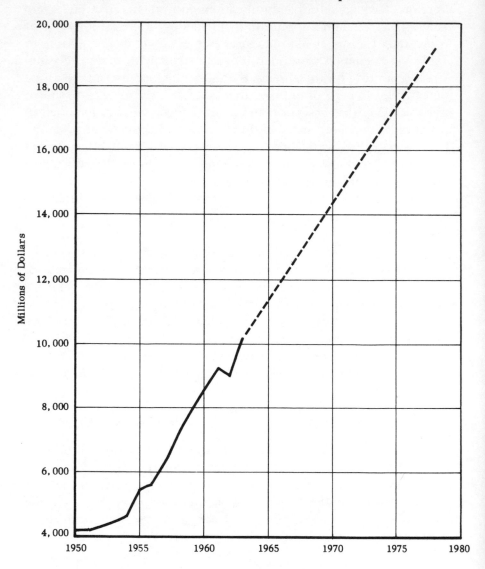

SOURCE: National income accounts in *Survey of Current Business*, July 1964.

a Excluding employment and construction spending.

One can see the principal functions of state and local governments
reflected in this bill of goods: maintaining highways and schools,
heating and lighting schools and public buildings, supplying police
and fire departments with vehicles and gasoline, feeding people in

TABLE IV-5. GOVERNMENT FINAL DEMAND, 1958, 1963, 1980

(millions of dollars)

Sector No.	Sector Name	All Federal 1958 (1)	Defense-like 1958 (2)	General Federal 1958 (3)	Defense-like 1963 (4)	Defense-like Détente 1980 (5)	Defense-like Cold War 1980 (6)	General Federal 1963 (7)	State & Local 1958 (8)
1	Livestock	−5	0	−5	0	0	0	−5	12
2	Crops	1,140	0	1,140	0	0	0	0	29
3	Forestry & fishery products	−135	0	−135	0	0	0	−140	0
4	Agricultural, forestry, & fishery services	42	7	36	9	8	9	55	−69
5	Iron ore mining	0	0	0	0	0	0	0	0
6	Non-ferrous ore mining	185	185	0	248	220	220	0	0
7	Coal mining	0	0	0	0	0	0	0	61
8	Petroleum mining	0	0	0	0	0	0	0	0
9	Minerals mining	10	10	0	13	12	13	0	−12
10	Chemical mining	10	10	0	13	12	13	0	12
11	New construction	Excluded from these columns							
12	Maintenance construction	1,030	820	210	1,024	920	1,024	0	3,381
13	Ordnance	3,230	3,230	0	3,920	2,400	4,150	10	4
14	Meatpacking	19	0	19	0	0	0	25	27
15	Tobacco	0	0	0	0	0	0	0	0
16	Fabrics & yarn	46	45	1	58	52	58	2	8
17	Rugs, tire cord, & miscellaneous textiles	5	5	0	6	6	6	1	0
18	Apparel	36	24	12	31	28	31	15	93
19	Household textiles & upholstery	98	83	15	106	95	106	20	0
20	Lumber & products, except wooden containers	−5	0	−5	0	0	0	−7	0
21	Wooden containers	0	0	0	0	0	0	0	0

(Table continued)

TABLE IV-5. GOVERNMENT FINAL DEMAND, 1958, 1963, 1980 (*continued*)

(millions of dollars)

Sector No.	Sector Name	All Federal 1958 (1)	Defense-like 1958 (2)	General Federal 1958 (3)	Defense-like 1963 (4)	Defense-like *Détente* 1980 (5)	Defense-like Cold War 1980 (6)	General Federal 1963 (7)	State & Local 1958 (8)
22	Household furniture	26	25	1	32	29	32	2	57
23	Office furniture	26	5	21	6	6	6	27	127
24	Paper & products, except containers	67	49	18	62	56	62	23	4
25	Paper containers	5	0	5	0	0	0	6	0
26	Printing and publishing	88	75	13	96	86	96	17	176
27	Basic chemicals	795	790	5	1,010	909	1,010	7	245
28	Plastics & synthetic materials	5	3	2	4	3	4	3	0
29	Drugs & cleaning & toilet preparations	130	55	75	70	63	70	100	180
30	Paint and allied products	5	5	0	6	6	6	0	0
31	Petroleum refining	700	680	20	870	782	870	26	384
32	Rubber & miscellaneous plastic products	114	110	4	141	127	141	5	74
33	Leather tanning	0	0	0	0	0	0	0	0
34	Shoes & other leather products	21	17	4	22	20	22	5	0
35	Glass & glass products	1	1	0	1	1	1	0	0
36	Stone & clay products	5	4	1	5	5	5	2	4
37	Iron & steel	110	96	14	123	110	123	18	0
38	Non-ferrous metals	335	335	0	300	270	300	0	0
39	Metal containers	15	15	0	19	17	19	0	0
40	Heating, plumbing, & structural metal products	15	15	0	19	17	19	0	0
41	Stampings, screw machine products, & bolts	88	55	33	70	63	70	43	4
42	Hardware, plating, wire products, & valves	126	96	30	123	110	123	39	45

#	Industry							
43	Engines & turbines	280	260	20	17	15	17	26	4
44	Farm machinery & equipment	17	12	5	15	14	15	6	16
45	Construction & mining machinery & equipment	78	72	6	130	120	130	8	20
46	Materials handling equipment	130	127	3	163	146	163	4	49
47	Metalworking machinery & equipment	265	250	15	15	14	15	20	4
48	Special industrial machinery	31	27	4	35	31	35	5	29
49	General industrial machinery & equipment	192	187	5	20	18	20	6	4
50	Machine shops & miscellaneous machinery	42	40	2	51	46	51	2	37
51	Office, computing & accounting machines	73	60	13	210	190	210	17	90
52	Service industry machines	62	54	8	69	62	69	10	20
53	Electric apparatus & motors	340	335	5	429	385	429	6	4
54	Household appliances	165	161	4	206	185	206	5	0
55	Electronic lighting & wiring equipment	86	86	0	110	99	110	0	8
56	Communication equipment	1,715	1,700	5	3,540	2,800	3,900	238	61
57	Electronic components	364	364	0	230	196	230	46	0
58	Batteries, X-ray, & engine electrical equipment	110	95	15	122	109	122	20	33
59	Motor vehicles	475	425	50	570	501	570	65	441
60	Aircraft & parts	7,800	7,800	0	9,260	5,590	10,220	290	0
61	Ships, trains, trailers, & cycles	634	630	4	900	450	900	165	37
62	Instruments and clocks	636	596	40	700	620	700	101	86
63	Optical & photographic equipment	130	127	3	160	144	160	10	16
64	Miscellaneous manufactured products	36	26	10	33	30	33	13	180
65	Transportation	1,400	1,300	100	1,664	1,500	1,664	130	404
66	Communication services	166	104	62	133	120	133	80	192
67	Radio & TV broadcasting	0	0	0	0	0	0	0	0
68	Electric utility services	102	82	20	105	94	105	26	293
69	Gas utility services	217	177	40	227	204	227	52	70
70	Water utility services	29	23	6	29	26	29	8	123
71	Wholesale & retail trade	640	620	20	794	713	794	26	183
72	Finance & insurance	0	0	0	0	0	0	0	192

(*Table continued*)

99

TABLE IV-5. GOVERNMENT FINAL DEMAND, 1958, 1963, 1980 (continued)

(millions of dollars)

Sector No.	Sector Name	All Federal 1958 (1)	Defense-like 1958 (2)	General Federal 1958 (3)	Defense-like 1963 (4)	Defense-like Détente 1980 (5)	Defense-like Cold War 1980 (6)	General Federal 1963 (7)	State & Local 1958 (8)
73	Real estate & rental	110	50	60	64	58	64	78	237
74	Hotels, personal & repair services	240	150	90	192	173	192	117	90
75	Business services	550	460	90	589	529	589	117	559
76	Research & development	465	465	0	1,160	1,043	1,160	0	0
77	Automobile repair services	125	95	30	122	109	122	39	82
78	Amusements & recreation	16	14	2	18	16	18	2	−45
79	Medical & educational services & non-profit institutions	630	230	400	294	264	294	1,000	314
80	Federal government enterprises	57	30	27	38	35	38	35	69
81	State & local government enterprises	110	0	110	0	0	0	142	4
82	Noncompetitive imports	2,630	2,300	330	1,800	1,600	1,800	600	4
83	Business travel	0	0	0	0	0	0	0	0
84	Office supplies	70	45	25	58	52	5	33	135
85	Dairy products	42	0	42	0	0	0	70	113
86	Canned & frozen foods	13	0	13	0	0	0	15	22
87	Grain mill products	85	0	85	0	0	0	70	53
88	Bakery products	0	0	0	0	0	0	0	11
89	Beverages	0	0	0	0	0	0	0	0
90	Miscellaneous food products	3	0	3	0	0	0	100	14

state institutions, salting icy streets, and so on. The second largest item, business services, includes advertising, accounting data processing, and legal services. It is difficult, however, to deduce changes in the proportions in the bill of goods from the moderate changes which have occurred in the published expenditures by function. As there appear to be no other indicators at present, we have assumed no change in the distribution of this spending among industries. The 1958 breakdown by industry is shown in column 8 of Table IV–5.

V

Exports and Imports

EXPORTS

Forecasting exports is a privilege we would forego if we could, for not only are they notoriously hard to predict in the detail in which we need them, sometimes fluctuating as much as 30 percent in a year, but it is also a bit out of keeping with the carefully constructed checks and balances in the rest of our system to simply toss in export projections which rest on nothing more than past trends and a few hunches about the future. Yet forecast them we must and on just such trends and hunches, though in the end we can at least check to be sure that export expansion approximately equals import expansion.

A thorough study of the foreign markets for each sector's products or the construction of a complete model of world trade would require time, resources, and competence which were not mine. Perhaps, however, an extensive study of these markets would be out of place in a book which puts its major emphasis on the interaction of the domestic sectors. In any event, the only objective of the slightly modified trend projections which we shall use for exports is to make the total output forecasts of the exporting industries usable for forecasting the sales of the industries supplying materials to these export industries. For example, we hope that, though our forecast of farm machinery exports is unlikely to command the confidence of the exporters, it is not so unrealistic that it vitiates the farm machinery output forecast as an indicator of steel sales to farm machinery. Since exports of farm machinery were about 12 percent of output in 1962, a percentage point error in the growth rate of exports would produce only about one-eighth of a percentage point error in the growth rate of the industry's steel consumption. Thus, for the purpose of this book, we can be content with rather rough export projections.

This objective for the export forecasts dictates that we must pay the most attention to the industries which have the largest shares of their output going to exports. Table V–1 lists the twenty industries

TABLE V–1. IMPORTANCE AND FORECASTS OF EXPORTS

	1958 Exports as Percent of Output[a]	Forecast Growth Rate to 1975 (percent per year)
Crops	7.5	6.5
Coal	12.1	5.0
Stone & clay mining	9.8	5.0
Tobacco	7.3	3.5
Basic chemicals	5.6	6.0
Plastics & synthetic materials	7.9	6.0
Engines & turbines	9.6	6.0
Farm machinery	7.3	6.0
Construction & mining machinery	23.0	3.0
Material-handling equipment	7.0	7.0
Metalworking machinery	9.0	8.5
Special industry machinery	14.6	7.0
General industrial machinery	7.3	7.0
Office & computing machinery	6.0	11.0
Service industry machinery	6.0	7.0
Electrical apparatus & motors	5.4	4.0
Motor vehicles	3.9	5.0
Ships, trains, trailers, & cycles	7.9	0.0
Instruments & clocks	5.1	15.0
Optical & photographic equipment	5.6	11.0
Transportation	6.7	7.0

[a] From *Survey of Current Business*, November 1964, p. 21.

in which exports exceeded 5 percent of output in 1958. By comparison, all merchandise and transportation exports were 4 percent of GNP in 1958. Motor vehicle exports are included in the list because, although less than 5 percent of output, the dollar amount is the largest of any sector except crops. Two-thirds of the sectors in the table fall into the machinery or instrument categories; crops, coal, chemicals, and transportation fill out the list. The influence of exports on the material requirements of all other industries is negligible.

The history of these principal exports over the nine years 1956–1964 together with the trend lines used to predict future growth are shown in Figure V–1. The growth rates used in the projections

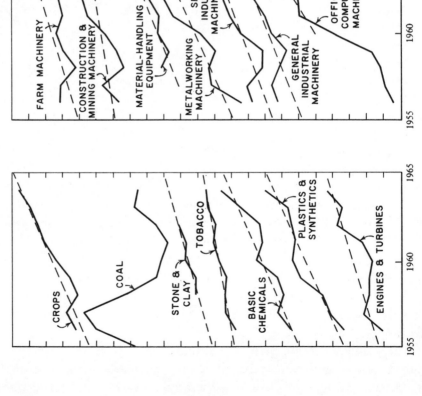

Fig. V-1. U.S. Exports, 1956–1964

Vertical Scale: 1 Division = 20% Change

104

appear in Table V–1 for the export-sensitive industries; the Master Table shows the rates for all industries. The indexes for the historical trends are based on current-dollar values. For the years 1958–1962, it is possible to find export figures corresponding quite exactly to the model sectors in the valuable new Census Bureau publication, *U.S. Commodity Exports and Imports as Related to Output, 1962 and 1961.* For earlier and later years, exports and imports are not available in a classification compatible with the Standard Industrial Classification used for domestic output. For the earlier years, the 1958 figure has been moved back by indexes for categories roughly but not exactly comparable to the model sectors; similarly, the 1962 figure has moved forward to 1964. For a few sectors, only the 1958–1962 series is shown in Figure V–1 because no "roughly comparable" series was readily available; these sectors are all small.

Exports of the industries not listed in Table V–1 have been extrapolated more or less mechanically from graphs similar to those of Figure V–1. For the export-sensitive industries, most of the trend projections have been tempered by or supported by independent information or conjecture. Among these considerations were the following:[1]

Crops. The 6.5 percent growth rate shown on Figure V–1 is a combination of an 8 percent growth rate in exports to Japan and to Europe outside the Common Market, a 4 percent growth to Common Market countries, and a 7 percent growth rate to the rest of the world. It is, of course, the Common Market's grain policy which is expected to slow down exports to its countries to about 4 percent per year, though American soya bean and meal exports should continue as the raw material of the expanding European livestock and poultry industry. The growth rates of exports to the rest of the world are expected to continue because of the growth of their economies and the difference in agricultural productivity between these countries and the United States. The Common Market countries presently buy about one-quarter of U.S. crop exports, the rest of Europe and Japan take another quarter, and the rest of the world imports the other half. The projected rate therefore comes out to be 6.5 percent per year $(6.5 = (\frac{1}{4})4 + (\frac{1}{4})8 + (\frac{1}{2})7)$.

Coal. The difficulty of forecasting coal exports appears immedi-

---

[1] The following comments draw heavily on an unpublished report by Arthur D. Little, Inc.

ately from the graph in Figure V–1. Political factors such as the Suez crisis or protection of the coal industries of the principal importing countries, most of which are West European, have played a large role in this erratic history. As a result, we have little basis for establishing a trend in the economically determined demand for coal exports. Nevertheless, it is safe to say that U.S. coal can compete in price in Europe for both electrical generation and steel production. The recent and expected future expansion of the European steel industry in locations accessible to seagoing commerce is conducive to coal exports for steelmaking. For electrical generation, the principal competitor of coal is fuel oil, and there might be some question of what effects the North Sea gas discoveries may have on the price of fuel oil. At present, it appears that the principal effects will be in the prices of naphtha and raw materials for chemical manufacturing rather than in fuel oil prices. We have therefore presumed that European industrial coal usage will grow at about the same rate as U.S. usage, 2.5 percent per year, while the U.S. share of the European market will also rise about 2.5 percent per year, for a total growth in U.S. coal exports of somewhere around 5 percent per year.

Basic chemicals and plastics and synthetic materials. During the last decade, exports of these items have expanded an average of 8 to 10 percent per year. During these years, the U.S. has enjoyed a relative technological advantage and a cheap source of raw materials on the Gulf Coast. Now, however, foreign companies are reaching comparable technological levels, building plants of comparable scale, and securing raw materials at comparable cost. A slackening of the growth rate would seem to be in prospect, though the expansion in the use of plastics and a continuation of international specialization argue for the maintenance of a high growth rate. We have projected 6 percent per year.

Capital goods. For nearly all types of machinery, exports account for a large and rapidly expanding portion of the market. Several factors combine to promise a continuation of their growth. First, trade barriers are low and are not likely to be raised, for most developing countries recognize that high tariffs on machinery would only hamper their industrialization programs. Second, the kinds of machines made in the United States and in the rest of the world often differ because of the high wage rates in this country. Machines designed for the American market therefore usually have more power and automatic controls and produce more per man-hour spent operating them than do typical European machines which serve the same general purpose. Diversity is the wellspring of trade, and manufacturers in low-wage countries find that, for particular applications, a more expensive, heavy-duty U.S. machine is more economical than the light or low-powered type of machine they usually buy. Conversely, of course, U.S. manufacturers often find imported machines fill a particular bill better than domestically made ones. The U.S. industry, therefore, should be able to sell well in the rapidly growing markets of the developing countries while simultaneously experiencing stiff import competition. Finally, the shift from stagnation to growth in the domestic demand for machinery should make possible swelling catalogues and specialties that catch the eye of the foreign purchaser. Though in the short term, good domestic business can lengthen delivery times and thereby diminish export sales, in the long run, when capacity has been adjusted to take care of the higher demand, it supports the export trade.

One comprehensive model[2] which projects world trading patterns to 1970 shows a growth of U.S. machinery exports by 10.2 percent per year between 1959 and 1970. This model, which was developed in the Netherlands, balances world exports and world imports in seven major industrial categories—one being machinery—and relates imports to the economic growth of the importing country. Its high rate of growth for U.S. machinery exports indicates that our high rates are not out of line with world demand or the product of an optimism confined to this side of the Atlantic.

IMPORTS

Two types of imports are distinguished in the model: those which are directly allocated (the so-called noncompetitive imports) and those which are allocated indirectly (the competitive imports). The directly allocated class consists of those items which are not produced in significant quantity in this country (such as coffee beans) plus the imports purchased directly by final-demand sectors (such as packaged biscuits), whether or not they are produced in this country. These directly allocated imports are handled by a special import row of the input-output matrix. Imported coffee beans, for example, appear

---

2 L. B. M. Mennes, "A World Trade Model for 1970," unpublished paper presented at the Rome meetings of the Econometric Society in 1965.

in this row as an input into the "miscellaneous food products" sector, which roasts and blends coffee; the imported biscuits appear as a sale at the intersection of the import row and the consumption column. Such directly allocated imports account for approximately half of the total imports. The workings of the model forecast them automatically; so it is not necessary to discuss them further here.

The indirectly allocated, or competitive, imports consist of raw and semi-manufactured materials which compete with domestic production, such as raw petroleum, iron and non-ferrous metal ores, chemical minerals, raw sugar, textiles, lumber, newsprint, refined metals, and machinery and instruments of all sorts. These commodities, in fact, constitute the bulk of this sort of imports. Such imports appear in the input-output table as negative entries in an import column where they reduce the total demand for the corresponding domestically produced commodity. That is, they are treated as negative exports. Therefore, they must, like the exports, be independently forecast. Barring special circumstances, however, it seems reasonable to suppose that the demand for the imports will grow at about the same rate as the demand for the domestically produced article. We have followed this supposition wherever there are no obvious special circumstances. The resulting growth rates appear in the "competitive import" column of the Master Table.

Several of these "obvious special circumstances" merit mention.[3] Because of a presumed high income elasticity of consumers for imported beverages, we expect their sales to continue growing at about 7 percent per year, as they have in the past. Similarly, imported bakery products, which account for only a crumb of the market at present, should continue to rise rapidly.

We expect a continuation of the slow trend to self-sufficiency in newsprint; so the growth rate of paper imports is put at 3 percent per year, one percentage point less than the paper industry's growth rate. The Mandatory Imports Program for petroleum ties imports into the area east of the Rockies to 12.2 percent of domestic production. Imports from Canada and into the West Coast, which are not under the Mandatory Program, should continue to increase somewhat faster than domestic production and bring the growth rate of imports up to about 5 percent per year against a growth in domestic production of 3.3 percent per year.

[3] Again I draw on the unpublished Arthur D. Little report.

Machinery imports will grow more rapidly than machinery output for the same reasons that their exports grow faster than output.

Imports of all ores are expected to grow faster than the domestic output and thus to continue increasing the U.S. dependence on imported raw materials. Similarly, leather imports should continue to increase because of the demand for greater variety in leathers, although, as in the past, the total demand for leather is not expanding.

The total expansion projected in exports approximately equals the expansion in total imports (both directly and indirectly allocated). Because we are forecasting in constant dollars, this approximate equality between export and import expansion is consistent with either an improved or a worsened balance of payments, according to how the foreign and domestic price levels move. Moreover, even at constant prices, a change of a few percentage points in exports or imports can change their difference, and therefore the balance of payments, by many more points, although the effect on industry outputs is negligible. In short, these forecasts are *not* forecasts of the balance of payments.

VI

The Input-Output Table

In the center of our forecasting system stands what is usually called an input-output table, a table showing how much each industry needs of the produce of other industries in order to produce one dollar's worth of its own output. The table is usually laid out as in Table I-1 of Chapter I, so that the inputs into a particular industry form a vertical *column*, while the sales of an industry to other industries form a horizontal *row*. A table which shows the sales in dollars from each industry to each other industry is termed a transactions or *flow* table, while the table which shows each column of this flow table divided by the output of the using industry—the requirements per dollar of output—is called the *coefficient* table. In this terminology, the "steel coefficient in the automobile column" is the value of the steel (in dollars) needed to make one dollar's worth of automobiles.

Our coefficient table is based upon the one prepared by the Department of Commerce for the year 1958.[1] Naturally, many of the coefficients will change by 1975; some of these changes can be fairly confidently predicted on the basis of engineering knowledge or economic trends. Probable changes in most of the significant coefficients have been studied and projected by Anne P. Carter, of the Harvard Research Project on the Structure of the American Economy, and by members of the staff of Arthur D. Little, Inc. I have relied entirely on their work in this field and therefore have neither the competence, right, nor desire to go into a full description of these projected coefficient changes here. Such a description can only

[1] *Survey of Current Business*, September 1965. Because the flow tables in this publication were not released by the Department of Commerce until a few weeks before this book went to press, I did not know, as I wrote it, precisely what the 1958 flows would be. I have written this book almost entirely in terms of index numbers to prevent an inadvertent comparison of a 1963 or 1975 flow with an "official" 1958 flow which may be different from the value I assumed on the basis of incomplete data.

be written by those who have done the work, and indeed the descriptions they have already written fill several volumes larger than this one. The extent of coefficient projection can be quickly seen from the Master Table. In all, some four hundred coefficients have trends; in addition, some which were studied were left constant. To give the reader some rough idea of the kind of work which went into these projections, the first section below describes and illustrates three general approaches to this work. The second section discusses some of the technical problems connected with handling secondary products in input-output forecasting.

COEFFICIENT PROJECTION

Though the methods which can be used to forecast changes in coefficients are as varied as the technical developments they reflect, to organize our discussion we may distinguish three categories which, for convenience, we may call technical projections, judicious extrapolations, and product-mix adjustments. The first works directly and quantitatively with engineering information; the second combines engineering judgment with a comparison of two (or more) past input-output tables, while the last makes almost no use of engineering knowledge but relies upon trends in the assortment of products produced by an input-output sector and upon more detailed input information than the table contains. Because technical projection is the most colorful when it can be done, we begin with an illustration in electrical generation.

TECHNICAL PROJECTION

Five sources of energy are used in the production of electricity—coal, oil, gas, water, and nuclear power. The input coefficients into the electricity column depend, of course, on the relative shares of each of the five and upon the thermal efficiency of each. The latter question is one to which engineers were able to address themselves fairly readily. On the basis of projections of efficiency, fuel prices, and capital costs, curves were drawn showing the relative costs of building a kilowatt of capacity for each type of generation in each future year. Different regions of the country had different curves because of the large regional differences in the relative prices of the fuels. For regions and years in which the cost of two kinds of plants, say, coal and nuclear, are about equal, we assumed that coal would get half of the newly built plants while nuclear power would capture the other half. Where nuclear generation has the edge, but not decisively enough to prevent special locational factors from swinging some new plants to coal, we assumed that 75 percent of the new construction would be nuclear and 25 percent coal-burning, while for wider cost spreads, all new units were assumed to be nuclear. Then, by splitting down the model's forecast of increments in electrical generation by regions, we calculated how many megawatts of new capacity of each type (coal, nuclear, etc.) would be installed in each year. Cumulating this investment produces the shares of each type in 1975. The resulting shares show nuclear power and gas gaining at the expense of the other sources as shown in the table below.

| | *Share in Generation* | |
Energy Source	1958	1975
Coal	54%	51%
Oil	7	5
Gas	17	22
Hydro	22	15
Nuclear	0	7
	100%	100%

Although only 7 percent of the generation will be nuclear by 1975, the calculations predict that nearly half of the capacity built in that year will be nuclear.

Trends were then introduced into the coefficients in the coal, oil, and gas utility rows of the electricity column to adjust for the combined effects of increasing thermal efficiency[2] and the changing composition of capacity. In the chemicals row, a coefficient had to be introduced for nuclear fuel. The 1958 table shows a zero entry, and so we had to make up one from technical information. By 1975, this cost is expected to be about .14 cents per kilowatt hour, or about one-third of the cost of nuclear generation. Adding to the cost of generation the average profits and the average costs of transmission and distribution of a kilowatt-hour of electricity gives the total price of nuclear power in 1975. Dividing this sum into .14 cents gives the share of nuclear fuels in this cost. Since 7 percent of 1975 production is expected to be nuclear, 7 percent of this share is the chemical coefficient in the electricity column of the 1975 table.

Though electrical generation was clearly the easiest industry in which to make direct technical projections, the approach was useful

[2] At this point and at countless others, Resources for the Future's book, *Resources in America's Future* (John Hopkins Press, 1963), proved very helpful.

in other, less clear-cut cases. For example, in the steel industry technical advice enabled us to estimate the input vectors into the various steelmaking processes—the open hearth, the electric furnace, and the basic oxygen process—and helped us to estimate the fraction of steel output which will be made by each process by 1975. On the last point, however, we found ourselves in the middle of a controversy among the experts. Some of them held that the ability of the oxygen process to use scrap is narrowly limited and that widespread use of this process will hold down the price of scrap so that the open hearth, with its much greater scrap-using ability, will continue to be economical. Other experts held that the first group underestimated the scrap-using potential of the basic oxygen process and that if scrap became cheaper relative to pig iron, the process could be modified to use more scrap. Furthermore, they argued, improved manufacturing methods are cutting down on prompt industrial scrap while new methods of pelletizing and magnetic separation of ores tend to keep down the price of pig iron.

This argument makes plain how quickly a discussion of technology can turn into a question of economics and relative prices. Though we were not really able to judge the discussion on its merits, we have leaned toward the views of the second group and have projected a large gain for the basic oxygen process. Within each process, moreover, we have projected declines in fuel use due to the speeding up of the whole process through the use of oxygen.

JUDICIOUS EXTRAPOLATION

Though there are other instances of the use of direct technical projection, its application remains limited by the disparity between the aggregates with which the economist must work if he is to include the whole economy in his system and the much more detailed products which the engineer can think about easily. More detailed input-output tables will facilitate this communication, but the barriers are likely to remain for a long time. The economist wants to know about the use of basic chemicals in rubber and plastic products; the engineer is ready to talk about the compounds used for treating stereo-type synthetic rubber. "You can't generalize," is often the advice the economist quickly gets when he seeks technical help. To get a conversation with an industry expert off to a more auspicious start than that, we have found it useful to begin by presenting him with the kind of generalization we want. For example, we might begin by saying to a specialist on machinery manufacture, "Our statistics show that between 1947 and 1958 the steel input into food, textile, paper-making, and printing machinery declined from 10 cents per dollar of output to 9 cents per dollar, while non-ferrous metals rose from 2 cents to 4.5 cents. What specific developments do you think were responsible for most of this change? Do you expect the rate of change to accelerate, diminish, or stay about the same over the next ten years?" This approach at least seemed to loosen the tongues of the specialists, and from their comments one could put together an informed guess about future trends. Sometimes, as in the case of the non-ferrous coefficient just mentioned, they felt the substitution possibilities causing the past rise had about been exhausted, and therefore they expected no further increase. In the case of the steel coefficient, they thought the decline would continue but at only about half its former rate. Such "judicious extrapolations" are rough at best and should not be supposed to be highly accurate. I believe, however, that they generally reflect the right direction and order of magnitude of coefficient change and will prove better than leaving the coefficients constant—the only really feasible alternative.

The "judicious extrapolation" approach required input-output tables for two different years. In the early 1950s, a large-scale, 450-sector table was made for the year 1947. Because of the detail and thorough documentation of this table, it was possible to make from it a 1947 table in the 1958 prices comparable with the 1958 table in sector definition and accounting conventions. It took many months of patient labor on the part of Anne Carter and her assistants at Harvard to produce the two comparable tables which provided the starting point for the "judicious extrapolations." Comparisons of the 1958 and 1947 tables are studied in numerous ways in a forthcoming article by Mrs. Carter. For a few coefficients, especially in the energy, fuels, and metals rows, it was possible to construct an annual series up to 1962 and from it to make a more reliable extrapolation than could be done from the two-point comparison.

PRODUCT-MIX ADJUSTMENTS

The third, and perhaps most widely used, method of forecasting coefficients hinges on the fact that certain parts of some heterogeneous sectors are expected to grow faster than other parts of the same sector. When coupled with differences in the input coefficients of the components of a sector, these differences in the growth rate of the components produce apparent changes in coefficients, though no technological change is involved. For example, the following table shows that the components of the plastics and synthetic materials sector have very different requirements for pulp and paper.

Pulp and Paper Coefficient for the Plastics and Synthetics Materials Sector

SIC Industry Number	Name	Paper-Row Coefficient	Share of Total 1958	Sector Output 1975
2821	Plastics	.02	.52	.63
2822	Rubber	.02	.15	.12
2823	Cellulosic fibers	.20	.14	.05
2824	Noncellulosic fibers	.02	.19	.20

The purchases of this sector from the paper sector consist mostly of wood pulp for use as a raw material. One of the four-digit subsectors, cellulosic fibers, uses pulp as its principal raw material and has a pulp coefficient ten times the size of that of the other subsectors. In 1958, the average coefficient for the whole plastics and synthetics sector came to about .046; but it is certain that by 1975 the output of cellulosic fibers will have declined in relation to the other products in this sector and lowered this average. The last column in the Master Table shows a rough guess of output proportions in 1975, a guess which implies an average paper-row coefficient of .029, only 63 percent of the 1958 coefficient.

On the basis of the detailed input information contained in the *Special Supplement on Materials Consumed* of the *1958 Census of Manufactures*, such product-mix adjustments were made for a number of industries. In some cases it was possible to adjust the detailed coefficients for expected technical changes before applying the anticipated changes in product mix. The extent of such technical projections was limited only by our resources and resourcefulness.

The need for hand adjustments for changes in product mix on the basis of published data would be automatically eliminated (and the work would be done much more precisely) if we had an input-output table which made full use of the detail our Censuses presently offer. Had we had four sectors instead of one for plastics and synthetics, the above adjustment would have been unnecessary. Such hand adjustments for shifts in the product mix *within* four-digit industries will continue to be necessary even for quite large tables, but it should not be necessary to resort to them except where they can reflect special information not available in the Census.

Prices and Paper Clips

Two special problems in the projection of input-output coefficients require a word of explanation, namely, the problem of prices and what might be called the paper-clip problem. As to the first, we have said in Chapter I that the forecasts are in constant dollars; we make no estimate of the rate of inflation in the future. In the coefficient-change studies, however, we have necessarily considered the effects of expected changes in *relative* prices. For example, in the electrical generation study, the projected price of coal influences the coefficient forecasts, but future coal usage is measured by its dollar value in 1958 prices, that is, by an almost physical output measure. This procedure works well enough for a fairly unchanging commodity, like coal, for which a price index can be relatively clearly defined. But what is a constant dollar's worth of electronic components? Prices of particular components have sometimes dropped 50 percent or more in just a few years simply because improvements in manufacturing curtail the loss on rejects. If we stick with the physical unit as the measure of output, we will have to change all of the input coefficients in the column of the producing industry though the product itself shows no change. If, on the other hand, we use "current-dollar" output, i.e., sales in the prices of the year in which they are made, no change at all may be necessary. Another argument for using current-dollar outputs is that physical units are often hard to specify. Isn't a transistor which does the job of an electronic tube the "same" product at a far lower price from the economic point of view? If so, the making of price indexes for electronic components becomes a hopeless task. We gave up on it and were guided instead (I am not sure how consistently) by the following general rule: Measure commodities which (like coal) have clearly defined price indexes in "constant" dollars; measure other commodities (like electronic components) in what "current" dollars will be if prices on basic materials do not change and wage rates increase $3\frac{1}{4}$ percent per year.[3]

The paper-clip problem concerns the many small items which are used by almost all industries but account for a negligible fraction of the total materials purchases of any one industry. Direct information on how many paper clips, say, the aircraft industry consumes is not available and is not likely to be collected. Rather than try to dis-

[3] The "noninflationary guidepost" rate.

tribute each such item separately, all office supplies products, wherever they are produced, have been treated in the input-output table as if they were sold to a "dummy" office supply column. The "output" of this column is then distributed among the industries. Paper clips and pencils, therefore, are assumed to be consumed in the same proportion in all industries.

The procedure is satisfactory enough for well-established items like paper clips. The difficulties start when the photocopier appears on the scene and increases its sales fivefold in five years. The paper it uses can be put into office supplies, though only at the expense of forecasting changes in all the coefficients of the office supply row and column. The machines themselves, however, belong in the capital equipment matrix, but in any one industry's capital spending they will form only a negligible fraction. All industries together, however, compose an important and very fast-growing market. The recent very rapid expansion in carpet sales to industry and institutions caused by the newly discovered low maintenance costs of rugs is another example of a similar market. In theory, these markets should be perfect for analysis by input-output because they spread over the whole economy. In practice, they are awkward for input-output because the factors which cause, say, the steel industry to invest large sums in new plants have little or nothing to do with what causes it to buy photocopiers or rugs. Moreover, they are markets which expand rapidly at first but then begin to feel the effects of saturation. In fact, these demands are probably as close as one is likely to come to private "autonomous" demand and therefore probably should be handled in a special final demand column just as defense purchases now are. In the present work, we became aware of the photocopier and rug problems only at the end of our work, when the relevant part of the *1963 Census of Manufactures* appeared. As a quick expedient, to redress the imbalance between 1963 actual output and that implied by the 1958 coefficients, we dumped all the excess rugs and photocopying machines into the office supplies column, thereby bringing the sum of this column to more than 1.0, but made no changes in the office supply row.

SECONDARY PRODUCTS

In the Master Table, a few small entries appear which may prove slightly puzzling without a word of explanation. For example, it appears that in 1975, 6 percent of the output of wooden containers will be used by the lumber industry. Now it takes only a casual acquaintance with the lumber industry to know that it uses scarcely any wooden boxes at all. What then are all these boxes doing in that cell of the table? The answer is that they are not boxes at all, but lumber products *other than* wooden containers which happen, however, to be made by plants whose primary business is making wooden containers. This somewhat strange arrangement is the result of inevitable problems with industrial classification and shortcuts in computer programing which could and should be eliminated.

The classification problems arise because many establishments produce items belonging to two different four-digit product categories, say, wooden boxes and lumber. An establishment will be classified in the box industry, or the lumber industry, or another four-digit industry according to which one has the highest fraction of its output. All of the products belonging to that four-digit industry are said to be "primary" to that establishment; all its other products are called "secondary." Some of the most important information used in making the input-output table is the purchases of specific materials by establishments. If the establishment makes more than one product, we simply do not know how the materials are divided among those products. Therefore, in what we call the *primary* input-output table, a column, say the lumber column, shows the inputs into all *establishments* whose *primary* product is lumber, whatever else they may produce. The lumber row of this table, however, shows the distribution of only lumber (and not of the other products, such as barrels, of establishments primarily engaged in sawing lumber). Moreover, this row includes *all* lumber, even the so-called "secondary" lumber which is produced by plants whose primary business is making something else, say, wooden boxes.

The question which this primary table does not answer and which must be answered before we can work back from final demands to industry outputs is: How will the total production of an item, say, lumber, be spread among the establishments classified in the various industries? What fraction of lumber will be "primary," that is, produced by establishments in the lumber column and what fraction will be "secondary," coming from establishments in the wooden container column, the crops column, and so on? The assumption we have used is that the percentage distribution of each material's production among primary and secondary producers will remain the same as it was in 1958. Because the secondary production is generally small relative to the primary, more complicated methods of treating the problem by statistical creation of "pure" producing industries did not seem to merit the labor they would have required.

This assumption, known as the "transfer along the row" method of dealing with secondary production, can be easily incorporated into the input-output calculations. We simply introduce an artificial flow, a transfer, from, say, the wooden container industry to the lumber industry in the amount of the lumber produced in wooden container establishments. The total output of an industry then becomes the sum of all output of establishments in that industry plus all such transfers into the industry. The introduction of these artificial or "secondary" flows has the advantage of avoiding special calculations for the secondary. Its disadvantage is that it confounds primary and secondary flows in the same table, so that in interpreting a flow one must always bear in mind that it may be in part secondary rather than primary.

In most cases, such as the "wooden-containers-to-lumber" flows, the secondary flow is rather easily recognized. Nevertheless, in future work I think it will be worthwhile to keep the division of an item's production among the various columns separate from the primary flows. The portion of the computer program which does this division of output among producers can also, at the same time, aggregate the sums of several rows into the output of one column. The convenience of having the same number of rows and columns therefore disappears. We would be perfectly free to have many more products (rows) than producing industries (columns). This is an interesting possibility which will come up again in the last chapter.

VII

Labor Force and Productivity

As Saturn, in Kepler's system, marks out the space within which all the lower planets must revolve, so the labor force forecast in our system delimits the field within which all the other forecasts must work out their places. The first section sets forth this forecast of the labor force, but how fast this forecast will let the economy grow depends also on how fast labor productivity increases. The second section, therefore, attempts to ascertain and project historical trends in labor productivity in each industry. The third section presents the employment forecasts by industry and indicates how faster growth of labor supply or productivity would affect the output and employment in the various industries.

For many business planning problems, the bounding role of the labor force constraint exhausts the significance of this chapter; but for many public uses of forecasts—for regional planning or for guiding national manpower development—it is important to know in which industries employment will grow fast and in which, slowly. For these purposes, the individual industry productivity projections must be carefully examined.

THE LABOR FORCE AND POPULATION FORECAST

The population forecast used in the labor force forecasts and in the consumption forecasts is the second highest of four alternative projections made by the U.S. Census Bureau.[1] The bureau considers it "a moderately high series in that it presumes only a modest drop from the levels of fertility in the last decade." The presumed drop reflects the notion that women in the 25–35 age groups in 1962 will, in comparison with women in these age groups five or ten years

[1] *Projections of the Population of the United States, by Age and Sex: 1964 to 1985,* Current Population Reports, Series P-25, No. 286, July 1964. Series B was used.

earlier, have fewer children in their remaining childbearing years because they had more when they were younger. Their completed fertility rates would still be in the range of 3.2 to 3.5 children per woman as compared to 2.4 for women aged 45 to 49 in 1962. According to this projection, the U.S. population will grow by 1.5 percent per year between 1965 and 1975.

From this population projection, a labor force "outlook" has been developed by the Bureau of Labor Statistics.[2] Because all the workers of 1975 have already been born, the principal uncertainties are how many women will want work, how long young men and women will go to school, and how soon men will retire. Separate participation rates were projected for each five-year age group of each sex. In some cases, these groups were further separated: Different rates were used for unmarried women, married women with a child under five, and married women without a child under five. People under 25 and in school have different rates from people under 25 and not in school. Farmers in the groups over 60 have higher participation rates than other men of the same age. In projecting trends in the labor force participation rates of each of these groups, it was "assumed that the change from 1948 to [1964] would continue but at a declining pace [so that, between 1964 and 1980] the change in rate would be about half the amount that had occurred in the preceding 16 years."[3] An alternative projection showed that if all the trends continued unabated, the 1980 labor force would be 3.5 percent higher and contain 3.7 million more women and 0.2 million fewer men. This alternative gives us a useful indication of the degree of uncertainty in the labor force projection.

This projection tells us the total number of people seeking work, while the model generates the number of jobs in private industry and agriculture. Therefore, if we start with the labor force, we must make the following adjustments to find the number of jobs the model's forecasts should create:

Subtract all government employees (except those in government enterprises, which are treated like private industries).
Subtract domestic servants.
Subtract unemployed persons.
Add number of second and third jobs held.

2 Sophia Cooper and Denis F. Johnston, "The Outlook for the Labor Force at Mid-Decade," a paper presented before the American Statistical Association, December 30, 1964.
3 *Ibid.*, p. 5.

TABLE VII-1. LABOR BALANCE: HISTORY, 1958–1963, AND FORECAST TO 1980

(in thousands)

	1958	1959	1960	1961	1962	1963	1970	1975	1980
+ Model employment	57,480	59,519	59,777	58,960	60,170	60,748	69,610	74,958	79,940
Model wage & salary workers[a]	43,529	45,214	45,850	45,395	46,625	47,444			
Model proprietors exc. agriculture[b]	6,551	6,903	6,593	6,423	6,694	6,674			
Model agriculture[c]	5,844	5,836	5,723	5,463	5,190	4,946			
Model government enterprises[d]	956	969	996	1,017	1,038	1,064			
Model unpaid family workers[e]	(600)	597	615	662	623	(620)			
+ Federal government[d]	4,291	4,195	4,199	4,295	4,557	4,495	4,630	4,880	4,930
Military[d]	2,632	2,543	2,516	2,598	2,800	2,723	2,700	2,700	2,700
Defense Department civilian[f]	1,098	1,088	1,047	1,042	1,068	1,063	1,000	1,000	1,000
Other federal	561	564	636	655	689	709	930	1,180	1,230
+ State & local[d]	5,507	5,700	5,986	6,179	6,473	6,753	8,820	10,570	12,990
Public education[d]	2,552	2,684	2,872	2,957	3,184	3,385	4,420	5,270	6,640
Other state & local[d]	2,552	3,016	3,114	3,222	3,289	3,368	4,400	5,300	6,350
+ Domestic service[d]	2,550	2,575	2,559	2,662	2,694	2,656	2,800	2,900	3,000
= Total jobs held	69,828	71,989	72,521	72,114	73,894	74,652	85,860	93,308	100,860
− Multiple job adjustment	3,195	3,856	3,326	2,746	3,221	3,106	3,200	3,300	3,400
= Total people working	66,633	68,133	69,195	69,368	70,673	71,546	82,660	90,008	97,460
+ Unemployment	4,681	3,813	3,931	4,806	4,007	4,166	3,332[g]	3,638[g]	3,948[g]
= Labor force (total)[c]	71,284	71,946	73,126	74,175	74,681	75,712	85,992	93,646	101,408

[a] Bureau of Labor Statistics, *Employment and Earnings Statistics*, March 1965, Table B–1, column 1 less column 11.
[b] National accounts, in *Survey of Current Business*, July 1964, persons engaged in production less full-time equivalent employees for all industries except farms.
[c] Labor force table in *Employment and Earnings*.
[d] National accounts, full- and part-time employees.
[e] *Employment and Earnings*, September 1963, p. 94.
[f] Bureau of the Census, *Statistical Abstract of the United States*.
[g] Four percent of projected civilian labor force in 1970, 1975, and 1980.

Table VII–1 shows the "model employment" calculated through these adjustments for 1958–1963 and projected for 1970, 1975 and 1980.

In the projection, the "exogenous" nonmodel employment was predicted along the following lines. The number of military personnel and Department of Defense civilian employees has been assumed to remain unchanged, while the number of other, nondefense federal employees is assumed to grow in line with its recent trend at about 4 percent per year. For the half of state and local government employees who work in public education, the forecasts are made by assuming a continuation of the upward trend in their number per child between the ages of 5 and 17 and then applying this number to the number of children of these ages in the population forecast discussed above. The result is a slackening in the rate of growth of employment in public education. Other state and local employment is assumed to continue growing along the steady trend it has followed in the past decade. Domestic service seems to have reversed its long decline; a slow increase is expected in the future. For reference, unemployment is set at 4 percent of the civilian labor force, and the number of second and third jobs held is assumed to increase slightly from the 1963 level. Figure I–1 (p. 5) shows the projection of private employment which results from these assumptions.

TRENDS IN LABOR PRODUCTIVITY

Our projections of labor productivity are all simple exponential extrapolations of historical trends from 1947 to 1963. In principle, all we have done is, for each industry, to calculate the number of man-hours worked in each year, divide them by the output of that year, plot the ratios on semilogarithmic graph paper, fit (by eye) a straight line through the points, and extrapolate it into the future. In so simple a scheme, there are only two major tasks: One is to get the historical series on man-hours and the other is, of course, to find an appropriate historical series on output.

Instead of actually computing man hours per year in each industry, we used what might be called "constant-hours man years." These were computed by the formula:

$$(1) \qquad M_{it} = \frac{H_i(t)}{H_i(1963)} \, P_i(t) + N_i(t),$$

where $H_i(t)$ = average weekly hours of production workers in industry i
in year t.

$P_i(t)$ = average number of production employees in industry i in
year t.

$N_i(t)$ = average number of nonproduction employees in industry
i in year t.

M_{it}, the "constant-hours man-years" is therefore just the number of nonproduction workers plus the *hour-adjusted* number of production workers. The *Employment and Earnings Statistics* of the Bureau of Labor Statistics enables us to construct such a series for the non-agricultural industries for 1958 and subsequent years. Prior to that date, the Standard Industrial Classification (SIC) was somewhat different; and the M_t series, therefore, cannot be carried back to 1947 for all industries in the model. Such a series back to 1947 can, however, be constructed for all the major (two-digit) industries.

For our choice of output indexes, there are two major contenders: the Federal Reserve Board Index of Production and the deflated value of shipments. The FRB indexes have the advantage that they are readily available and represent a thorough effort to measure the growth of physical volume of output. But for our present purposes, the crucial question is whether a given historical output series is comparable with the future outputs which will be generated by the forecasting system. Now the forecasts are determined very largely by the consumption projections, and these, in turn, are based upon functions estimated from the personal consumption expenditure series in the national accounts. These series are derived, in concept if not always in practice, by deflating the shipments of manufacturing industries by appropriate portions of the Wholesale Price Index and splitting the result between consumption and intermediate use. Thus, in the end, we see that the historical output series with which the forecasts are comparable are the price-deflated shipments for manufacturing industries. This measure of output shows growth noticeably different from the FRB indexes in a number of industries; the FRB indexes generally grow faster.

Unfortunately, such deflated shipments series are not readily available. For the years 1947 to 1958, series on such deflated shipments by SIC four-digit industries were made available to us by the Office of Business Economics. We then grouped these to match the model industries as closely as possible. For 1958 and subsequent years, we constructed such indexes by deflating the shipments of establishments in the model sector by appropriate portions of the Wholesale Price Index. Where there was no appropriate price index, we used the undeflated shipments.

For the nonmanufacturing industries, we used a variety of sources. For mining and gas and electric utilities, we used the FRB indexes; in construction, we used the output series in the national accounts. For transportation, trade, finance and insurance, we took the series on gross national product originating in the sector. For each service industry, we used national income in that industry (from the national accounts) adjusted for price changes by a deflator constructed by comparing the constant-dollar GNP originating in all services with the total national income in all the service industries. In agriculture, we used the Department of Agriculture's index of output per man-hour directly, that is, we did not estimate separate employment and output series. The USDA figures appear for crops and livestock separately in *Agricultural Statistics*. For the remaining handful of industries, such as agricultural services, rather than concoct some output index even less reliable than those above, we specified the rate of productivity change directly.

For the manufacturing industries, we also constructed output series for the major (two-digit) industries by aggregating the outputs of the appropriate model sectors with weights proportional to their employment in 1963.

For each sector for which output indexes were available, we then plotted on semilogarithmic paper the ratio of output to constant-hours man-years. For manufacturing sectors where this latter series was not available back of 1958, the index of the ratio over the 1947–1958 period for the two-digit industry of which that sector was a part was filled in on the graphs.

The productivity growth rates derived from these graphs are listed in Table VII–2, in the second column. In steady, noncyclical industries, there was usually not much uncertainty about where the trend line should be drawn. The points define the line quite unambiguously in agriculture, transportation, communications, trade, finance, amusements, medicine and education, electric and gas utilities, coal mining, the food industries, textiles, apparel, shoes, lumber, furniture, paper, printing, chemicals, rubber and plastic products, petroleum refining, non-ferrous metals, motor vehicles, and instruments. Fortunately, these industries provide the bulk of our employment; errors in productivity estimates for the remaining industries

TABLE VII–2. EMPLOYMENT GROWTH, ELASTICITY, AND PRODUCTIVITY

		Percent Growth per Year of			Output-Employment Elasticities
		Output	Labor Productivity	Employment	
1	Livestock	2.3	4.2	−1.9	0.74
2	Crops	3.2	8.0	−4.8	0.70
3	Forestry and fishery products	3.2	3.0	0.2	1.37
4	Agricultural services	3.0	1.0	2.0	0.78
5	Iron ore mining	3.8	3.8	0.0	1.18
6	Non-ferrous ore mining	2.5	6.8	−4.3	0.84
7	Coal mining	2.5	7.3	−4.8	0.71
8	Petroleum mining	2.9	4.5	−1.6	1.00
9	Minerals mining	2.8	4.2	−1.4	0.77
10	Chemical mining	3.4	3.3	0.0	0.97
11	New construction	3.9	2.1	1.8	0.85
12	Maintenance construction	3.1	0.0	3.1	0.69
13	Ordnance	−1.3	3.3	−4.6	0.00
14	Meatpacking	2.4	4.2	−1.8	0.77
15	Dairy products	2.1	2.4	−0.3	0.45
16	Canned and frozen foods	4.1	3.8	0.3	0.94
17	Grain mill products	3.5	0.9	2.6	0.52
18	Bakery products	3.6	1.3	2.3	0.56
19	Beverages	4.5	2.4	2.1	1.55
20	Miscellaneous food products	4.8	1.9	2.9	1.04
21	Tobacco	3.1	0.0	3.1	0.43
22	Fabrics and yarn	3.3	4.5	−1.2	1.53
23	Rugs, tire cord, miscellaneous textiles	3.2	5.0	−1.8	1.88
24	Apparel	3.7	2.5	1.2	1.56
25	Household textiles and upholstery	4.0	2.5	1.5	1.24
26	Lumber and products, except containers	3.3	4.5	−1.2	1.37
27	Wooden containers	1.5	4.6	−3.1	0.92
28	Household furniture	3.8	1.1	2.7	1.05
29	Office furniture	3.7	2.5	1.2	0.80
30	Paper and products, except containers	4.5	1.4	3.1	0.97
31	Paper containers	3.9	1.4	2.5	0.89
32	Printing and publishing	4.0	2.7	1.3	1.67
33	Basic chemicals	5.0	6.2	−1.2	0.77
34	Plastics and synthetics	5.2	5.0	0.2	1.03
35	Drugs, cleaning, and toilet items	4.3	3.9	0.4	0.64
36	Paint and allied products	2.3	3.4	−1.1	0.87
37	Petroleum refining	3.4	3.7	−0.3	0.86
38	Rubber and plastic products	3.9	2.6	1.3	0.87
39	Leather tanning	0.0	3.4	−3.4	1.36
40	Shoes and other leather products	2.6	0.0	2.6	1.37
41	Glass and glass products	3.3	3.6	−0.3	0.95
42	Stone and clay products	3.9	1.8	2.1	1.09
43	Iron and steel	2.8	4.9	−2.1	0.72
44	Non-ferrous metals	3.6	2.7	0.9	0.72
45	Metal containers	3.0	0.0	3.0	0.98
46	Heating, plumbing, structural metal	3.8	0.0	3.8	0.89
47	Stampings, screw machine products	2.3	0.0	2.3	0.63

Table VII-2. Employment Growth, Elasticity, and Productivity (*continued*)

		Percent Growth per Year of			Output-Employment Elasticities
		Output	Labor Productivity	Employment	
48	Hardware, plating, wire products, valves	3.4	0.0	3.4	0.74
49	Engines and turbines	4.1	1.4	2.7	0.46
50	Farm machinery and equipment	3.9	0.0	3.9	0.24
51	Construction and mining machinery	3.4	1.2	2.2	0.38
52	Material-handling equipment	3.8	4.0	−0.2	0.33
53	Metalworking machinery and equipment	4.1	0.0	4.1	0.00
54	Special industrial machinery	4.2	0.0	4.2	0.00
55	General industrial machinery	4.0	1.6	2.4	0.20
56	Machine shops and miscellaneous machinery	2.3	0.0	2.3	0.52
57	Office and computing machines	5.5	0.8	4.7	0.41
58	Service industry machines	3.6	0.4	3.2	0.70
59	Electric apparatus and motors	3.4	2.5	0.9	0.31
60	Household appliances	2.7	3.5	−0.8	0.81
61	Electric lighting and wiring equipment	3.8	0.7	3.1	0.75
62	Communication equipment	1.8	2.5	−1.3	0.16
63	Electric components	3.5	2.8	0.8	0.44
64	Batteries, X-ray, and engine electric equipment	3.7	3.3	0.4	0.66
65	Motor vehicles	3.8	3.6	0.2	0.95
66	Aircraft and parts	−0.5	0.0	−0.5	0.07
67	Ships, trains, trailers , and cycles	2.5	1.8	0.7	0.68
68	Instruments and clocks	5.5	4.5	1.0	0.72
69	Optical and photographic equipment	4.8	4.1	0.7	0.94
70	Miscellaneous manufactured products	4.1	2.3	1.8	1.18
71	Transportation	3.7	4.0	−0.3	0.92
72	Communication	4.5	6.3	−1.8	0.82
73	Radio, TV broadcasting	4.0	2.6	1.3	0.97
74	Electric utility	5.4	6.5	−1.1	0.88
75	Gas utility	5.3	7.0	−1.7	0.78
76	Water utility	4.1	0.0	4.1	0.85
77	Wholesale and retail trade	3.7	1.4	2.3	1.01
78	Finance and insurance	4.9	1.0	3.9	1.13
79	Real estate and rental	4.4	1.0	3.4	1.07
80	Hotels, personal and repair services	4.2	2.4	1.8	1.55
81	Business services	3.9	0.0	3.9	0.97
82	Research and development	0.3	0.0	0.3	0.21
83	Automobile repair services	3.7	0.0	3.7	1.17
84	Amusements and recreation	3.0	3.4	−0.6	1.73
85	Medical and educational institutions	4.9	0.0	4.9	1.36
86	Federal government enterprises	4.1	0.0	4.1	1.01
87	State and local government enterprises	4.2	0.0	4.2	0.87
88	Imports	3.9			
89	Business travel and entertainment	3.8			
90	Office supplies	3.9			

can have little effect on the total consumption needed to produce full employment. The graphs for these remaining industries, however, often leave considerable uncertainty about the rate of productivity change, and their employment projections must likewise be considered uncertain.

For iron and steel, which has a particularly volatile graph, we have connected the points for the years 1955–1956 with those for 1961–1963, both periods of relatively high output. This line implies the high rate of 4.9 percent per year increase in productivity, but it must be admitted that it is nowhere near the points for the years before 1954 or 1957–1960. Most machinery industries, and the aircraft industry, have erratic curves that show little or no decisive trend in recent years. Where in doubt, we have relied most heavily upon the 1958–1963 points for projecting the trends.

It scarcely seems necessary to point out that these productivity measures do not say what is causing the increase in productivity— automation or economies of large-scale production or better educated workers or a higher proportion of workers in high-wage jobs or still other factors. Using other measures of labor input which incorporate quality changes, one gets different, generally lower rates of productivity change. But the labor force forecast does not come in such quality units, and the principal function of these productivity trends is to allow us to compute employment comparable with the labor force. All the trends in automation, education, and shifting job structures in each industry are simply assumed to continue into the future. In particular, we have not investigated the effect of capital investment by an industry on its rate of change of productivity. It seems reasonable to suppose that a spurt in an industry's expansion, bringing with it an influx of new equipment, would quicken the rate of its productivity growth. Our model is well suited to handle such an effect if it can be measured; but at the moment, such a study must be left for the future.

In making up the employment-output ratios for the base year, 1962, the 1962 employment (including self-employed and unpaid family workers) in each industry was first adjusted, if necessary, to its "trend" value by multiplying by the ratio of the trend line to the 1962 point on the productivity graphs. Then, to assure comparability with forecast outputs, 1962 outputs were calculated by taking the 1963 outputs "forecasted" by the model and moving them back to 1962 by the 1963-1962 output index described above. The 1962 output derived in this way often differed from the 1962 output derived by moving 1958 outputs—those of the year for which the input-output table was made—forward to 1962 by the output indexes. The differences reflected changes in input-output coefficients or final demand composition which we had been unable to locate in spite of considerable attention to these matters. Using the former output, however, assures almost perfect agreement between the employment the model "forecasts" for 1963 and observed employment in that year. The ratio of the adjusted 1962 employment over the 1962 output so derived provided the base-year employment-output ratio for each industry. In each subsequent year, it was changed by the percentages shown in the first column of Table VII–2.

EMPLOYMENT FORECASTS

The rates of growth of productivity, employment, and output are exhibited in Figure VII–1. In the bar for each industry, the left vertical line marks the employment growth rate while the right vertical line marks the output growth rate. The length of the space between them, which is shaded, therefore indicates the rate of growth of productivity. The right edge of the shaded areas reveals the growth profile of production, the left edge of the shaded areas shows the employment profile, and the size of the shaded areas depicts the distribution of productivity increases in the economy.

High rates of productivity growth appear in crops (8.0 percent), gas (7.0 percent), electric utilities (6.5 percent), coal mining (7.3 percent), chemicals (3.9–6.2 percent), textiles (4.5 percent), lumber (4.5 percent), and steel (4.9 percent). Material handling and batch processing lend themselves especially well to automation, and it is therefore not surprising to note that in all these industries, relatively homogeneous articles account for much of the output. Moreover, it argues well for the continuation of the past productivity trends that some of the fastest growth rates reflect little more than new applications of old ideas. Engineering time and thought are required to put them into practice, and engineering time flows at about a constant rate from year to year.

The high rate of productivity growth in communications (6.2 percent) may appear to be all the result of one basic innovation, the dial telephone. Now that that innovation has about run its course, productivity might be expected to slow down in the next decade.

FIG. VII–1. Productivity, Employment, and Output Growth Rates

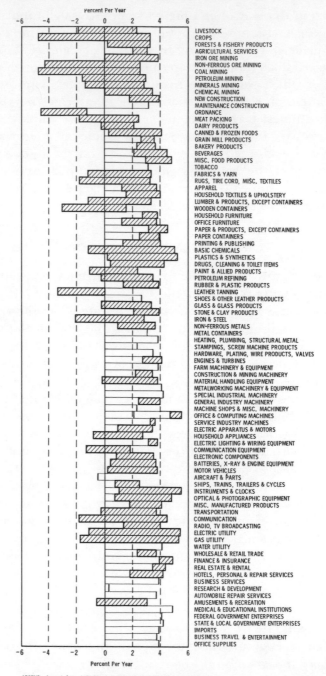

Percent Per Year

LIVESTOCK
CROPS
FORESTS & FISHERY PRODUCTS
AGRICULTURAL SERVICES
IRON ORE MINING
NON-FERROUS ORE MINING
COAL MINING
PETROLEUM MINING
MINERALS MINING
CHEMICAL MINING
NEW CONSTRUCTION
MAINTENANCE CONSTRUCTION
ORDNANCE
MEAT PACKING
DAIRY PRODUCTS
CANNED & FROZEN FOODS
GRAIN MILL PRODUCTS
BAKERY PRODUCTS
BEVERAGES
MISC. FOOD PRODUCTS
TOBACCO
FABRICS & YARN
RUGS, TIRE CORD, MISC. TEXTILES
APPAREL
HOUSEHOLD TEXTILES & UPHOLSTERY
LUMBER & PRODUCTS, EXCEPT CONTAINERS
WOODEN CONTAINERS
HOUSEHOLD FURNITURE
OFFICE FURNITURE
PAPER & PRODUCTS, EXCEPT CONTAINERS
PAPER CONTAINERS
PRINTING & PUBLISHING
BASIC CHEMICALS
PLASTICS & SYNTHETICS
DRUGS, CLEANING & TOILET ITEMS
PAINT & ALLIED PRODUCTS
PETROLEUM REFINING
RUBBER & PLASTIC PRODUCTS
LEATHER TANNING
SHOES & OTHER LEATHER PRODUCTS
GLASS & GLASS PRODUCTS
STONE & CLAY PRODUCTS
IRON & STEEL
NON-FERROUS METALS
METAL CONTAINERS
HEATING, PLUMBING, STRUCTURAL METAL
STAMPINGS, SCREW MACHINE PRODUCTS
HARDWARE, PLATING, WIRE PRODUCTS, VALVES
ENGINES & TURBINES
FARM MACHINERY & EQUIPMENT
CONSTRUCTION & MINING MACHINERY
MATERIAL HANDLING EQUIPMENT
METALWORKING MACHINERY & EQUIPMENT
SPECIAL INDUSTRIAL MACHINERY
GENERAL INDUSTRY MACHINERY
MACHINE SHOPS & MISC. MACHINERY
OFFICE & COMPUTING MACHINES
SERVICE INDUSTRY MACHINES
ELECTRIC APPARATUS & MOTORS
HOUSEHOLD APPLIANCES
ELECTRIC LIGHTING & WIRING EQUIPMENT
COMMUNICATION EQUIPMENT
ELECTRONIC COMPONENTS
BATTERIES, X-RAY & ENGINE EQUIPMENT
MOTOR VEHICLES
AIRCRAFT & PARTS
SHIPS, TRAINS, TRAILERS & CYCLES
INSTRUMENTS & CLOCKS
OPTICAL & PHOTOGRAPHIC EQUIPMENT
MISC. MANUFACTURED PRODUCTS
TRANSPORTATION
COMMUNICATION
RADIO, TV BROADCASTING
ELECTRIC UTILITY
GAS UTILITY
WATER UTILITY
WHOLESALE & RETAIL TRADE
FINANCE & INSURANCE
REAL ESTATE & RENTAL
HOTELS, PERSONAL & REPAIR SERVICES
BUSINESS SERVICES
RESEARCH & DEVELOPMENT
AUTOMOBILE REPAIR SERVICES
AMUSEMENTS & RECREATION
MEDICAL & EDUCATIONAL INSTITUTIONS
FEDERAL GOVERNMENT ENTERPRISES
STATE & LOCAL GOVERNMENT ENTERPRISES
IMPORTS
BUSINESS TRAVEL & ENTERTAINMENT
OFFICE SUPPLIES

Percent Per Year

LEGEND: In each bar: Left side of shaded area marks employment growth rate.
Right side of shaded area marks output growth rate.
Shaded area is equal to productivity growth rate.

SOURCE: Table VII–1.

But, although dialing is now almost universal, telephone productivity has not slackened its growth in recent years. One reason, perhaps, is that the productivity of "plant" workers (repairmen, linemen, etc.) as well as that of operators has been increasing rapidly all along. Between 1955 and 1959, the operating revenue per plant worker increased 5 percent per year.[4] We therefore have projected a continuation of the historical trend.

Productivity generally grows more slowly in the machine-making industries, where the processes have been harder to automate. The cost savings resulting from advances in the techniques of electronic manufacturing, such as the use of printed circuits and micro parts have been passed on to purchasers through price reductions and do not show up in labor productivity when we use the output measures discussed in the preceding chapter.

Since there is some uncertainty about the level of total employment in the future—both because the assumption of 4 percent unemployment is somewhat arbitrary and because of the uncertainty about labor force participation—it is desirable to know how the outputs of the various industries would be affected by achieving a higher or lower level of employment through regulation of the growth of consumption. The fourth column of Table VII–2 presents such information in the form of "output-employment" elasticities, the percentage by which each industry's output (and employment) increases when total "model" employment is increased 1 percent through an increase in consumption. These elasticities represent, in a sense, the transformation of the income elasticities of our consumption study back through the economy to the industry outputs. It is not surprising, therefore, to see the high output-employment elasticities occurring in the industries that make high-elasticity consumer items. For these industries, the output-employment elasticities will be somewhat higher than the consumption-income elasticity, because some industries, especially the defense and export-dependent machinery sectors, respond very little to consumption. Total consumption must rise somewhat more than 1 percent to get private employment up 1 percent. Thus, the highest output-employment elasticity, the 1.88 in the rugs and tire cord industry, exceeds the consumer's income elasticity of 1.85 for rugs, the principal product of the industry. The other high output-employment elasticities oc-

---

[4] Number of plant workers from statement of Paul A. Gorman in *New Views on Automation* Joint Economic Committee, 86th Cong., 2nd. Sess.

cur in service industries such as amusements and recreation (1.73), hotels and personal services (1.55), medical and educational institutions (1.36), and in industries related to clothing, such as apparel (1.56), fabrics (1.53), and shoes (1.37). The high elasticities of lumber (1.37) and, hence, of forestry (1.37) reflect the response of residential construction, the largest user of lumber. The biggest employer of all, wholesale and retail trade, has the neutral elasticity of 1.01.

With the aid of these elasticities, one can quickly deduce the pattern of outputs which our system would forecast if we required it to produce a slightly higher or lower level of employment than that specified in Table VII–1.

VIII

Prospect

If authors could, like composers, repeat the opening strains at the end of the piece, then we would certainly write here *da capo al segno* and send the reader back to repeat Chapter I. The second time through, those passages which may have seemed at first brief announcements would now sound like encompassing summaries. The aspirations stated for the system would sound different against the background of what it really provides. But the most important theme to be emphasized in the repetition is that the special value of the parts of this system lies not in their merits—if any—as individual consumption, or investment, or export, or technical change, or labor productivity forecasts, but in their forming a coherent picture of the whole economy in more detail than we have ever before had.

In my own view, the present forecasts represent an advance over what was previously available and, at the same time, fall far short of their potential. No part of the system is really satisfactory, though some are worse than others. Like a pilot plant, the model produced some useful output but is more valuable for what its builders learn in the process of construction and operation. Though I hope not to let my own experience rust away unused, some indication of the possible developments which now appear to be the most useful may be of interest to anyone considering using or making this kind of forecasts in the future. These reflections fall under three general headings, improvements in input-output tables, development of short-run forecasts to go with the long-run ones, and improvements in the investment equations.

INPUT-OUTPUT TABLES

The previous chapters have dealt with the problems which were foreseen in advance, systematically attacked, and more or less subdued. But for every hour spent on them, at least another hour must have been spent on the unforeseen problems, which, like neglected scratches, seemed to get infected, fester, and cause days of discomfort. Foremost among these neglected scratches was the need for a 1963 input-output table as the base of the forecasts. Forecasting 1975 in the middle of 1965 from the base of a recession year, 1958, seven years earlier seemed just a bit too ridiculous to tolerate, even though the input-output table for that year was not fully published until after this work was essentially complete. Instead, 1963 was chosen as the base year for the forecasts because it was the most recent year for which we had relatively complete statistics. At first, I supposed that using our coefficient projections to bring the 1958 table up to 1963 and then applying estimates of 1963 final demand would give a pretty good 1963 table to serve as a base for the forecast to 1975. The tale of woes which sprang from that supposition need not be chronicled here. Time and again the figures in this 1963 table failed to agree with published statistics. Reconciling one number or index with another, searching (often in vain) for precise statistical definitions, revising punched cards, and tracing through all the other changes required by one revision all consumed endless exasperating hours. This experience has convinced me that anyone going into the regular business of input-output forecasting should start by developing a way of producing current tables consistent with the principal current sources of information on the economy. These tables need not embody the kind of basic research which goes into making a full benchmark table like those for 1947 or 1958; rather the current tables should rely upon these basic tables for the structure of input columns and make only such mechanical modifications as are necessary to maintain consistency with the principal sources of current information such as the *Annual Survey of Manufactures, Current Industrial Reports,* foreign trade statistics, the national accounts, and certain trade association reports. Because the sources of data remain much the same from year to year, much of this job could and should be programed for a computer. As soon as some data become available, a "first edition" current table could be produced and subsequently revised as more facts become known. It should be possible to produce a fairly good table within a year after the end of the year to which it refers.

The idea of statistical accounts which agree with current information but also rest on work for an earlier, benchmark year is by no means new. Indeed, the national accounts which appear every July are of just this nature. To an outsider, in fact, it seems apparent that making current input-output tables and making current national accounts could be combined to their mutual benefit.

Production of such "current" tables for past years would also yield a comprehensive set of statistical time series for industry output, personal consumption, investment, exports, and government demands. At present, we have no series on industry outputs in constant dollars which is fully compatible with our constant-dollar series on final demands. The output series produced by the forecasting system are therefore not fully comparable to the historical output series used to estimate employment and investment requirements, and the reliability of the investment and employment projections consequently suffers. Extension of our statistical system in this direction is much needed.

Much of our current economic information consists of production statistics for particular products. To be able to use these in keeping the input-output table up to date, we must have a table which distinguishes many more rows than does the present one. Such an increase in the detail of the table will also help us with what seems to be the most frequent source of difficulty in applying the present table to business problems, namely, that many of the 90 sectors of the model contain such a variety of products that they do not match the normal ideas of a "line of business." For example, boilers and structural metal products appear in the same row of the table, although their manufacture is two very different businesses. By judicious subdivision of the present sectors, the worst of these problems could be eliminated with about 200 sectors. Fortunately, there seems to be good reason to expect that the 1963 table will be published in this much detail. There is actually, of course, little reason not to go much further and distinguish 300 or 400 *rows,* though somewhat fewer columns may be adequate. Much of the 1958 table was, in fact, made by distributing the output of individual products (at the four-, five-, or six-digit SIC level) among the four-digit industries, which are the smallest groupings for which the Census reports materials used. Four-digit detail in the columns is, therefore, as much as can be hoped for, but some rows might well refer to smaller product categories. As far as computation is concerned, full use could easily be made of this extra detail. It would be quite possible to keep the same efficient, iterative procedure for working back from final demands to industry outputs even if we had a table with many more rows than columns, provided, of course, that we knew what columns produced what fractions of the total sales in each row.

Current tables in greater product detail should also improve the coefficient projections by making it possible to spot trends already in progress more readily and to quantify new technical developments more exactly than at present. Subdivision of some of the present columns would reduce the need for product-mix projections by hand. The study of technical change should become a continuing project; it requires constant watching of the current press and going behind the usual news stories to quantify the developments of which they tell.

SHORT-TERM AND REGIONAL FORECASTS

The forecasts developed in this book are all long term. The forecast for one year ahead makes no use of the "leading indicators" which tell us a great deal about the next twelve months but nothing about the fifth year in the future. Current input-output tables will make it useful to include at the beginning of the long-term forecast a serious one- or two-year forecast. Such short-range forecasts will entail several changes in the structure of the system. Investment and construction for the year after the base year, as well as for the base year, will be largely predetermined. Inventory changes will have to be taken seriously rather than being given their present summary treatment. Together with these changes, it will probably be desirable to go over to a different mechanism for the generation of investment. In the present forecasts, we have made each industry's investment at any time depend upon the rate of change of its output at that same time.[1] This simultaneity was dictated by our desire to have our forecasts consistent with their being believed by business, for if a company believed that its sales will increase at such-and-such a rate, it would surely try to have the capacity ready to meet them. Econometric studies find, however, that industrial investment lags behind increases in sales. To make realistic forecasts for the two years just ahead, such a lag will definitely have to be used; and if we use the investment equations with a lag for these years, we may as well keep it for the later years. Eliminating this simultaneity will also simplify the computing scheme and make it unnecessary to go back

[1] By a minor change, we could have made investment dependent upon future changes in output, also.

to revise investment in the light of the outputs it implies, because the implied output will now be later in time than the outputs which prompted the investment.

In the short-range forecasts, we will not be allowed to make one of the basic assumptions of the long-range system, namely, that federal tax policy will be adjusted to insure a specific level of employment. Rather, we shall have to consider tax policy as fixed and ask what level of employment it implies. To answer this question with our model, we shall have to consider the connection from employment back to income, which we have not needed so far. As an easier, if less satisfactory, alternative we can, of course, use income forecasts from one of the several aggregate econometric models now in operation and apply our model only to break it down by industry.

Input-output forecasting also seems well suited to enter the regional forecasting field. The crux of many regional problems is what industries will locate in a region or which ones the region should try to attract. By its very nature, this problem requires detailed forecasts of the markets to which an industry sells and detailed knowledge of its material requirements. A related question to which input-output is applicable is determining the requirements of a specified industrial development program for public services such as power, transportation, water, or schools.

INVESTMENT EQUATIONS

Of the various parts of the model, the treatment of investment stands at the front of the line waiting for improvement. In the last half-dozen years, much good work has been done on investment, but none of it has produced really satisfactory ways of forecasting. The aggregate time series on investment have been run through computers in so many different ways that it seems unlikely that much more knowledge can be squeezed out of them. Cross-sectional studies across companies have also given disappointing results. One body of data, however, remains largely unexploited, namely, the investment reported in the *Annual Surveys of Manufactures*. The reports on which the survey is based contain annual investment for fifteen years by a large number of establishments classified by four-digit industry. The sales, employment, and costs of labor and of materials for these establishments are also available. If any statistics will permit us to determine capital requirements for growth, these are they, although organizing and using them will be no simple matter. Because they relate to fairly specific types of plants, it will be possible to interpret the numbers in the light of qualitative knowledge of the industries. Particular attention to new or greatly enlarged establishments should help define the requirements for expansion, while comparison with slow-growing establishments should reveal replacement requirements. This information, unfortunately, is hard to match with financial data on the company owning the establishment.

The capital coefficients in the present study are probably too low for the next decade, for they are based on a period of lower profits and therefore scarcer investment funds than now prevail. The availability of funds seems definitely to influence expenditures and should be taken into account in future studies, though to use such a variable as "profitability" to full effect, we must be able to forecast it. Forecasting profits will require refinement of input-output techniques, for they are, as is well known, by no means proportional to output in the short run.

In addition, as soon as we start trying to forecast profits, we find ourselves in the midst of the larger problem of forecasting prices or, at least, relative prices. Formally, one can easily compute what changes in *relative* prices are implied by the projected changes in input-output coefficients and labor-output ratios provided that, say, the Wholesale Price Index remains constant, wages increase in the same proportion in all industries, and profits and depreciation per unit of output remain constant. Such price forecasts would be useful in making the coefficient projections, and in stating forecasts in current dollar amounts for financial planning. We have not made such price forecasts in the present study because we have no reliable background against which to interpret them, no comprehensive set of outputs over a series of years in both current and "constant" dollars, in which "constant" dollars have a statistical definition comparable to the output forecasts.

The same *Annual Survey* data should also permit a sound approach to the problems of how new investment affects labor productivity. There is no shortage of production function estimates purporting to describe the substitution between labor and capital, but the estimates are all so indirect, contradictory, and so subject to disturbance by extraneous elements that it is difficult to put much trust in them.

The labor productivity field remains wide open; so does the problem of distinguishing between the many kinds of labor and of forecasting skill requirements.

I could continue detailing directions in which all the other parts of the model need improvement, but it is surely already clear that we stand in no danger of building a fully satisfactory system soon. I feel, however, that we stand on the threshold of exciting developments in making and using consistent forecasts.

APPENDIX

Mathematical Methods Used in
Generating the Forecasts

Two aspects of the computer program used to produce the forecasts deserve mention: first, the solution of the static input-output equations for industry outputs; and, second, the iterative procedure for simultaneous determination of outputs and investment.

SOLUTION OF STATIC INPUT-OUTPUT EQUATIONS

When the vector of final demands, $f(t)$, has been calculated for one particular year, t, and the matrix $A(t)$ of input-output coefficients has been brought up to date by the linear time trends in some of its coefficients, we have to solve the equation

$$x(t) = A(t) \, x(t) + f(t)$$

for the vector $x(t)$ of the gross outputs of the industries. We used a modified version of the Seidel iterative process. In its simplest version this process consists of taking as the initial approximate solution, $x^{(0)} = f$. Successively better approximations are then calculated by the formula

$$x_i^{(k+1)} = \left[\sum_{j=1}^{i-1} a_{ij} x_j^{(k+1)} + \sum_{j=i+1}^{n} a_{ij} x_j^{(k)} + f_i \right] / (1 - a_{ii})$$

where $x^{(k)}$ is the kth approximation to the solution and the a_{ij}, x_j, and f_i are elements of A, x, and f, respectively. In words, we start with $x^{(0)} = f$, then adjust the first element of x, x_1, so that the first equation is satisfied. Then with that value of x_1 and the old values of $x_3, \ldots, x_n$ fixed, we adjust x_2 so that the second equation is satisfied, and so on through x_n. Then we start over with x_1 again, and continue the process until the difference between two successive approximations, $x^{(k)}$ and $x^{(k+1)}$ is as small as desired. The method can be proved to converge for the input-output A matrix.[1] Note that if the matrix A is triangular, that is, if all

[1] The clearest proof I know of is in B. P. Demidovich and I. A. Maron, *Osnovy Vychislitel'noy Matematiki*, Moscow, 1960, pp. 323–326.

the elements above the principal diagonal are zero, then one pass through the equations produces the solution: $x^{(1)} = Ax^{(1)} + f$. Generally speaking, the more nearly triangular A is, the faster the process converges. We have modified the procedure in three ways to accelerate its convergence. First, instead of adjusting variables in the order in which they come in the published matrix, we took them in a more nearly triangular order. For example, we took bakery products first, then meatpacking and dairy products, then livestock raising, then grain mill products (which include both animal feeds and flour), and then crop raising. With this arrangement, we reduced from eight to seven the average number of iterations needed to obtain outputs accurate to $1 million (five significant figures). Second, we noticed that by adjusting a few outputs more than once as we went through the list, we could save another iteration, bringing the total down to six. Finally, by using $x(t - 1)$ as the initial solution for $x(t)$, we brought the iteration count down to five, and by using $x^{(0)}(t) = x(t - 1) + [x(t - 1) - x(t - 2)]$, we got it down to two for the years after 1965.

The saving in computer time by use of the Seidel method over the use of the Gauss-Jordan matrix-inversion method can be approximated by the relation

$$T_s \gtrsim \left(\frac{i}{n} \right) T_I$$

where T_s is time required for the Seidel method, T_I is the time for the inversion, i is the number of iterations required by the Seidel process, and n is the dimension of the A matrix. In our case, therefore, more than forty-five times as much computer time would have been required had we used standard matrix inversion routines. Moreover, since the A matrix changes slightly each year, it is very important to keep the whole matrix in core storage. Inversion routines destroy the matrix on which they work, and there is not room to keep a duplicate in memory. The Seidel process does not change the matrix in the process of solution and is therefore, for this reason also, much more economical than the inversion process.

SIMULTANEOUS DETERMINATION OF OUTPUTS

The fundamental system of equations which the forecasting model must solve is of the form

(1) $$x(t) = A(t)\,x(t) + DB(t)\,x(t) + f(t)$$

where $x(t)$ is the vector of industry outputs at time t, $A(t)$ is the matrix of input-output coefficients projected to time t, D is the differential operator, $B(t)$ is the matrix of capital requirements per unit of output [so $DB(t)\,x(t)$ is expansion investment], and $f(t)$ is the vector of all final demands except expansion investment. This $f(t)$ vector depends, of course, on the projection of disposable income in Step 2 of Chapter I. Given a particular f(t), how can we solve (1) for x(t)?

Under the title "The Leontief Dynamic System," equation (1) has provoked a considerable literature proporting to show that the solutions of it are unstable. These demonstrations begin by supposing that x(o) is fixed and that (1) should therefore be solved for $\dot{x}$(o), the derivative of x(t) with respect to time. So interpreted, (1) is unstable. But since it is difficult indeed to imagine an economy which decided on the rates of growth of its industries in such a fashion, these demonstrations are quite irrelevant economically. On the other hand, equation (1) is quite sufficient to determine the unique smooth equilibrium growth path, x(t), which satisfies (1), though it may not have exactly the observed initial value at time t = 0.

In simplest terms, all that equation (1) requires of the solution x(t) is that when the investment implied by x(t) is added to f(t), the resulting demand will, by ordinary static input-output calculations, give rise to those same outputs x(t). The natural iterative procedure for solving (1) is therefore to choose an initial course of outputs, call it $x^{(0)}$, for a series of years t = 1, . . . , T, and use it to determine the values of capital stocks required—$B(t)x^{(0)}(t)$—for those years. To this series, a linear operator D* is then applied to approximate the course of investment—$DB(t)x^{(0)}(t)$—by $D*B(t)x^{(0)}(t)$ for all values of t. Finally, this course of investment is substituted into (1) and the required course of outputs, $x^{(1)}(t)$, is calculated by $x^{(1)}(t) = A(t)x^{(1)}(t) + D*B(t)x^{(0)}(t) + f(t)$. This $x^{(1)}(t)$, the second approximation to x(t), gives a new course of outputs which may, of course, differ from $x^{(0)}(t)$, the one originally assumed. It may be used to find $x^{(2)}(t)$, and $x^{(2)}(t)$, to find $x^{(3)}(t)$ and so on, by the recursive relation

$$\text{(2)} \qquad x^{(k)}(t) = A(t)x^{(k)}(t) + D*B(t)x^{(k-1)}(t) + f(t).$$

Does this process converge? We shall show that it will for an appropriate choice of the differential operator D*. Namely, if a polynomial in t of sufficiently low degree is fitted by least squares to B(t)x(t) and the derivatives of this polynomial used for D*B(t)x(t), then the complete system becomes a set of linear equations. The calculations reported below indicate that the above iterative process will converge to the unique solution of these equations. The smoothing imposed by the polynomial rules out all the unstable solutions of (1) and leaves us with only the economically relevant smooth growth path. Our calculations will allow us to estimate the degree of polynomial which can be used. It turns out that fitting a cubic (so that the investment curve will be quadratic) is a safe procedure for forecast periods of four years or over. Fitting a fourth-degree polynomial is safe with eight or more periods; fifth-degree polynomials may not be safely convergent unless more than twelve forecast periods are used.

To see how these safe areas may be ascertained, we note first that the coefficients of a polynomial in t fitted by least squares to a series of T observations, $s = [s(1), \ldots, s(T)]$, are linear combinations of the components of s. Furthermore, since the value of the derivative of a polynomial at any specified value of t is a linear combination of the coefficients, it follows that the values of the derivative of the polynomial at each point of time are a linear combination of the observations in the vector s. Thus

(3) $$D^*s(t) = c(t)s; \quad t = 1, \ldots, T,$$

where $c(t)$ is a row vector. Letting C be the T-by-T matrix with rows $c(1), \ldots, c(T)$, we may write (3) as

(4) $$D^*s = Cs.$$

We can now express the process described by (2) as the iterative solution of linear equations. The conditions of convergence of this solution procedure are known and can be applied to yield the results mentioned. First, to express (2) as a system of linear equations, let us use the following notations:

$$X = \begin{pmatrix} x(1) \\ \vdots \\ x(T) \end{pmatrix}, \quad F = \begin{pmatrix} f(1) \\ \vdots \\ f(T) \end{pmatrix}, \quad \hat{A} = \begin{pmatrix} A(1) & & 0 \\ & \ddots & \\ 0 & & A(T) \end{pmatrix},$$

$$\hat{B} = \begin{pmatrix} B(1) & & 0 \\ & \ddots & \\ 0 & & B(T) \end{pmatrix}, \quad \hat{C} = \begin{pmatrix} \hat{c}_{11} & \hat{c}_{12} & \cdots & \hat{c}_{1T} \\ \vdots & \vdots & & \vdots \\ \hat{c}_{T1} & \hat{c}_{T2} & \cdots & \hat{c}_{TT} \end{pmatrix},$$

where $\hat{c}_{ij}$ is an n-by-n diagonal matrix with all its diagonal elements equal to C_{ij}. Thus, all the nonzero elements of $\hat{C}$ lie on the principal diagonal and oblique stripes parallel to it and separated (both horizontally and vertically) by $n - 1$ zero elements. With this notation, the system (2) becomes

(5) $$X^{(k)} = \hat{A}X^{(k)} + \hat{C}\hat{B}X^{(k-1)} + F$$

or

(6) $$X^{(k)} = (I - \hat{A})^{-1}\hat{C}\hat{B}X^{(k-1)} + (I - \hat{A})^{-1}F,$$

and we know that the process will be convergent if $|dcr(I - \hat{A})^{-1}\hat{C}\hat{B}| < 1$, where "dcr" means "dominant characteristic root."

Now $dcr(I - \hat{A})^{-1}\hat{C}\hat{B} = dcr\,\hat{C}\hat{B}(I - \hat{A})^{-1}$ and $\hat{B}(I - \hat{A})^{-1}$ is block-diagonal. Let us write it as

$$\hat{Q} = \hat{B}(I - \hat{A})^{-1} = \begin{pmatrix} Q(1) & & 0 \\ & \ddots & \\ 0 & & Q(T) \end{pmatrix}.$$

We shall assume that $Q(1) = Q(2) = \ldots = Q(T) = Q$.
Then

$$\hat{C}\hat{B}(I - \hat{A})^{-1} = \hat{C}\hat{Q} = \begin{pmatrix} c_{11}Q & c_{12}Q & \cdots & c_{1T}Q \\ \vdots & \vdots & \vdots & \vdots \\ c_{T1}Q & c_{T2}Q & \cdots & c_{TT}Q \end{pmatrix}$$

and

$$(\hat{C}\hat{Q})^2 = \begin{pmatrix} c^2_{11}Q^2 & c^2_{12}Q^2 & \cdots & c^2_{1T}Q^2 \\ \vdots & \vdots & \vdots & \vdots \\ c^2_{T1}Q^2 & c^2_{T2}Q^2 & \cdots & c^2_{TT}Q^2 \end{pmatrix} = \hat{C}^2\hat{Q}^2,$$

where c_{ij} is element i,j of C^2. Likewise, we can show that $(\hat{C}\hat{Q})^r = \hat{C}^r\hat{Q}^r$ for any positive integer, r.
Now

$$|dcr\,(I - \hat{A})^{-1}\,\hat{C}\hat{B}\,| = |dcr\,\hat{C}\hat{Q}| = \sqrt[r]{|dcr\,(\hat{C}\hat{Q})^r|} \leq \sqrt[r]{||(\hat{C}\hat{Q})^r||} = \sqrt[r]{||\hat{C}^r\hat{Q}^r||}$$

$$\leq \sqrt[r]{||\hat{C}^r||} \cdot \sqrt[r]{||\hat{Q}^r||}.$$

where $||\ ||$ denotes the matrix norm defined by $||A|| = \max_j \Sigma_{i=1} |a_{ij}|$, for any matrix A. Using this norm, it is easily seen that $||\hat{C}^r|| = ||C^r||$. The values of $\sqrt[r]{||C^r||}$ for $r = 8$ are presented in Table A–1 for various values of T and degrees of polynomial. To use the table, we need only have some idea of the value of $\lim_{r \to \infty} \sqrt[r]{||\hat{Q}^r||}$.

TABLE A–1. VALUES OF $||C^8||^{1/8}$ FOR POLYNOMIALS OF VARYING DEGREE APPLIED TO FORECASTS OF VARYING LENGTH

Length of Forecast (T)	Degree of Polynomial					
	1	2	3	4	5	6
4	0.	.013	.091			
5	0.	.014	.061	.550[a]		
6	0.	.010	.048	.393	1.231	
8	0.	.007	.029	.224	0.536	
10	0.	.005	.016	.179	0.427	.888
12	0.	.006	.024	.149	0.333	.725

[a] This D* corresponds to that used by the author in an article in *Econometrica*, October 1963. The series used in that article would result from the present iterative method using $X^{(0)} = 0$. Although the value in the table shows that our sufficient condition for convergence is not met, the process did, in fact, converge satisfactorily, at least as far as it was carried.

But[2]

$$\lim_{r \to \infty} \sqrt[\tau]{||\hat{Q}^r||} = |\operatorname{dcr} \hat{Q}| = |\operatorname{dcr} (I - \hat{A})^{-1}B|$$

Now the reciprocal of dcr $(I - A)^{-1}B$ is maximum rate of balanced growth of a closed economy with technology given by the A and B matrix.[3]

Since the A matrix we have is for an open economy, this rate turns out to be rather high, about 30 percent per year; giving a value of $\operatorname{dcr}(I-A)^{-1}B$ of about 3. Hence, if $\sqrt[8]{||C^8||} < .3$, we can be fairly certain of convergence. Table A–1 thus leads to the conclusion mentioned above about usable polynomials.

I have not been able to remove the assumption that Q(t) is constant and still get such strong results, but it is unlikely that small changes in Q would upset a strongly convergent process.

In the forecasts, we had linear trends in A(t) and used a third-degree polynomial. We always found rapid convergence at about the rate Table A–1 would lead us to expect. It is important to note that the above results hold only when s(t) is deduced for *all* the values of t for which x(t) enters the series to which the polynomial is fitted. In the forecasts, 1963 investment was known in advance; therefore, 1963 outputs were not included in the series to which the polynomials were fitted. When we tried including them, the process did not converge.

[2] The first equality follows from Theorem 3.1 of Richard S. Varga, *Matrix Iterative Analysis*, Englewood Cliffs, N.J., Prentice-Hall, 1962, p. 65.

[3] See R. Dorfman *et al., Linear Programming and Economic Analysis*, New York, McGraw-Hill, 1959, p. 345. (B in their notation is Q here.)

INDEX

Master Table

The table on the following pages shows the growth rates and relative size of the markets for each of the ninety producing industries in the economy. These industries are listed down the left margin of the table; the markets, including intermediate use by these same industries, equipment investment, construction, government purchases, exports, and consumption, appear across the top of the table. For each industry there are two rows. The first shows the fraction of the sales of the industry (to customers other than itself) which will go to the various markets in 1975. These fractions are in thousandths; a "." represents a zero, while a "o" stand for a fraction less than .0005. The second row for each industry shows the growth rates of the various markets where they differ from the growth rate shown at the top of the column for that consuming industry or type of demand. Where there is no difference, the second row is blank. A double entry in a cell, therefore, marks a market for which a coefficient change is projected. The bottom pair of rows shows the distribution and growth rates of employment.

Growth-Volume Table for Forecast of the American Economy, 1963–1975

Intermediate Demands

Buyer (columns):
1 LIVESTOCK · 2 CROPS · 3 FORESTRY AND FISHERY PRODUCTS · 4 AGRICULTURAL SERVICES · 5 IRON ORE MINING · 6 NON-FERROUS ORE MINING · 7 COAL MINING · 8 PETROLEUM MINING · 9 MINERALS MINING · 10 CHEMICAL MINING · 11 NEW CONSTRUCTION · 12 MAINTENANCE CONSTRUCTION · 13 ORDNANCE · 14 MEAT PACKING · 15 DAIRY PRODUCTS · 16 CANNED AND FROZEN FOODS · 17 GRAIN MILL PRODUCTS · 18 BAKERY PRODUCTS · 19 BEVERAGES · 20 MISC FOOD PRODUCTS · 21 TOBACCO · 22 FABRICS AND YARN · 23 RUGS, TIRE CORD, MISC. TEXTILES · 24 APPAREL · 25 HOUSEHOLD TEXTILES AND UPHOLSTERY · 26 LUMBER + PRODUCTS, EXC CONTAINERS · 27 WOODEN CONTAINERS · 28 HOUSEHOLD FURNITURE · 29 OFFICE FURNITURE · 30 PAPER + PRODUCTS EXCEPT CONTAINERS · 31 PAPER CONTAINERS · 32 PRINTING AND PUBLISHING · 33 BASIC CHEMICALS · 34 PLASTICS AND SYNTHETICS · 35 DRUGS, CLEANING + TOILET ITEMS · 36 PAINT AND ALLIED PRODUCTS · 37 PETROLEUM REFINING

GROWTH RATES (by column 1–37):
23, 32, 32, 30, 38, 25, 25, 29, 28, 34, 39, 31, −13, 24, 21, 41, 35, 36, 45, 48, 31, 33, 32, 37, 40, 33, 15, 38, 37, 45, 39, 40, 50, 52, 43, 23, 34

(Stacked cell values are shown as top / bottom. A centred dot · denotes a negligible / blank entry.)

Seller ↓ / Buyer →	1	2	3	4	5	6	7	8	9	10	11	12	13	14	15	16	17	18	19	20	21	22	23	24	25	26	27	28	29	30	31	32	33	34	35	36	37
1 LIVESTOCK	247/35	44/−25	6	12	·	·	·	·	·	·	·	·	·	554/14	189/13	11	0	·	·	30	·	·	·	·	·	·	·	·	·	·	·	·	·	·	0	·	·
2 CROPS	225	28/24	9	22	·	·	·	·	·	·	·	·	·	0	3	66/166	166	2	9	86/36	38	56	1/19	0/27	1/443	·	·	·	·	·	·	·	1	·	0/23	·	·
3 FORESTRY AND FISHERY PRODUCTS	·	·	11	1	·	·	·	·	·	·	·	·	·	35	·	·	·	·	·	14	·	·	·	·	·	9	·	·	·	·	·	·	12	·	·	·	·
4 AGRICULTURAL SERVICES	263/698	·	15	1	·	·	·	·	·	·	·	·	·	·	·	231	·	·	·	·	·	1/443	·	90	6	·	·	·	·	·	·	·	·	·	·	·	·
5 IRON ORE MINING	·	·	·	·	56	10	·	·	0	0	·	·	·	·	·	·	·	·	·	·	·	·	·	·	·	·	·	·	·	·	·	·	57	·	·	·	·
6 NON-FERROUS ORE MINING	·	·	·	·	46/237	237	1	·	1	0	·	0	0	·	·	·	·	·	·	·	·	·	·	·	0	0	·	·	·	·	·	·	75	·	1	0	·
7 COAL MINING	3	0	·	·	4/48	1	207	·	1	0	·	0	0	2	4	4	4	0	2	9	1	9	1	0	1	1	·	1	3	25/−4	1	3	30/19	20	3	3	5
8 PETROLEUM MINING	·	43	·	3	·	·	1	22	7	7	·	84	1	·	0	0	1	0	2	1	1	0	0	1	·	0	·	0	0	30	1	2	3	1	·	4	829/829
9 MINERALS MINING	0	·	·	·	·	0	1	·	7	53	·	0	·	0	0	0	1	0	3	1	0	1	0	·	0	0	·	0	0	30	·	711/47	18	1	3	0	38
10 CHEMICAL MINING	41	41	0	·	2	2	0	·	1	53	·	·	4	4	0	4	4	0	·	1	0	1	0	1	0	0	·	0	3	30	·	711/47	711/47	1	0	1	2
11 NEW CONSTRUCTION	·	·	·	·	·	·	·	·	·	·	·	·	·	·	·	·	·	·	·	·	·	·	·	·	·	·	·	·	·	·	·	·	·	·	·	·	·
12 MAINTENANCE CONSTRUCTION	11	22	0	0	0	0	0	0	0	0	·	0	0	2	2	4	2	2	3	3	0	1	0	1	0	3	·	0	0	3	1	3	1	2	0	0	1
13 ORDNANCE	·	·	·	·	·	·	·	·	·	·	·	·	44/31	·	·	·	·	·	·	·	·	·	·	·	·	·	·	·	·	·	·	·	·	·	·	·	·
14 MEAT PACKING	·	·	·	·	·	·	·	·	·	·	·	·	·	78/14	·	5	1	11/31	13	13	·	·	·	·	0	·	·	2	·	·	·	·	1	·	1/23	·	·
15 DAIRY PRODUCTS	·	·	3	·	·	·	·	·	·	·	·	·	·	5	135	7	3	8/31	0	10	·	·	0	·	·	·	·	·	·	·	·	·	1	4	·	·	·
16 CANNED AND FROZEN FOODS	·	·	4	·	·	·	·	·	·	·	·	·	·	·	48	48	·	·	6	5	·	·	·	·	·	·	·	·	·	·	·	·	·	·	·	·	·
17 GRAIN MILL PRODUCTS	338/33	·	·	1	·	·	·	·	·	·	·	·	·	1	1	9	38/31	184/31	40/40	41/42	·	·	·	·	·	·	·	·	·	·	·	·	·	·	·	·	·
18 BAKERY PRODUCTS	·	·	·	·	·	·	·	·	·	·	·	·	·	·	·	·	·	·	·	·	·	·	·	·	·	·	·	·	·	·	·	·	·	·	·	·	·

SECTOR NUMBER	1	2	3	4	5	6	7	8	9	10	11	12	13	14	15	16	17	18	19	20	21	22	23	24	25	26	27	28	29	30	31	32	33	34	35	36	37
GROWTH RATES	23.	32.	.	.	30.	38.	25.	25.	29.	28.	34.	39.	31.-13.	24.	21.	41.	35.	36.	45.	48.	31.	33.	32.	37.	40.	33.	15.	38.	37.	45.	39.	40.	50.	52.	43.	23.	34.
19 BEVERAGES	1	.	.	.	.	.	.	.	.	.	.	.	.	.	.	1	.	.	.	62	5	.	.	.	.	.	.	.	.	.	.	.	.	.	.	.	.
20 MISC FOOD PRODUCTS	14	0	.	.	.	.	.	.	.	.	.	.	.	.	.	52	47	35/31	15	249	.	.	.	.	.	0	.	0	.	7	0	.	12/45	2	17	4	1
21 TOBACCO	.	.	.	.	.	.	.	.	.	.	.	.	.	.	.	.	2	.	.	0	.	.	.	.	.	.	.	.	.	0	0	.	.	.	.	.	C
22 FABRICS AND YARN	.	1	.	.	.	0	0	.	.	.	.	.	.	0	0	0	0	0	.	0	0	508	51	548/35	145	0	.	0	0	10	.	.	0	0	1	0	0
23 RUGS, TIRE CORD, MISC. TEXTILES	2	11	6	4	.	.	.	1	0	.	.	.	.	.	.	0	0	.	.	0	.	113/35	96/41	37	90/43	1	.	15/22	8/21	9	.	9	1	0	0	0	0
24 APPAREL	.	.	.	.	.	.	.	.	.	.	.	.	.	0	1	0	0	0	0	0	.	1	1	218/39	2	.	.	0	0	1	0	0	0	0	0	0	1
25 HOUSEHOLD TEXTILES AND UPHOLSTERY	2	13	.	.	.	.	.	.	.	.	.	0	9	.	.	12	21	.	2	2	.	14	4	76	74/46	.	.	2	.	12	0	0	16	.	.	0	1
26 LUMBER + PRODUCTS, EXC CONTAINERS	0	0	.	.	.	0	-23	1	0	0	.	65	.	8/-11 -18	37/-5	45	18	27/10	48	39/22	0	0	0	0	0	381	29	67/33	12/27	151/50	.	.	7	0	.	0	1
27 WOODEN CONTAINERS	166/-3	.	.	0	.	.	.	.	.	.	.	.	.	.	.	.	.	.	21	.	21	.	.	.	0	60	37	1	0	21	7	0	13	4	.	.	1
28 HOUSEHOLD FURNITURE	.	.	.	.	.	.	.	.	.	.	.	11	.	.	.	.	.	.	.	.	.	.	2	0	2	5	1	15	12	0	.	4	.	.	.	.	.
29 OFFICE FURNITURE	.	.	.	.	.	.	.	.	.	.	.	.	.	.	.	.	.	.	.	.	.	.	.	.	5	2	0	18	23	1	.	4	0	0	.	.	.
30 PAPER + PRODUCTS EXCEPT CONTAINERS	.	1	0	0	0	0	0	0	1	0	.	6	0	1	2	4	16	5	.	15	5	2	2	1	3	5	1	2	5	251/47	171	290/51	15/45	19/28	4/20	1	5
31 PAPER CONTAINERS	3	1	3	1	.	.	0	1	0	1	.	2	8	64	89/59	35	11	34	19	13	22	4	25	7	.	9	0	16	7	89	40	19	23	9	62/47	4	8
32 PRINTING AND PUBLISHING	0	1	0	0	0	0	0	0	0	0	.	0	0	2	1	2	1	1	2	1	1	1	0	1	0	2	0	0	0	10	2	148	3	0	66	0	0
33 BASIC CHEMICALS	2	200/78	0	0	1	13/15	1/12	1	1/-3	.	.	5	0	3	3	3	3	2	1	4	0	12	3	3	0	4	0	0	37/55	1	18/50	252/55	165/55	59/34	26	52/55
34 PLASTICS AND SYNTHETICS	.	.	.	.	.	.	.	.	.	.	.	.	.	0	0	0	0	0	2	.	186/45	74/44	32/49	.	.	0	.	0	33/76	5/80	69/64	64	27	3	44/43	2
35 DRUGS, CLEANING + TOILET ITEMS	3	.	.	.	.	0	0	0	0	.	.	0	.	2	1	0	14	0	1	1	3	3	0	0	.	0	.	0	4	.	.	35/59	11/59	65	.	.	6
36 PAINT AND ALLIED PRODUCTS	.	.	1	0	.	0	0	.	.	.	.	349/6	1	0	1	0	1	1	3	0	1	2	1	0	0	23	0	45/33	14/33	2	5/80	38	25	5	10	2	4
37 PETROLEUM REFINING	2	47/24	1	0	0	1/44	3	3	3	.	.	22	0	3	2	3	1	3	3	0	0	2	0	0	0	5	0	1	43/8	49/43	1/8	19	61/53	5	5	1	74
38 RUBBER AND PLASTIC PRODUCTS	2	19	1	0	.	1	2	3	0	1	.	8/-70	2	2	105/2	105	1/86	7/86	3	.	3	6	3	10	.	7	0	25/56	4/84	55/89	72	2	15	14	29/89	1	1
39 LEATHER TANNING	.	.	.	.	.	.	.	.	.	.	.	0	0	.	.	.	1	.	.	.	.	0	87	0	.	.	0	0	4	.	.	.	0	0	.	.	.
40 SHOES AND OTHER LEATHER PRODUCTS	0	1	0	0	0	0	0	0	0	0	.	0	0	0	0	0	1	.	3	.	0	0	0	5	3	0	.	0	3	1	0	0	0	0	0	0	C
41 GLASS AND GLASS PRODUCTS	1	.	.	0	0	.	0	.	.	.	.	35	1	40/28	96/28	96	0	117/35	18	18	.	11	0	0	0	4	.	22/56	34/56	0	3	0	11	0	59/35	4	1
42 STONE + CLAY PRODUCTS	0	3	.	.	0	1	0	13	.	.	.	75	0	0	0	0	1	0	0	0	0	0	0	0	.	5	0	1	0	9	0	0	7	0	2	2	5
43 IRON AND STEEL	.	.	.	.	2	4/-6	-1/-6	0	1	1	.	19/-24	-2	0	0	0	1	.	0	0	0	0	3	0	0	0	1	6/42	11/42	0	0	0	7	0	0	1	0
44 NON-FERROUS METALS	0	0	.	.	0	1	2	0	0	.	.	34/-5	19/-5	1	2	2	1	1	2	1	1	0	0	.	.	1	.	4	3/42	2	0	2	22/27	0	0	0	C
45 METAL CONTAINERS	2	7	.	.	0	0	0	0	.	0	.	.	33	13	337/10	337	3	2	199/50	104	.	.	0	.	.	0	.	.	.	8	0	0	56	4	74/57	30/14	54
46 HEATING, PLUMBING, STRUCTURAL METAL	.	.	.	.	0	0	1	0	0	.	.	96	1	.	.	.	.	.	.	.	.	.	0	.	.	0	.	2	.	0	.	0	0	0	0	0	0

Intermediate Demands

Buyer / Seller

Sector Number	Seller	1 LIVESTOCK	2 CROPS	3 FORESTRY AND FISHERY PRODUCTS	4 AGRICULTURAL SERVICES	5 IRON ORE MINING	6 NON-FERROUS ORE MINING	7 COAL MINING	8 PETROLEUM MINING	9 MINERALS MINING	10 CHEMICAL MINING	11 NEW CONSTRUCTION	12 MAINTENANCE CONSTRUCTION	13 ORDNANCE	14 MEAT PACKING	15 DAIRY PRODUCTS	16 CANNED AND FROZEN FOODS	17 GRAIN MILL PRODUCTS	18 BAKERY PRODUCTS	19 BEVERAGES	20 MISC FOOD PRODUCTS	21 TOBACCO	22 FABRICS AND YARN	23 RUGS, TIRE CORD, MISC. TEXTILES	24 APPAREL	25 HOUSEHOLD TEXTILES AND UPHOLSTERY	26 LUMBER + PRODUCTS, EXC CONTAINERS	27 WOODEN CONTAINERS	28 HOUSEHOLD FURNITURE	29 OFFICE FURNITURE	30 PAPER + PRODUCTS EXCEPT CONTAINERS	31 PAPER CONTAINERS	32 PRINTING AND PUBLISHING	33 BASIC CHEMICALS	34 PLASTICS AND SYNTHETICS	35 DRUGS, CLEANING + TOILET ITEMS	36 PAINT AND ALLIED PRODUCTS	37 PETROLEUM REFINING
	GROWTH RATES	23.	32.	32.	30.	38.	25.	25.	29.	28.	34.	39.	31.	-13.	24.	21.	41.	35.	36.	45.	48.	31.	33.	32.	37.	40.	33.	15.	38.	37.	45.	39.	40.	50.	52.	43.	23.	37.
47	STAMPINGS, SCREW MACHINE PRODUCTS	5	5					3	1	0	0	6	4	5	3	5	5			-8	4	1			3	0	6	0	5	3	6	1	1	4	1	7	0	1
48	HARDWARE, PLATING + VALVES, WIRE PRODUCT	3	6	3	1			2	7			8	8	4	1	3	4	1		-57	2	1	1		3	1	10	0	33	42	21	2	4	9	10	10	0	28
49	ENGINES AND TURBINES								7	0	0			1																				0	1			
50	FARM MACHINERY AND EQUIPMENT	2	78							0				1			0	0			1						0		0	0	0			0	0	0	0	
51	CONSTRUCTION + MINING MACHINERY					10	14/44	43/54	11	26/36	5	7	7	0			1				1						3		1	1	3	1	0	0	3	2	0	1
52	MATERIAL HANDLING EQUIPMENT					129	0	7		17	3	7	7	0													3		2		1	1	0	7	2	0	0	0
53	METALWORKING MACHINERY + EQUIPMENT					0	0	2	2	0	0	0	0	-8			0	0		0	0			0	0	0	4	0	3	1	11	1	0	3	2	0	0	1
54	SPECIAL INDUSTRIAL MACHINERY						1	1	2	1	0	4	4	1			1			1	1		20	0	0	0	2	0	0	2	2	5	0	4	3	1	0	1
55	GENERAL INDUSTRIAL MACHINERY					0	1	1	17	1	0			0			0	0		0	1		0	0	0	0	0	0	3	0	2	0	0	3	1	0	0	1
56	MACHINE SHOPS + MISC MACHINERY	1	2							0	0	154	154	1			1			1	1			0	0	0	2		1	1	3	0	2	4	1	0	0	0
57	OFFICE AND COMPUTING MACHINES								0	0	0						0			0	0		0		0	0	0	0	0	6	1	0	2	0	1	0	0	0
58	SERVICE INDUSTRY MACHINES									0	4	9	9	4			0	0	0	1	0			0	0	0	0		0	6	1	2	1	3	1	1	1	0
59	ELECTRIC APPARATUS AND MOTORS					0	1	1	5	0	1	14	14/17	13/-5			0			1	2		0		0	0	0	0	0	3	1	0	4	4	1	1	0	0
60	HOUSEHOLD APPLIANCES									0	0	17	17	0						0					0	0	0	0	0	0	0	0	0	0	0	0	0	0
61	ELECTRIC LIGHTING AND WIRING EQUIP	0	0	0	0	0	0	1	1	0	0	47	47	15/-5			1	1		1	2		0		1	0	4	0	0	1	6	0	1	1	1	0	0	0
62	COMMUNICATION EQUIPMENT								1			3	3	31/5			1			1	2		0		0	0	0	0	0	0	0	0	1	0	1	0	0	1
63	ELECTRONIC COMPONENTS						0	1	3	0	4			1				0							0	0	0		0	0	0	0	0	0	1	0	0	0
64	BATTERIES, X-RAY + ENGINE ELEC EQUIP	3	12				0	0	1	0	0	3	3	8			1	0		1	1		0		0	0	1		2	0	0	0	0	0	1	0	0	0

SECTOR NUMBER	1	2	3	4	5	6	7	8	9	10	11	12	13	14	15	16	17	18	19	20	21	22	23	24	25	26	27	28	29	30	31	32	33	34	35	36	37
GROWTH RATES	23.	32.	32.	30.	38.	25.	25.	28.	29.	28.	34.	39.	31.-13.	24.	21.	41.	35.	36.	45.	48.	31.	33.	32.	37.	40.	33.	15.	38.	37.	45.	39.	40.	50.	52.	43.	23.	34.
65 MOTOR VEHICLES	1	2	.	.	0	0	0	0	0	.	.	.	.	.	.	.	.	.	.	.	.	.	.	.	.	0	0	0	0	.	0	0	0	.	.	.	0
66 AIRCRAFT AND PARTS	.	1	7	.	1	.	2	.	.	.	.	.	79	1	.	.	.	.	.	.	.	.	0	.	.	0	0	0	0	.	0	3	0	.	.	.	0
67 SHIPS, TRAINS, TRAILERS + CYCLES	.	1	.	0	0	0	0	.	.	.	.	.	3	.	.	.	.	.	.	.	.	.	.	.	0	2	0	0	0	1	0	0	0	0	.	.	0
68 INSTRUMENTS AND CLOCKS	.	1	.	.	0	0	0	0	0	.	2	2	14 5	0	.	.	.	.	.	.	1	0	0	0	1	0	.	0	1	1	0	0	1	1	5	0	0
69 OPTICAL + PHOTOGRAPHIC EQUIPMENT	.	.	.	.	.	.	.	.	.	.	.	.	1	.	.	.	.	.	.	.	.	.	.	0	.	.	0	0	0	2	.	0	1	0	0	0	0
70 MISC MANUFACTURED PRODUCTS	0	0	0	0	0	0	0	0	0	.	0	7	1	0	.	.	0	.	.	.	1	0	3	46	.	2	0	3	4	2	1	39	3	7	0	0	1
71 TRANSPORTATION	12	8	.	0	1	1	0	2	0	0	9	.	1	21 22	10 3	11	5	9 13	12	16	1	9 38	32 38	4 28	1 38	12	2	2	1	15 48	4	8 46	16	6	1	19 19	19
72 COMMUNICATION	3	6	.	0	0	0	0	0	0	.	1	1	1	3	2	2	1	1	2	3	0	2	0	4	1	2	0	2	1	3	1	16	6	1	1	1	2
73 RADIO, TV BROADCASTING	.	.	.	.	.	.	.	.	.	.	.	.	.	.	.	.	.	.	.	.	.	.	.	.	.	.	.	.	.	.	.	.	.	.	.	.	.
74 ELECTRIC UTILITY	4	4 36	.	0	0	0	1	3	2	0	13	1	1	3	2	2	1	1	2	5	3	7	1	3	1	3	1	1	1	12 62	1	4	37	2	.	0	46 44
75 GAS UTILITY	1	1	.	56	0 56	2 44	14	2	0	.	.	.	0	3	2	2	2	1	2	3	3	2	0	0	36	0	0	0	.	16 74	1	.	28	3	1	0	21
76 WATER UTILITY	1	46	0	0	0	0	0	4	0	0	4	.	0	4	2	2	1	2	2	4	0	3	0	2	1	2	0	3	0	21	0	2	16	3	2	0	10
77 WHOLESALE AND RETAIL TRADE	7	9	.	0	0	0	1	1	1	0	0	13	1	6 13	3 13	3	1	1	1	5	3	4 38	38 38	5 28	30	3	0	2	1	5 48	2	4 46	5	1	2	1	37 37
78 FINANCE AND INSURANCE	5	10	.	1	0	1	1	3	1	0	2	1	1	3	2	2	1	1	2	3	0	2	1	4	0	2	0	1	1	3	1	5	6	2	2	0	4
79 REAL ESTATE AND RENTAL	3	19 12	1	0	1	1	1	18	1	0	1	0	0	1	1	1	1	0	1	1	1	3	0	3	1	1	0	1	0	1	1	8	3	1	1	1	2
80 HOTELS,PERSONAL + REPAIR SERVICES	.	.	.	.	0	0	0	0	0	.	.	.	0	0	0	0	0	0	0	1	0	0	0	0	0	0	0	0	0	0	0	2	0	0	0	.	0
81 BUSINESS SERVICES	1	28	5	0	0	0	0	11	0	0	2	1	2	12	9 30	8	4	5	36 50	16 52	7	4	1	5	1	2	0	2	1	6	1	24	8	3	42	1	12
82 RESEARCH AND DEVELOPMENT	.	.	.	.	.	.	.	.	.	.	.	.	.	0	1	1	0	0	1	1	.	3	.	1	.	2	.	2	1	3	.	.	44	22	.	.	8
83 AUTOMOBILE REPAIR SERVICES	5	6	.	.	0	0	0	0	0	.	3	3	4	7	7	4	0	0	0	2	0	3	1	0	0	8	0	1	0	3	0	2	3	0	.	0	2
84 AMUSEMENTS AND RECREATION	.	.	.	.	0	0	0	0	0	.	0	0	0	0	0	0	0	0	0	0	0	0	0	0	0	0	0	0	0	0	0	0	0	0	8	0	.
85 MEDICAL AND EDUCATIONAL INSTITUTIONS	4	0	.	0	0	0	0	0	0	.	0	0	0	0	0	0	0	0	0	0	0	0	0	1	0	0	0	0	0	0	0	1	0	0	0	0	1
86 FED GOVMT ENTERPRISES	1	1	0	0	0	0	0	0	0	.	0	1	1	0	1	1	0	0	0	0	0	1	1	1	1	0	0	0	0	3	1	24	9	7	4	1	7
87 STATE AND LOCAL GOVMT ENTERPRISES	0	0	0	0	0	0	0	0	0	.	0	0	0	1	1	1	0	0	0	0	0	0	1	0	0	0	0	1	0	4	0	1	2	0	0	0	1
88 IMPORTS	1	24	.	0	.	0	.	.	0	.	.	.	.	35	.	.	.	.	.	206	.	.	.	.	.	.	.	.	.	.	.	0	6	.	.	1	.
89 BUSINESS TRAVEL AND ENTERTAINMNT	2	3	0	0	1	1	1	8	1	.	5	7	10	6	6	6	3	4	6	6	1	6	1	14	3	8	4	4	2	5 -1	4	45	37	2	7	3	4
90 OFFICE SUPPLIES	0	1	0	0	0	0	0	2	0	.	1	2	4	2	2	3	1	2	2	4	0	3	1	1	1	2	0	2	1	4	2	30	10	0	2	1	3
EMPLOYMENT	25.20. -19.-48.	2. 4.	2.	0.-0. -43.-48.	0.-16.	0.-14.	0.-1.	0.-16.	0.-14.	0. 18.	0. 51. 31.-46.	24.-2. -12.-18.	3.-4. -3.	3.-3.	3. 26.	3.: 25. 23. 21.	4. 29. -12.-18.	2. 5. 31.-12.	2. 7. -12.-31.	1. 21. -12.-12.	2. 12. 15.-30.	5. 27.	9. 3. 12. 31.	2. 9. -25. 3.	15. 5. 13.-12.	3. 4.-11. 2.-3.	-3.

Growth-Volume Table for Forecast of the American Economy, 1963–1975

Intermediate Demands

Seller / Buyer	RUBBER AND PLASTIC PRODUCTS	LEATHER TANNING	SHOES AND OTHER LEATHER PRODUCTS	GLASS AND GLASS PRODUCTS	STONE + CLAY PRODUCTS	IRON AND STEEL	NON-FERROUS METALS	METAL CONTAINERS	HEATING, PLUMBING, STRUCTURAL METAL	STAMPINGS, SCREW MACHINE PRODUCTS	HARDWARE, PLATING, VALVES, WIRE PRODUCT	ENGINES AND TURBINES	FARM MACHINERY AND EQUIPMENT	CONSTRUCTION + MINING MACHINERY	MATERIAL HANDLING EQUIPMENT	METALWORKING MACHINERY + EQUIPMENT	SPECIAL INDUSTRIAL MACHINERY	GENERAL INDUSTRIAL MACHINERY	MACHINE SHOPS + MISC MACHINERY
SECTOR NUMBER	38	39	40	41	42	43	44	45	46	47	48	49	50	51	52	53	54	55	56
GROWTH RATES	39.	-0.	26.	33.	39.	28.	36.	30.	38.	23.	34.	41.	39.	34.	38.	41.	42.	40.	23.
1 LIVESTOCK	.	.	.	.	.	.	.	.	.	.	.	.	.	.	.	.	.	.	.
2 CROPS	.	.	.	.	0	.	.	.	.	.	.	.	.	.	.	.	.	.	.
3 FORESTRY AND FISHERY PRODUCTS	.	0	.	.	.	.	.	.	.	.	.	.	.	.	.	.	.	.	.
4 AGRICULTURAL SERVICES	.	.	.	.	.	.	.	.	.	.	.	.	2	.	.	.	.	.	.
5 IRON ORE MINING	.	.	.	.	7	844 38	18	.	.	.	.	.	.	.	.	0	.	.	.
6 NON-FERROUS ORE MINING	.	.	.	0	4	6	736 26	.	.	.	2	.	.	.	.	.	.	.	.
7 COAL MINING	3 -11	1	.	2	17 -14	180 2	8	0	1	1	1	1	1	1	.	.	0	0	0
8 PETROLEUM MINING	.	.	.	.	.	.	.	.	.	.	.	.	.	.	.	.	.	.	.
9 MINERALS MINING	5	.	.	18	345	27 12	3	.	1	.	1	.	0	0	.	.	.	7	0
10 CHEMICAL MINING	13	1	.	1	36	11	3	.	.	.	0	.	.	.	.	.	.	.	.
11 NEW CONSTRUCTION	.	.	.	.	.	.	.	.	.	.	.	.	.	.	.	.	.	.	.
12 MAINTENANCE CONSTRUCTION	0	0	0	0	0	7	0	0	1	0	0	0	0	0	0	1	0	0	0
13 ORDNANCE	.	0	.	.	.	0	1	.	0	1	0	.	2	0	.	0	1	0	0
14 MEAT PACKING	.	.	.	.	.	.	.	.	.	.	.	.	.	.	.	.	.	.	.
15 DAIRY PRODUCTS	.	.	.	.	.	.	.	.	.	.	.	.	.	.	.	.	.	.	.
16 CANNED AND FROZEN FOODS	.	.	.	.	.	.	.	.	.	.	.	.	.	.	.	.	.	.	.
17 GRAIN MILL PRODUCTS	.	.	.	.	.	.	.	.	.	.	.	.	.	.	.	.	.	.	.
18 BAKERY PRODUCTS	.	.	.	.	.	.	.	.	.	.	.	.	.	.	.	.	.	.	.

Seller / Buyer	OFFICE AND COMPUTING MACHINES	SERVICE INDUSTRY MACHINES	ELECTRIC APPARATUS AND MOTORS	HOUSEHOLD APPLIANCES	ELECTRIC LIGHTING AND WIRING EQUIP	COMMUNICATION EQUIPMENT	ELECTRONIC COMPONENTS	BATTERIES, X-RAY + ENGINE ELEC EQUIP	MOTOR VEHICLES	AIRCRAFT AND PARTS	SHIPS, TRAINS, TRAILERS + CYCLES	INSTRUMENTS AND CLOCKS	OPTICAL + PHOTOGRAPHIC EQUIPMENT	MISC MANUFACTURED PRODUCTS	TRANSPORTATION	COMMUNICATION	RADIO, TV BROADCASTING	ELECTRIC UTILITY
SECTOR NUMBER	57	58	59	60	61	62	63	64	65	66	67	68	69	70	71	72	73	74
GROWTH RATES	55.	36.	34.	27.	38.	18.	35.	37.	38.	-5.	25.	55.	48.	41.	37.	45.	40.	54.
1 LIVESTOCK	.	.	.	.	.	.	.	.	.	.	.	.	.	.	0	.	.	.
2 CROPS	.	.	.	.	.	.	.	.	.	.	.	0	.	0	2	.	.	.
3 FORESTRY AND FISHERY PRODUCTS	.	.	.	.	.	.	.	.	.	.	.	.	.	2	1	.	.	.
4 AGRICULTURAL SERVICES	.	.	.	.	.	.	.	.	.	.	.	.	.	.	.	.	.	.
5 IRON ORE MINING	.	.	2	.	.	.	.	2	.	.	.	.	.	.	.	.	.	.
6 NON-FERROUS ORE MINING	.	.	.	.	4	.	.	2	.	.	.	2	.	.	.	.	.	.
7 COAL MINING	.	0	1	1	.	1	0	.	11	1	1	.	2	1	-1 -163	.	.	231 43
8 PETROLEUM MINING	.	.	.	.	.	.	.	.	.	.	.	.	.	.	.	.	.	.
9 MINERALS MINING	.	.	.	.	.	.	.	0	0	.	0	0	.	0	1	.	.	.
10 CHEMICAL MINING	.	.	.	.	.	.	.	.	.	.	.	.	.	0	1	.	.	.
11 NEW CONSTRUCTION	.	.	.	.	.	.	.	.	.	.	.	.	.	.	.	.	.	.
12 MAINTENANCE CONSTRUCTION	0	0	0	0	0	1	0	0	6	1	0	0	0	1	70 29	23	1	25 39
13 ORDNANCE	2	.	3	0	0	74	12	.	3	104 -35	.	69	1	0	.	.	.	.
14 MEAT PACKING	.	.	.	.	.	.	.	.	.	.	.	0	.	0	2	.	.	.
15 DAIRY PRODUCTS	.	.	.	.	.	.	.	.	.	.	.	1	.	.	3	.	.	.
16 CANNED AND FROZEN FOODS	.	.	.	.	.	.	.	.	.	.	.	0	.	.	2	.	.	.
17 GRAIN MILL PRODUCTS	.	.	.	.	.	.	.	.	.	.	.	0	.	.	1	.	.	.
18 BAKERY PRODUCTS	.	.	.	.	.	.	.	.	.	.	.	0	.	.	2	.	.	.

SECTOR NUMBER	38	39	40	41	42	43	44	45	46	47	48	49	50	51	52	53	54	55	56	57	58	59	60	61	62	63	64	65	66	67	68	69	70	71	72	73	74
GROWTH RATES	39.	-0.	26.	33.	39.	28.	36.	30.	38.	23.	34.	41.	39.	34.	36.	41.	42.	40.	23.	55.	36.	34.	27.	38.	18.	35.	37.	38.	-5.	25.	55.	48.	41.	37.	45.	40.	54.
19 BEVERAGES	·	·	·	·	·	·	·	·	·	·	·	·	·	·	·	·	·	·	·	·	·	·	·	·	·	·	·	·	·	·	·	·	1	·	·	·	·
20 MISC FOOD PRODUCTS	0	0	·	·	·	·	0	·	·	·	·	0	0	0	0	·	·	·	·	·	0	·	·	·	·	·	·	·	0	0	0	·	0	1	·	·	·
21 TOBACCO	·	·	·	·	·	·	·	·	·	·	·	·	·	·	·	·	·	·	·	·	·	·	·	·	·	·	·	·	·	·	0	·	0	·	·	·	·
22 FABRICS AND YARN	18 29	0	9	·	·	2	2	·	0	·	1	0	0	0	0	0	1	0	0	0	0	0	1	0	0	0	0	8	0	0	4 34	0	15	1	0	·	·
23 RUGS, TIRE CORD, MISC. TEXTILES	153 18	0	14	0	0	1	2	·	0	0	0	0	0	0	0	0	0	0	0	0	1	0	0	1	0	0	48	1	2	1	5	0	17	7	2	1	·
24 APPAREL	2	0	0	1	0	0	1	·	0	0	1	0	0	0	0	0	0	0	0	0	0	0	0	0	0	0	0	1	1	0	1	0	0	0	0	·	·
25 HOUSEHOLD TEXTILES AND UPHOLSTERY	1	0	0	0	1	0	1	·	1	0	0	0	1	0	0	0	0	0	0	0	0	1	1	1	0	0	75	0	1	1	·	3	6	3	1	·	·
26 LUMBER + PRODUCTS, EXC CONTAINERS	2	·	4	6	2	3	2	0	3	3	0	0	1	1	0	3	1	3	·	3	1	1	2	0	0	3	3	3	2	14	·	0	19	2	0	·	·
27 WOODEN CONTAINERS	0	3	2	38	35	9	·	3	27	5	9	1	2	1	0	0	0	0	0	4	25 10	0	39 1	0 29 -21	6	0	0	0	·	·	5	·	7	55	·	·	·
28 HOUSEHOLD FURNITURE	0	0	0	0	·	0	0	0	3	0	2	·	0	0	0	0	0	0	0	1	1	0	1	0	0	0	0	0	0	7	1	·	1	0	·	·	·
29 OFFICE FURNITURE	1	0	0	0	0	0	0	·	10	·	5	·	1	0	0	0	0	1	0	1	1	1	0	0	0	0	4	0	10	10	16	0	4	·	1	·	·
30 PAPER + PRODUCTS EXCEPT CONTAINERS	3	0	2	1	16	4	3	1 18	2	2	2	0	0	0	0	0	0	0	0	2	1	4	0	1	3	4	0	10	0	1	60	8 57	13	3	·	1	·
31 PAPER CONTAINERS	15	0	8	43 32	19	4	2	6 19	9	8	9	2	1	1	0	0	0	2	0	5	5	5	8	13 46	10	5	3	8	2	1	10 45	4	60	2	·	1	·
32 PRINTING AND PUBLISHING	2	0	1	0	1	2	1	0	0	0	1	0	1	0	0	0	0	0	1	1	0	0	0	1	0	0	0	1	0	1	0	0	3	6	11	1	0
33 BASIC CHEMICALS	24 34	2	0	6	12	21 36	10 49	0	2	1	5	1	10	6 30	3 41	0	0	0	3	0	1	1	1	1	10 94	3 42	4	4	1	1	11 57	4	3	3	0	34 146	·
34 PLASTICS AND SYNTHETICS	190 42	95 123	·	14	·	1	18 28	0	0	2	1	0	0	0	0	0	0	0	0	1	6	0	1	9 48	9	0	16 91	16 91	1	12 78	·	0	22	0	·	·	·
35 DRUGS, CLEANING + TOILET ITEMS	1	2	0	7	5	2	2	23	0	0	1	0	0	0	0	0	0	2	0	0	0	0	0	0	0	0	0	3	0	0	2	0	2	2	0	0	·
36 PAINT AND ALLIED PRODUCTS	1	0	0	0	6	9	5	23 15	11	7	2	6	1	3	2	0	0	2	1	8	10	10	12	8	2	1	0	59 27	4	18	2	0	29	26	·	·	·
37 PETROLEUM REFINING	-9 -9	0	0	0	6 73	21 73	3	0	1	1	2	1	1	1	1 38	1	1	1	1	1	1	1	0	0	1	0	10	4	1	1	1	0	1	90 31	1	0	11 45
38 RUBBER AND PLASTIC PRODUCTS	31	1	19	1	10	7	2	4	3	3	6	1	10	36 30	2	2	5 44	5	0	83 62	6 62	4 16	23 53	40 40	14 36	3	10 107	16 91	7	4 11 78	11 63	32 38	28	34	1	0	·
39 LEATHER TANNING	12 145 651 -9	·	·	·	·	0	·	0	2	2	1	5	5	1	0	1	9	2	1	0	1	1	2	1	3	0	0	17	0	3	9	0	82	7	·	·	·
40 SHOES AND OTHER LEATHER PRODUCTS	4	0	90	·	0	0	0	0	0	0	0	0	0	0	0	0	0	0	0	0	0	2	0	0	0	0	0	0	0	0	0	0	0	16	0	0	0
41 GLASS AND GLASS PRODUCTS	23	0	46 28	3	0	0	0	0	15	0	1	0	0	0	0	0	0	0	0	3	3	3	3	28 27	16 -27	1	1 133	0	0	0	2	35	3 14	3	0	0	·
42 STONE + CLAY PRODUCTS	4	1	1	9 135	23 7	8	8	1	8	4	7	2	2	3	1	6 59	2	6	4	4 10	4 10	4 10	4	2	4	4	2 12	2 12	5	4	3	6 35	14	2	1	·	·
43 IRON AND STEEL	1	·	1	135	320 33	10	50 12	135 31	50	90	13 31	20 26	34 32	33	21 35	20 39	32 38	17 11	23 22	19 27	16 18	16 18	11 31	5 33	3 32	148 26 -50	148 26 -50	10 -50	25 12	7 47	1 35	1	12 19	12 19	·	·	·
44 NON-FERROUS METALS	2	0	0	1	2	44 455 36 37	455 103	99 43	3 24	59 36	2 45	2	16	38	16	19	19	15 38	6 34	14 28	16 19	16 19	17 41	18 41	17 10	23 61	64 61 -1	64 61 -1	13 44	26 44	8 47	37	6	·	·	·
45 METAL CONTAINERS	·	·	·	·	·	0	·	·	7	2	6	·	·	0	0	1	0	0	0	0	0	0	0	0	0	0	0	0	0	0	0	0	0	0	0	·	·
46 HEATING, PLUMBING, STRUCTURAL METAL	0	·	0	0	5	0	0	1	23	3	7	0	1	6 40	2	2	4	9	0	7	2	6	1	1	0	0	3	3	1	19	1	·	0	0	·	·	·

GROWTH-VOLUME TABLE FOR FORECAST OF THE AMERICAN ECONOMY, 1963–1975 (continued)

Intermediate Demands — Buyer / Seller

Seller \ Buyer (Sector No.)	36 RUBBER AND PLASTIC PRODUCTS	39 LEATHER TANNING	40 SHOES AND OTHER LEATHER PRODUCTS	41 GLASS AND GLASS PRODUCTS	42 STONE + CLAY PRODUCTS	43 IRON AND STEEL	44 NON-FERROUS METALS	45 METAL CONTAINERS	46 HEATING, PLUMBING, STRUCTURAL METAL	47 STAMPINGS, SCREW MACHINE PRODUCTS	48 HARDWARE, PLATING, VALVES, WIRE PRODUCT	49 ENGINES AND TURBINES	50 FARM MACHINERY AND EQUIP MENT	51 CONSTRUCTION + MINING MACHINERY	52 MATERIAL HANDLING EQUIPMENT	53 METALWORKING MACHINERY + EQUIPMENT	54 SPECIAL INDUSTRIAL MACHINERY	55 GENERAL INDUSTRIAL MACHINERY	56 MACHINE SHOPS + MISC MACHINERY	57 OFFICE AND COMPUTING MACHINES	58 SERVICE INDUSTRY MACHINES	59 ELECTRIC APPARATUS AND MOTORS	60 HOUSEHOLD APPLIANCES	61 ELECTRIC LIGHTING AND WIRING EQUIP	62 COMMUNICATION EQUIPMENT	63 ELECTRONIC COMPONENTS	64 BATTERIES, X-RAY + ENGINE ELEC EQUIP	65 MOTOR VEHICLES	66 AIRCRAFT AND PARTS	67 SHIPS, TRAINS, TRAILERS, CYCLES	68 INSTRUMENTS AND CLOCKS	69 OPTICAL, PHOTOGRAPHIC EQUIPMENT	70 MISC MANUFACTURED PRODUCTS	71 TRANSPORTATION	72 COMMUNICATION	73 RADIO, TV BROADCASTING	74 ELECTRIC UTILITY
GROWTH RATES	39.	-0.	26.	33.	39.	26.	36.	30.	38.	23.	34.	41.	39.	34.	38.	41.	42.	40.	23.	55.	36.	34.	27.	38.	18.	35.	37.	38.	-5.	25.	55.	48.	41.	37.	45.	40.	54.
47 STAMPINGS, SCREW MACHINE PRODUCTS	8	0	0	·	3	34	31	8	29	41	46/45	32/12	21/35	6/8	6/33	29/33	11/35	14	2	2/28	27/22	24/20	47/23	15/19	32/21	24/33	10/24	240/10	35/-	12/4	19/4	2/18	24	5	·	·	·
48 HARDWARE, PLATING, VALVES, WIRE PRODUCT	14	0	3	1	15	49	19	1	42/35	15	45/36	-0/-1	20/26	7/36	7/23	13/38	9	13	5	3	26/9	27	19/11	7	10/-3	4	1	174/42	-12/-15	13/31	10/24	4	17	1	·	·	12/22
49 ENGINES AND TURBINES	0	·	·	·	·	1	0	0	19	3	3	4/101	50/26	44	2	4	1	30	4	·	2	45	·	·	·	·	0	58	7	46/11	0	·	0	45	1	·	·
50 FARM MACHINERY AND EQUIP MENT	0	·	·	0	0	·	·	·	·	·	4	3/12	41	23	2	3	1	4	·	·	·	0	·	0	0	·	1	13	1	1	1	·	1	·	·	·	·
51 CONSTRUCTION + MINING MACHINERY	0	0	·	·	·	5	0	0	9	0	6	7/9	9/32	63	20	3	8	11	2	·	2	2	·	0	0	0	1	4	0	8	1	0	0	12	0	·	·
52 MATERIAL HANDLING EQUIPMENT	0	·	·	·	2	2	1	·	7	1	6	2	1	15	42	13	13	28	0	0	2	2	0	4	0	·	0	5	3	13	0	·	0	·	·	·	·
53 METALWORKING MACHINERY + EQUIPMENT	1	0	·	1	2	30	20	6	12	10	43	7/45	11/43	13	2	59/38	19	19	8/34	8	·	16/36	6	4	0	5	7/47	80	44/-0	5	15/45	2	1	0	·	·	0
54 SPECIAL INDUSTRIAL MACHINERY	2	·	·	·	2	7	1	0	10	·	5	1	1	2	2	3	62	9	3	6	9	11	2	0	1	0	1	2	1	0	3	6	2	4	0	·	0
55 GENERAL INDUSTRIAL MACHINERY	2	0	·	1	1	14	9	4	25	3	13	14/32	37/46	48/39	22/44	32/38	50/50	78	3	6	2	7	2	3	3	3	7	40	22	13	9	2	2	5	·	·	·
56 MACHINE SHOPS + MISC MACHINERY	15	·	·	·	·	97	27	7	26	10	14	51/49	32/52	10	14	19	10	18	98	6	2	2	7	·	5	3	10/9	134	61	9	32	1	10	5	·	·	·
57 OFFICE AND COMPUTING MACHINES	·	·	·	·	·	·	·	·	1	1	0	0	0	0	0/1	0/102	1	1	0	97	54	1	·	·	3	5	0	·	·	1	·	0	5	1	·	·	·
58 SERVICE INDUSTRY MACHINES	0	·	·	0	0	0	1	·	31	3	4	·	0	1	1	3/137	7	16	0	0	·	1	42	1	2	·	0	16	2	4	4	0	5	6	0	·	0
59 ELECTRIC APPARATUS AND MOTORS	1	0	0	0	1	15	7	0	19	3	5	7	3	5/17	14/49	23/44	27/20	42	1/25	10/25	41	68	26	16	24/22	22	8/12	12	5	22	60/79	6	7	6	6	·	0
60 HOUSEHOLD APPLIANCES	1	·	0	·	0	1	9	2	18	2	4	0	3	0	2	2	·	·	0	0	47	7	11	11	1	1	1	1/0	1	5	2	0	3	3	0	·	·
61 ELECTRIC LIGHTING AND WIRING EQUIP	5	0	0	2	4	7	25	0	7	6	6	6	0	1	1	1	4	2	0	6	6	36	11	41	24/-7	11	26	48	4	5	8	3	1	2	19	5	·
62 COMMUNICATION EQUIPMENT	1	·	·	·	·	·	·	·	0	0	0	0	·	0	0	0	0	4	0	4	1	1	0	1	71	16	1	1/28	78/14	1	1	0	0	2	19	5	·
63 ELECTRONIC COMPONENTS	1	·	·	0	0	0	1	·	1	1	1	1	0	0	1	1	3	3	2	51/62	0	50/42	12/119	3/455	455	65	10/57	7	15	0	97/88	0	5	2	2	·	0
64 BATTERIES, X-RAY + ENGINE ELEC EQUIP	1	0	·	0	0	33	·	·	0	1	1	21	11	2	1	·	2	0	1	·	2	2	1	44	2	1	43/260	260	18	3	3	5	3	44	3	·	0

SECTOR NUMBER	38	39	40	41	42	43	44	45	46	47	48	49	50	51	52	53	54	55	56	57	58	59	60	61	62	63	64	65	66	67	68	69	70	71	72	73	74
GROWTH RATES	39.	-0.	26.	33.	39.	28.	36.	30.	38.	23.	34.	41.	39.	34.	38.	41.	42.	40.	23.	55.	36.	34.	27.	38.	18.	35.	37.	38.	-5.	25.	55.	48.	41.	37.	45.	40.	54.
65 MOTOR VEHICLES	0	0	0	·	0	0	2	1	0	2	2	3	2	1	1	10	0	0	1	0	1	0	0	0	0	·	3	421	3	2	4	·	0	4	·	·	·
66 AIRCRAFT AND PARTS	3	·	0	·	0	·	0	·	2	1	1	3	1	0	0	3	2	10	1	0	2	2	2	0	1C	0	0	2	241 / -3	1	14	0	1	24	2	0	0
67 SHIPS, TRAINS, TRAILERS + CYCLES	1	0	·	·	1	4	2	·	18	1	1	5	1	1	1	3	3	2	1	2	0	8	2	1	0	2	7	1	67	67	2	0	4	87	2	0	3
68 INSTRUMENTS AND CLOCKS	2	0	1	0	1	1	3	·	13	1	4	0	1	1	0	1	1	4	1	2	61	12	18 / 30	1	7	3	1	0	25 / -3	1	70	5	1	4	0	0	16
69 OPTICAL + PHOTOGRAPHIC EQUIPMENT	1	0	1	0	0	1	0	0	1	1	0	0	0	100 / 135	0	0	0	3	0	0	0	0	2	0	8	0	0	1	8	0	15	55	60	0	0	0	0
70 MISC MANUFACTURED PRODUCTS	6	0	2	0	3	2	3	0	1	3	3	0	0	0	5	2	0	0	1	1	0	1	2	2	8	0	0	4	2	1	5	1	60	8	2	0	·
71 TRANSPORTATION	5	C	1	32 / 35	14	31 / 33	6 / 30	21	5 / 34	2	3	39	1 / 30	0	0	3	3	3	2	54	34	32 / 32	1	1 / 16	1 / 13	1	17	4	3	2	2	1	3	80 / 44	1	0	3
72 COMMUNICATION	2	0	1	1	2	5	3	0	3	1	2	0	1	1	0	3	3	3	0	1	1	1	1	1	2	1	0	5	3	1	2	1	3	40 / 64	9	6	3
73 RADIO, TV BROADCASTING	·	·	·	·	·	·	·	·	·	·	·	·	·	·	·	·	·	·	·	·	·	·	·	·	·	·	·	·	·	·	·	·	·	·	·	3	·
74 ELECTRIC UTILITY	5	C	1	2	9 / 50	37 / 73	11 / 37	1	3	2	3	0	1	0	0	2	2	1	2	1	1	1	1	8	0	1	7	1	2	1	2	1	1	53 / 53	3	0	43 / 46
75 GAS UTILITY	4 / 93	0	·	8	18 / 47	61 / 73	12 / 40	1	2	1	1	0	0	0	0	1	3	0	0	0	0	1	0	·	C	0	3	3	1	0	0	0	1	44	2	0	54 / 39
76 WATER UTILITY	3	C	0	1	2	17	4	0	1	1	2	0	1	0	0	0	0	1	0	0	1	1	0	1	1	1	6	1	3	1	1	0	1	9	4	0	16
77 WHOLESALE AND RETAIL TRADE	3	0	1	31 / 35	7 / 33	2 / 7 / 33	3	21 / 34	3	2	3	39 / 30	1	1	1	1	1	2	0	54 / 54	34 / 34	32 / 32	18 / 30	2	13 / 16	0	1	8	13 / 25	2	2	1	4	10	3	0	·
78 FINANCE AND INSURANCE	2	0	1	1	3	5	3	1	3	1	1	2	0	0	1	1	1	1	0	1	1	1	0	·	1	0	4	0	1	1	1	0	2	27	2	1	3
79 REAL ESTATE AND RENTAL	1	0	0	0	1	1	1	0	1	0	1	0	0	0	0	1 / 38	1	1	0	0	0	0	0	0	1	0	1	1	0	1	0	1	1	16	3	1	1
80 HOTELS, PERSONAL + REPAIR SERVICES	1	0	1	0	1	2	1	0	1	0	1	1	0	0	0	1	1	0	0	1	1	1	1	0	1	0	2	·	0	1	1	0	1	10	1	0	·
81 BUSINESS SERVICES	7	0	3	1	4	6	3	1	4	1	4	1	2	1	1	2 / 38	2	2	0	3	1	1 / 42	11	1	7	1	27	1	3	1	3	5	5	23 / 42	8	3	6
82 RESEARCH AND DEVELOPMENT	·	·	·	3	·	20	7	·	3	·	·	14	·	·	·	·	·	·	·	·	·	·	·	·	·	3	·	19	10	·	·	4	·	·	·	·	·
83 AUTOMOBILE REPAIR SERVICES	0	0	0	0	3	1	0	0	2	1	0	0	0	0	0	0	0	0	0	0	0	0	0	0	C	0	0	0	0	0	0	0	1	105	2	0	2
84 AMUSEMENTS AND RECREATION	0	0	0	0	0	0	0	0	0	0	0	0	0	0	3	0	0	0	0	0	0	0	0	0	C	0	0	0	0	0	0	0	0	6	1	85	·
85 MEDICAL AND EDUCATIONAL INSTITUTIONS	0	0	0	0	0	1	0	0	0	0	0	0	0	0	0	0	0	0	0	0	0	0	0	0	0	0	0	0	0	0	0	0	0	1	0	0	0
86 FED GOVMT ENTERPRISES	2	1	1	2	3	1	1	2	2	0	1	1	0	0	0	1	1	1	1	0	1	1	0	0	4	0	1	0	11	2	2	1	3	23 / 66	11	0	13
87 STATE AND LOCAL GOVMT ENTERPRISES	0	0	0	0	2	3	3	1	0	0	0	0	0	0	0	0	0	0	0	0	0	0	0	0	0	0	0	1	0	0	0	0	0	177	1	0	29
88 IMPORTS	-13 / -10	0	·	·	1	·	2	·	·	·	·	·	·	·	·	2	1	·	·	·	0	·	0	·	1	·	0	0	0	0	0	11	58	7	·	·
89 BUSINESS TRAVEL AND ENTERTAINMENT	9	0	2	3	10 / -14	6	7	1	10	5	3	3	3	5	2	7	5	8	2	12	4	15	4	4	19	10	3	17	5	5	19	3	11	20	8	5	6
90 OFFICE SUPPLIES	4	2	1	3	5	5	3	0	3	2	1	1	1	2	1	2	3	1	3	1	1	1	1	1	1	1	7	4	2	6	1	5	5	29	30	1	·
EMPLOYMENT	7 / 13-34	0 / 26	6 / 26	2 / -3	8 / 21-21	9 / 9	9 / 30	5 / 36	9 / 38	3 / 23	8 / 34	27	3 / 39	22	1 / -2	6 / 41	4 / 42	4 / 24	3 / 23	4 / 47	2 / 32	9 / -8	2 / -8	8 / 31-13	2 / 4	4 / 8	2 / 4	10 / -5	8 / -5	3 / 7	7 / 10	3 / 16	2 / 7	3 / -3	8 / -18	13 / 13	-11 / -4

GROWTH-VOLUME TABLE FOR FORECAST OF THE AMERICAN ECONOMY, 1963–1975

Buyer / Seller

Intermediate Demands																Capital Equipment																				
75 GAS UTILITY	76 WATER UTILITY	77 WHOLESALE AND RETAIL TRADE	78 FINANCE AND INSURANCE	79 REAL ESTATE AND RENTAL	80 HOTELS, PERSONAL + REPAIR SERVICES	81 BUSINESS SERVICES	82 RESEARCH AND DEVELOPMENT	83 AUTOMOBILE REPAIR SERVICES	84 AMUSEMENTS AND RECREATION	85 MEDICAL AND EDUCATIONAL INSTITUTIONS	86 FED GOVMT ENTERPRISES	87 STATE AND LOCAL GOVMT ENTERPRISES	88 IMPORTS	89 BUSINESS TRAVEL AND ENTERTAINMENT	90 OFFICE SUPPLIES	1 AGRICULTURE	2 PETROLEUM EXTRACTION	3 OTHER MINING	4 TRADE, CONSTRUCTION, MEDICINE, EDUCATION, & OTHER SERVICES	5 FOOD	6 TOBACCO	7 TEXTILES	8 APPAREL	9 LUMBER	10 FURNITURE	11 PAPER	12 PRINTING	13 CHEMICALS	14 PETROLEUM REFINING	15 RUBBER & PLASTIC PRODUCTS	16 SHOES & LEATHER	17 STONE, CLAY, & GLASS	18 STEEL	19 NON-FERROUS METALS	20 FABRICATED METAL PRODUCTS	21 NON-ELECTRICAL MACHINERY
GROWTH RATES 53.	41.	37.	49.	44.	42.	39.	3.	37.	30.	49.	41.	42.	39.	38.	39.	36.	38.	30.	41.	34.	23.	20.	10.	14.	40.	64.	43.	39.	69.	24.	20.	34.	30.	43.	18.	21. / 44.

Sector	75	76	77	78	79	80	81	82	83	84	85	86	87	88	89	90
1 LIVESTOCK					63					1	0	0		4	2	
2 CROPS					34 / -2						0		0		3	
3 FORESTRY AND FISHERY PRODUCTS					1										10	
4 AGRICULTURAL SERVICES			123		4								0			
5 IRON ORE MINING	24			4	4					2		1				
6 NON-FERROUS ORE MINING	4		0		5		20		6		0					
7 COAL MINING	3 / 26		3	4	7				6		0	28	41			
8 PETROLEUM MINING	152		0		14			0					2			
9 MINERALS MINING			3		6						0					
10 CHEMICAL MINING			0		2							0				
11 NEW CONSTRUCTION																
12 MAINTENANCE CONSTRUCTION	16	1	53	10 / 266 / 18		2	2		7	7	55	1	67			
13 ORDNANCE		4			2	2		0				0	0			
14 MEAT PACKING			14			2		0			5	6	0		51	
15 DAIRY PRODUCTS			15		2	2		0			0	7	0		57	
16 CANNED AND FROZEN FOODS			13		1	0		3			4	5	0		37	
17 GRAIN MILL PRODUCTS			3		0	0		0			1	2	0		13	
18 BAKERY PRODUCTS			12		1	0		0			4	5	0		44	

SECTOR NUMBER	75	76	77	78	79	80	81	82	83	84	85	86	87	88	89	90	1	2	3	4	5	6	7	8	9	10	11	12	13	14	15	16	17	18	19	20	21
GROWTH RATES	53.	41.	37.	49.	44.	42.	39.	3.	37.	39.	49.	41.	42.	39.	38.	39.	36.	38.	30.	41.	34.	23.	20.	10.	14.	40.	64.	43.	39.	69.	24.	20.	34.	30.	43.	18.	44.
19 BEVERAGES	.	8	4	.	1	.	.	.	.	.	3	4	0	.	29	.	.	.	.	.	.	.	.	.	.	.	.	.	.	.	.	.	.	.	.	.	.
20 MISC FOOD PRODUCTS	.	.	.	.	.	0	.	.	.	.	2	2	0	.	16	.	.	.	.	.	.	.	.	.	.	.	.	.	.	.	.	.	.	.	.	.	.
21 TOBACCO	.	.	1	.	0	.	.	.	.	.	0	4	.	4	35	35	.	.	.	.	.	.	.	.	.	.	.	.	.	.	.	.	.	.	.	.	.
22 FABRICS AND YARN	.	.	1	.	2	17	.	.	.	0	0	.	.	.	.	.	.	.	.	.	.	.	.	.	.	.	.	.	.	.	.	.	.	.	.	.	.
23 RUGS, TIRE CORD, MISC. TEXTILES	.	.	11	11	3	10	7	0	7	1	12	4	1	1	.	.	.	.	.	16	1	.	.	.	.	.	.	.	.	.	.	.	.	0	0	0	1
24 APPAREL	.	.	4	0	2	8	0	.	0	.	4	.	0	.	1	.	.	.	.	.	.	.	.	.	.	.	.	.	.	.	.	.	.	.	.	.	4
25 HOUSEHOLD TEXTILES AND UPHOLSTERY	.	.	17	15	1	52	10	0	7	2	17	1	.	.	1	.	.	.	.	.	.	.	.	.	.	.	.	.	.	.	.	.	.	.	.	.	.
26 LUMBER + PRODUCTS, EXC CONTAINERS	.	.	11	.	4	1	.	.	.	.	1	.	.	.	0	.	.	.	0	.	.	.	.	.	.	.	.	.	.	.	.	.	.	.	.	.	.
27 WOODEN CONTAINERS	.	176	2	.	6	.	.	.	.	.	.	.	.	.	.	.	.	.	.	.	.	.	.	.	.	.	.	.	.	.	.	.	.	.	.	.	.
28 HOUSEHOLD FURNITURE	.	.	4	.	1	3	.	.	.	.	.	.	.	.	.	.	.	.	.	30	1	.	.	.	.	.	.	.	.	.	.	.	.	0	0	0	1
29 OFFICE FURNITURE	.	.	10	.	1	2	.	.	.	.	.	.	.	.	.	.	.	2	2	435	9	1	3	3	3	.	8	17	2	4	1	.	7	6	2	10	24
30 PAPER + PRODUCTS EXCEPT CONTAINERS	.	.	48	12	1	14	7	0	0	0	10	3	0	.	0	35	.	.	.	.	.	.	.	.	.	.	.	.	.	.	.	.	.	.	.	.	.
31 PAPER CONTAINERS	.	.	98	8	2	5	.	0	.	.	7	2	.	.	.	.	.	.	.	.	.	.	.	.	.	.	.	.	.	.	.	.	.	.	.	.	.
32 PRINTING AND PUBLISHING	0	0	20	39	5	1	482	0	1	1	32	3	1	1	1	68	.	.	.	.	.	.	.	.	.	.	.	.	.	.	.	.	.	.	.	.	.
33 BASIC CHEMICALS	0	0	8	.	6	7	1	.	0	.	0	.	2	.	1	.	.	.	.	.	.	.	.	.	.	.	.	.	.	.	.	.	.	.	.	.	.
34 PLASTICS AND SYNTHETICS	.	.	1	.	2	.	0	.	0	.	0	.	0	.	.	.	.	.	.	.	.	.	.	.	.	.	.	.	.	.	.	.	.	.	.	.	.
35 DRUGS, CLEANING + TOILET ITEMS	.	.	18	2	4	25	4	.	1	0	106	-	0	0	5	.	.	.	.	.	.	.	.	.	.	.	.	.	.	.	.	.	.	.	.	.	.
36 PAINT AND ALLIED PRODUCTS	.	.	16	.	7	0	.	.	40	.	1	.	0	.	.	.	.	.	.	.	.	.	.	.	.	.	.	.	.	.	.	.	.	.	.	.	.
37 PETROLEUM REFINING	2 24	0	53	7	25	9	8	0	2	0	6	0	2	.	12	0	.	.	.	.	.	.	.	.	.	.	.	.	.	.	.	.	.	.	.	.	.
38 RUBBER AND PLASTIC PRODUCTS	0	0	33	9	6	9	9	.	36	0	11	2	1	0	1	.	.	.	.	6	.	.	.	.	.	.	.	.	.	.	.	.	.	0	0	0	0
39 LEATHER TANNING	.	.	5	.	2	8	0	.	6	.	0	2	.	.	0	.	.	.	.	.	.	.	.	.	.	.	.	.	.	.	.	.	.	.	.	.	.
40 SHOES AND OTHER LEATHER PRODUCTS	0	0	8	1	2	3	0	.	0	.	4	1	0	.	12	.	.	.	.	1	.	.	.	.	.	.	.	.	.	.	.	.	.	.	.	.	.
41 GLASS AND GLASS PRODUCTS	.	.	52	.	3	1	2	.	45	.	4	4	.	.	10	.	.	.	.	.	.	.	.	.	.	.	.	.	.	.	.	.	.	.	.	.	.
42 STONE + CLAY PRODUCTS	.	.	19	.	3	8	.	.	6	.	0	2	0	.	0	.	.	.	.	.	.	.	.	.	.	.	.	.	.	.	.	.	.	.	.	.	.
43 IRON AND STEEL	.	.	1	.	2	.	.	.	0	.	0	0	0	.	0	.	.	.	.	.	.	.	.	.	.	.	.	.	.	.	.	.	.	.	.	.	.
44 NON-FERROUS METALS	.	.	2	.	2	1	2	.	.	.	1	.	.	.	.	.	.	.	.	.	5	.	.	.	.	.	.	.	.	.	.	.	.	.	.	.	.
45 METAL CONTAINERS	.	.	4	.	1	.	.	0	.	.	4	.	.	.	.	.	.	.	0	1	3	0	.	.	.	.	.	5	3	.	1	0	1	2	2	1	1
46 HEATING, PLUMBING, STRUCTURAL METAL	.	.	12	.	1	.	.	.	.	.	4	.	.	.	.	.	.	2	0	4	.	3	1	0	0	0	4	5	3	3	1	0	1	2	2	1	1

Column group: Intermediate Demands (sectors 75–82), Capital Equipment / Buyer (sectors 83–90, 1–21). Seller sectors are listed in the rows (47–64).

Column legend (sector number → buyer):
75 GAS UTILITY · 76 WATER UTILITY · 77 WHOLESALE AND RETAIL TRADE · 78 FINANCE AND INSURANCE · 79 REAL ESTATE AND RENTAL · 80 HOTELS,PERSONAL + REPAIR SERVICES · 81 BUSINESS SERVICES · 82 RESEARCH AND DEVELOPMENT · 83 AUTOMOBILE REPAIR SERVICES · 84 AMUSEMENTS AND RECREATION · 85 MEDICAL AND EDUCATIONAL INSTITUTIONS · 86 FED GOVMT ENTERPRISES · 87 STATE AND LOCAL GOVMT ENTERPRISES · 88 IMPORTS · 89 BUSINESS TRAVEL AND ENTERTAINMNT · 90 OFFICE SUPPLIES · 1 AGRICULTURE · 2 PETROLEUM EXTRACTION · 3 OTHER MINING · 4 TRADE, CONSTRUCTION, MEDICINE, EDUCATION, & OTHER SERVICES · 5 FOOD · 6 TOBACCO · 7 TEXTILES · 8 APPAREL · 9 LUMBER · 10 FURNITURE · 11 PAPER · 12 PRINTING · 13 CHEMICALS · 14 PETROLEUM REFINING · 15 RUBBER & PLASTIC PRODUCTS · 16 SHOES & LEATHER · 17 STONE, CLAY, & GLASS · 18 STEEL · 19 NON-FERROUS METALS · 20 FABRICATED METAL PRODUCTS · 21 NON-ELECTRICAL MACHINERY

Seller	75	76	77	78	79	80	81	82	83	84	85	86	87	88	89	90	1	2	3	4	5	6	7	8	9	10	11	12	13	14	15	16	17	18	19	20	21
GROWTH RATES	53	41	37	49	44	42	39	3	37	30	49	41	42	39	38	39	36	38	30	41	34	23	20	10	14	40	64	43	39	69	24	20	34	30	43	18	44
47 STAMPINGS, SCREW MACHINE PRODUCTS	•	•	14	•	2	•	•	•	•	•	•	•	•	•	•	•	•	•	•	•	•	•	•	0	•	•	•	•	•	•	•	•	•	•	•	•	2
48 HARDWARE, PLATING, VALVES, WIRE PRODUCT	15	1	11	•	•	•	•	•	18	•	•	•	•	•	•	•	1	•	1	10	1	•	•	0	•	•	1	•	3	1	•	0	15	1	1	•	•
49 ENGINES AND TURBINES	•	•	7	•	3	62	•	•	•	•	•	•	•	•	•	•	6	2	5	20	3	•	2	0	3	0	10	10	10	3	2	•	2	5	2	2	2
50 FARM MACHINERY AND EQUIPMENT	•	•	8	•	3	65	•	•	•	•	•	•	•	•	•	494	•	•	•	75	•	•	•	0	3	0	•	•	1	•	3	0	0	0	1	0	0
51 CONSTRUCTION + MINING MACHINERY	•	13	13	•	3	•	7	•	•	•	•	•	•	•	•	22	22	124	94	131	•	•	1	1	6	1	6	2	12	•	4	•	15	1	1	14	21
52 MATERIAL HANDLING EQUIPMENT	•	12	12	•	4	•	5	•	0	•	•	•	•	•	•	•	•	1	30	95	21	•	1	1	7	1	8	2	2	1	4	•	1	17	5	14	21
53 METALWORKING MACHINERY + EQUIPMENT	•	4	4	•	9	5	•	•	0	•	•	•	•	•	•	•	•	•	•	28	•	•	•	1	2	•	•	8	•	2	6	•	1	51	18	40	41
54 SPECIAL INDUSTRIAL MACHINERY	•	9	9	•	4	•	•	•	0	•	•	•	•	•	•	21	21	•	5	63	69	3	43	8	24	2	83	52	62	2	15	3	16	7	3	0	2
55 GENERAL INDUSTRIAL MACHINERY	•	8	8	•	2	•	•	0	•	•	•	•	•	•	•	9	9	29	3	33	6	1	0	0	0	0	22	0	69	5	11	0	14	27	9	3	7
56 MACHINE SHOPS + MISC MACHINERY	•	18	18	•	7	•	0	78	•	•	•	•	•	•	•	•	•	1	•	6	•	•	•	0	0	0	0	0	0	0	3	0	0	2	2	7	•
57 OFFICE AND COMPUTING MACHINES	•	14	14	•	2	158	•	1	•	•	•	•	•	•	•	1	1	•	0	181	12	1	2	1	2	1	1	7	9	4	3	1	1	4	2	5	17
58 SERVICE INDUSTRY MACHINES	•	16	16	•	6	17	41	1	1	•	•	•	•	•	•	8	8	0	1	33	2	0	1	0	2	•	0	4	9	4	1	0	4	1	0	4	3
59 ELECTRIC APPARATUS AND MOTORS	0	0	5	•	36	1	0	1	•	•	•	0	•	0	•	2	•	1	369	35	2	0	1	1	0	•	0	2	2	0	0	•	1	1	0	4	5
60 HOUSEHOLD APPLIANCES	•	0	8	•	3	36	•	•	•	8	8	•	•	8	•	2	2	•	1	26	•	0	•	1	0	•	0	•	2	0	1	•	1	7	3	0	0
61 ELECTRIC LIGHTING AND WIRING EQUIP	•	•	8	•	1	3	0	14	14	•	0	0	•	5	•	0	•	0	1	5	•	0	0	1	0	0	0	1	1	0	1	0	7	1	3	4	4
62 COMMUNICATION EQUIPMENT	•	•	9	•	2	1	•	•	•	•	2	0	2	•	•	0	0	0	0	32	1	•	0	0	0	0	1	0	1	0	0	•	0	0	0	0	0
63 ELECTRONIC COMPONENTS	•	3	3	•	4	71	0	71	•	•	•	•	•	9	•	2	2	2	2	31	•	•	0	0	0	0	1	0	1	•	0	0	0	0	0	0	0
64 BATTERIES, X-RAY + ENGINE ELEC EQUIP	0	0	32	1	2	2	3	71	71	9	•	•	1	•	•	2	2	2	31	31	•	•	0	0	0	0	0	•	0	0	0	0	0	0	•	•	1

SECTOR NUMBER	75	76	77	78	79	80	81	82	83	84	85	86	87	88	89	90	1	2	3	4	5	6	7	8	9	10	11	12	13	14	15	16	17	18	19	20	21
GROWTH RATES	53.	41.	37.	49.	44.	42.	39.	3.	37.	30.	49.	41.	42.	39.	38.	39.	36.	38.	30.	41.	34.	23.	20.	10.	14.	40.	64.	43.	39.	69.	24.	20.	34.	30.	43.	18.	44.
65 MOTOR VEHICLES	.	.	11	.	1	.	.	.	56	.	0	0	1	.	.	.	27	2	2	112	5	0	0	0	1	0	1	1	1	2	3	1	1	0	0	0	2
66 AIRCRAFT AND PARTS	.	.	.	3	2	3	.	.	.	.	.	20	1	.	.	.	0	0	4	1	.	0	0	1	0	2	2	0	3	3	0	2	2	0	0	0	.
67 SHIPS, TRAINS, TRAILERS + CYCLES	.	.	4	.	2	2	6	.	3	.	7	.	.	.	.	6	20	5	8	19	3	.	1	1	2	5	2	10	3	.	2	2	5	2	1	.	.
68 INSTRUMENTS AND CLOCKS	.	.	8	2	2	12	.	.	3	.	163	.	1	.	.	.	1	4	0	67	12	.	1	0	5	0	5	0	10	2	1	0	5	2	1	0	0
69 OPTICAL + PHOTOGRAPHIC EQUIPMENT	.	.	37	.	2	55	15	.	.	10	41	.	6	67	.	1	6	0	0	54	.	.	1	1	6	8	4	0	.	2	.	1	0	0	0	0	0
70 MISC MANUFACTURED PRODUCTS	.	.	23	5	2	43	45	.	13	13	7	8	37	.	.	8	8	0	0	40	.	.	0	0	37	.	0	0	0	0	0	0	0	0	0	0	0
71 TRANSPORTATION	.	.	14	9	13	3	4	.	2	1	5	.	2	90	.	.	2	.	0	6	1	0	1	.	90	.	2	0	1	0	0	0	0	0	0	0	0
72 COMMUNICATION	2	0	95	45	21	61	61	.	5	3	21	1	2	.	.	.	.	.	1	.	.	.	2	.	.	.	1	0	1	.	.	.	.	.	0	.	.
73 RADIO, TV BROADCASTING	.	.	.	.	9	.	982	.	.	.	.	.	.	.	.	.	.	.	.	.	.	.	.	.	.	.	.	.	.	.	.	.	.	.	.	.	.
74 ELECTRIC UTILITY	7	0	20	6	11	5	14	.	6	2	16	5	.	.	.	.	5	.	1	16	1	0	0	0	4	.	5	1	1	1	3	0	1	1	0	1	1
75 GAS UTILITY	546	.	33	3	6	5	7	.	3	1	8	0	9	.	.	.	.	.	1	.	.	.	.	.	.	.	0	.	.	.	.	.	.	.	.	.	1
76 WATER UTILITY	.	.	92	9	20	34	14	.	2	2	15	2	2	.	.	.	.	.	.	.	.	.	.	.	.	.	.	.	.	.	.	.	.	.	.	.	.
77 WHOLESALE AND RETAIL TRADE	.	.	17	3	11	5	5	0	7	1	5	1	0	1	1	.	2	0	1	16	1	0	0	0	0	1	1	2	0	3	3	0	1	1	1	0	1
78 FINANCE AND INSURANCE	2	0	65	256	40	8	12	0	8	5	13	5	2	1	.	.	.	.	1	.	.	.	2	.	.	.	0	1	0	.	.	.	.	.	.	.	.
79 REAL ESTATE AND RENTAL	0	0	84	21	9	15	11	.	5	4	30	1	1	1	.	.	4	30	1	1	1	2	1	.	.	.	.	.	.	.	.	.	.	.	.	.	.
80 HOTELS, PERSONAL + REPAIR SERVICES	.	.	20	.	23	30	11	.	.	.	12	4	2	1	86	.	.	12	4	.	2	1	1	.	.	.	.	.	.	.	.	.	.	.	.	.	.
81 BUSINESS SERVICES	6	0	193	48	52	12	23	0	6	.	27	2	2	.	.	.	.	65	2	2	2	.	1	.	.	.	.	.	.	.	.	.	.	.	.	.	.
82 RESEARCH AND DEVELOPMENT	.	.	.	.	.	.	.	.	.	.	65	2	.	.	.	.	.	.	.	.	.	.	.	.	.	.	.	.	.	.	.	.	.	.	.	.	.
83 AUTOMOBILE REPAIR SERVICES	.	.	113	13	16	15	17	.	17	.	8	5	1	.	.	.	17	.	310	11	8	5	1	.	.	.	.	.	.	.	.	.	.	.	.	.	1
84 AMUSEMENTS AND RECREATION	.	.	26	2	26	.	9	0	.	310	27	.	.	4	33	.	.	9	.	27	.	.	.	.	.	.	.	.	.	.	.	.	.	.	.	.	.
85 MEDICAL AND EDUCATIONAL INSTITUTIONS	.	.	4	6	1	0	0	.	0	0	13	4	0	.	1	.	8	13	0	13	1	5	2	1	.	.	.	.	.	.	.	.	.	.	.	.	.
86 FED GOVMT ENTERPRISES	.	.	250	97	69	2	173	1	1	1	5	2	1	.	.	.	250	97	2	173	.	1	1	.	.	.	.	.	.	.	.	.	.	.	.	.	.
87 STATE AND LOCAL GOVMT ENTERPRISES	1384	.	91	21	106	4	2	.	5	.	0	4	0	.	.	.	91	21	.	2	.	4	0	0	.	.	.	.	.	.	.	.	.	.	.	.	1
88 IMPORTS	.	.	4	14	.	.	.	.	.	10	1	20	.	.	.	.	4	14	.	.	10	20	0	.	.	.	.	.	.	.	.	.	.	.	.	.	.
89 BUSINESS TRAVEL AND ENTERTAINMNT	5	0	239	8	.	21	33	0	4	11	78	5	2	.	.	.	239	8	.	33	11	78	2	17	.	.	.	.	.	.	.	.	.	.	.	.	.
90 OFFICE SUPPLIES	.	.	156	115	19	13	185	2	.	4	74	14	17	.	.	.	156	115	19	13	185	2	.	4	74	14	17	.	.	.	.	.	.	.	.	.	.
EMPLOYMENT	2.	1.	25.	53.	15.	49.	43.	1.	10.	3.	100.	15.	8.	0.	0.	0.	0.	0.	0.	0.	0.	0.	0.	0.	0.	0.	0.	0.	0.	0.	0.	0.	0.	0.	0.	0.	0.
EMPLOYMENT (line 2)	17.	41.	23.	39.	34.	18.	39.	3.	37.	-5.	49.	41.	42.																								

GROWTH-VOLUME TABLE FOR FORECAST OF THE AMERICAN ECONOMY, 1963–1975

Column groups: **Investment** (sectors 22–29), **Construction** (sectors 1–19), **Ultimate Use** (Imports, Exports, State & Local Governments, Federal Government, Consumption).

Investment buyer sectors: 22 ELECTRICAL MACHINERY · 23 MOTOR VEHICLES · 24 OTHER TRANSPORTATION EQUIP. · 25 INSTRUMENTS · 26 MISC. MANUFACTURING · 27 TRANSPORTATION · 28 COMMUNICATIONS · 29 UTILITIES

Construction buyer sectors: 1 RESIDENTIAL · 2 INDUSTRIAL · 3 OFFICES & WAREHOUSES · 4 STORES, RESTAURANTS, GARAGES · 5 SOCIAL & RELIGIOUS · 6 FARM (NON-RESIDENTIAL) · 7 RAILROAD · 8 GAS UTILITY · 9 ELECTRIC UTILITY · 10 TELEPHONE · 11 OIL & GAS WELLS · 12 ALL OTHER PRIVATE · 13 MILITARY · 14 WATER & SEWAGE · 15 HIGHWAY · 16 PUBLIC SERVICE ENTERPRISES · 17 CONSERVATION & DEVELOPMENT · 18 EDUCATION · 19 ALL OTHER PUBLIC

(Cells generally contain two stacked figures, shown below as a / b. A · indicates a negligible/blank entry.)

Seller (sector)	22	23	24	25	26	27	28	29	1	2	3	4	5	6	7	8	9	10	11	12	13	14	15	16	17	18	19	IMPORTS	EXPORTS	STATE & LOCAL GOVTS	FEDERAL GOVT	CONSUMPTION
GROWTH RATES	27.	50.	1.	37.	48.	37.	25.	48.	43.	33.	57.	51.	57.	-15.	29.	39.	44.	37.	38.	38.	-16.	31.	33.	32.	31.	6.	37.	0.	0.	0.	0.	0.
1 LIVESTOCK	·	·	·	·	·	·	·	·	·	·	·	·	·	·	·	·	·	·	·	·	·	·	·	·	·	·	·	-14 / -29	29 / 41	1 / 45	-9 / 45	76 / 17
2 CROPS	·	·	·	·	·	·	·	·	·	·	·	·	·	·	·	·	·	·	·	·	·	·	·	·	·	·	·	-9 / 41	150 / 65	2 / 41	·	114 / 14
3 FORESTRY AND FISHERY PRODUCTS	·	·	·	·	·	·	·	·	·	·	·	·	·	·	·	·	·	·	·	·	·	·	·	·	·	·	·	-203 / 41	64 / 102	·	-79 / 45	175 / 16
4 AGRICULTURAL SERVICES	·	·	·	·	·	·	·	·	·	·	·	·	·	·	·	·	·	·	·	·	·	·	·	·	·	·	·	·	0	-66 / 41	42 / 39	·
5 IRON ORE MINING	·	·	·	·	·	·	·	·	·	·	·	·	·	·	·	·	·	·	·	·	·	·	·	·	·	·	·	-360 / 36	29	·	·	·
6 NON-FERROUS ORE MINING	·	·	·	·	·	·	·	·	·	·	·	·	·	·	·	·	·	·	·	·	·	·	·	·	·	·	-1	-182 / 36	-28	111 / 15	·	·
7 COAL MINING	·	·	·	·	·	·	·	·	·	·	·	·	·	·	·	·	·	·	·	·	·	·	·	·	·	·	-1	-1	154 / 150	46 / 41	·	89 / -4
8 PETROLEUM MINING	·	·	·	·	·	·	·	·	·	·	·	·	·	·	·	·	·	·	·	·	·	·	·	·	·	·	·	-160 / 52	-0 / -36	·	·	·
9 MINERALS MINING	·	·	·	·	·	·	·	·	·	0	6	·	2	13 / 19	·	1	1	0	32 / 46	5	7	23	217 / 11	2	25	4	·	-103 / 46	23 / 50	-11 / 41	-5	3 / 2
10 CHEMICAL MINING	·	·	·	·	·	·	·	·	·	·	·	·	·	·	·	·	·	·	·	·	·	·	·	·	·	·	·	-289 / 77	98 / 42	24 / 41	11 / -5	9 / 2
11 NEW CONSTRUCTION	·	·	·	·	·	·	·	·	470	28	85	28	43	7	4	6	32	22	35	7	12	27	121	10	29	25	10	·	0	·	·	·
12 MAINTENANCE CONSTRUCTION	·	·	·	·	·	·	·	·	·	·	·	·	·	·	·	·	·	·	·	·	·	·	·	·	·	·	·	·	·	277 / 41	33 / -6	·
13 ORDNANCE	·	·	·	·	·	·	·	·	·	·	·	·	·	·	·	·	·	·	·	·	·	·	·	·	·	·	·	·	6 / 42	·	628 / -26	82 / 80
14 MEAT PACKING	·	·	·	·	·	·	·	·	·	·	·	·	·	·	·	·	·	·	·	·	·	·	·	·	·	·	·	-9 / 37	-9 / 31	20 / 41	2 / 45	858 / 25
15 DAIRY PRODUCTS	·	·	·	·	·	·	·	·	·	·	·	·	·	·	·	·	·	·	·	·	·	·	·	·	·	·	·	-6 / 38	117 / 21	21 / 41	10 / 45	801 / 15
16 CANNED AND FROZEN FOODS	·	·	·	·	·	·	·	·	·	·	·	·	·	·	·	·	·	·	·	·	·	·	·	·	·	·	·	-19 / 71	117 / 42	33 / 41	2 / 45	880 / 41
17 GRAIN MILL PRODUCTS	·	·	·	·	·	·	·	·	·	·	·	·	·	·	·	·	·	·	·	·	·	·	·	·	·	·	·	-2	152 / 41	10 / 41	45 / 41	270 / 35
18 BAKERY PRODUCTS	·	·	·	·	·	·	·	·	·	·	·	·	·	·	·	·	·	·	·	·	·	·	·	·	·	·	·	·	0	·	·	923 / 35

SECTOR NUMBER	22	23	24	25	26	27	28	29	1	2	3	4	5	6	7	8	9	10	11	12	13	14	15	16	17	18	19	0	0	0	0	0	-0	-0	-0
GROWTH RATES	27.	50.	1.	37.	48.	37.	25.	48.	43.	33.	57.	51.	57.	-15.	29.	39.	44.	37.	38.	30.	-16.	31.	33.	32.	31.	6.	37.	6.	0.	0.	0.	0.	0.	-0	
19 BEVERAGES	•	•	•	•	•	•	•	•	•	•	•	•	•	•	•	•	•	•	•	•	•	•	•	•	•	•	•	•	-8 / 72	1	•	•	941 / 45		
20 MISC FOOD PRODUCTS	•	3	•	•	•	•	•	•	•	•	•	•	•	•	•	•	•	•	1	•	•	•	•	•	•	•	•	-93 / 42	58 / 36	42 / 41	•	8 / 45	680 / 51		
21 TOBACCO	•	•	•	•	•	•	•	•	•	•	•	•	•	•	•	•	•	•	•	•	•	•	•	•	•	•	•	-4 / 31	122 / 135	•	•	•	831 / 30		
22 FABRICS AND YARN	•	•	•	•	•	•	•	•	•	•	•	•	•	•	•	•	•	•	•	•	•	•	•	•	•	•	•	-77 / 62	21 / 32	41 / 41	•	-4 / 39	105 / 39		
23 RUGS,TIRE CORD, MISC. TEXTILES	0	0	0	0	•	2	•	1	0	•	•	•	•	•	•	•	•	•	•	•	•	•	•	•	•	•	•	-227 / 52	19 / 31	•	•	8 / 44	2 / 325		
24 APPAREL	•	•	•	•	•	•	•	•	•	•	•	•	•	•	•	•	•	•	•	•	•	•	•	•	•	•	•	-9 / 81	13 / 52	9 / 41	•	2 / 14	924 / 37		
25 HOUSEHOLD TEXTILES AND UPHOLSTERY	•	•	•	•	•	•	•	•	•	•	•	•	•	•	•	•	•	•	•	•	•	•	•	•	•	•	•	-11 / 81	11 / 52	•	•	29 / 43	553		
26 LUMBER + PRODUCTS, EXC CONTAINERS	0	4	•	•	•	4	•	•	436 / 38	4 / 34	8 / 23	14 / 44	-6 / -31	•	•	•	•	5	2	1	2	4	7 / 11	1	1	12 / -7	•	-1 / 20	24 / 40	-45 / 16	•	-1 / 16	18		
27 WOODEN CONTAINERS	•	•	•	•	•	•	•	•	•	•	•	•	•	•	•	•	•	•	•	•	•	•	•	•	•	•	•	-43 / 31	4	•	•	•	•		
28 HOUSEHOLD FURNITURE	1	•	0	0	0	4	1	1	65	•	•	•	1	•	•	•	•	•	•	•	•	•	•	1	•	•	•	•	•	22 / 41	•	-5 / 38	-1 / 27		
29 OFFICE FURNITURE	9	5	•	5	4	24	19	8	23	36	4	1	38	•	•	8	•	0	•	•	•	3	•	1	20	2	•	-94 / 31	6	•	•	20 / 38	772 / 77 / 42		
30 PAPER + PRODUCTS EXCEPT CONTAINERS	•	•	•	•	•	•	•	•	19	4	0	1	1	•	•	•	•	•	•	•	•	•	•	•	•	•	•	-31 / 42	-1 / 6	•	•	-45 / 33	5 / 93 / 11 / 39		
31 PAPER CONTAINERS	•	•	•	•	•	•	•	•	•	•	•	•	•	•	•	•	•	13	•	•	3	•	•	•	•	•	•	-15 / 161	16 / 72	18 / 41	•	5 / 4	230 / 43		
32 PRINTING AND PUBLISHING	•	•	•	•	•	•	•	•	3	0	1	•	1	•	•	1	0	•	•	•	0	0	•	0	0	•	•	-63 / 91	94 / 60	23 / 41	•	39 / -6	14 / 34		
33 BASIC CHEMICALS	•	•	0	•	•	•	•	•	•	•	•	•	•	•	•	0	•	3	0	0	0	3	•	0	0	0	•	-10 / 92	106 / 90	•	•	15 / 44	2		
34 PLASTICS AND SYNTHETICS	•	•	•	•	•	•	•	•	•	0	1	•	•	•	•	1	0	•	•	•	0	1	1	•	0	5	•	-21 / 91	26 / 27	33 / 41	•	19 / 47	624		
35 DRUGS,CLEANING + TOILET ITEMS	•	•	•	•	•	•	•	•	85	5	6	3	8	1	0	0	0	0	0	1	1	2	0	0	•	•	1	-32 / 12	10	•	•	2 / 38	8		
36 PAINT AND ALLIED PRODUCTS	0	0	0	0	0	0	0	0	32	2	41	35	•	37	•	29	•	0	0	0	0	14 / 24	0	0	-17	•	3	-51 / 52	-12 / -36	32 / 41	•	30 / -4	462 / 38		
37 PETROLEUM REFINING	0	0	0	0	0	0	0	0	16 / 44	2 / 41	5 / 43	5 / 48	2	-1	-3	31 / 43	5	28	0	0	1	10 / 37	1	1	3	•	•	-26 / 91	16	12 / 41	•	10 / -4	175 / 30		
38 RUBBER AND PLASTIC PRODUCTS	•	•	•	•	•	•	•	•	69 / 57	9 / 31	6 / 53	6	0	0	0	11 / 9	25	1	0	1	1	1	2	2	2	•	•	-121 / 21	40 / 21	40 / 21	•	20 / -6	1 / 22		
39 LEATHER TANNING	•	•	•	•	•	•	•	•	•	•	•	•	•	•	•	•	•	•	•	•	•	•	•	•	•	•	•	-138 / 46	71 / 32	•	•	•	•		
40 SHOES AND OTHER LEATHER PRODUCTS	•	•	•	•	•	•	•	•	•	•	•	•	•	•	0	•	2	•	•	•	•	•	1	5	•	•	•	-23 / 72	7	•	•	7 / 6	908 / 27		
41 GLASS AND GLASS PRODUCTS	•	•	0	0	0	0	0	•	16	3	4	2	4	•	•	•	•	0	0	0	0	1	1	0	5	•	•	-26 / 20	30 / 31	30 / 31	•	0	66 / 35		
42 STONE + CLAY PRODUCTS	•	•	•	•	•	•	•	•	272 / 45	51 / 48	59 / 67	40 / 67	66 / 64	-3 / 37	31 / 29	5	2	6 / 50	3	0	11	27	43 / 41	1	9	31 / 13	•	-51 / 46	25 / 31	13 / 41	•	1 / 15	32 / 32		
43 IRON AND STEEL	•	•	•	•	•	•	•	•	35 / 29	24	5 / 48	5	1	-1	-31 / 43	31 / 43	0	28	0	1	1	10	39 / 37	0	2	-3	•	0 / -31	24 / 26	24 / 26	•	6 / 2	2 / 30		
44 NON-FERROUS METALS	•	•	•	•	•	•	•	•	69 / 57	9 / 31	6 / 53	6	0	0	0	9	25	•	0	0	1	1	1	2	2	2	•	-121 / 21	40 / 21	40 / 21	•	20 / -6	1 / 22		
45 METAL CONTAINERS	•	•	•	•	•	•	•	•	•	•	•	•	•	•	•	•	•	•	•	•	•	•	•	•	•	•	•	-10 / 29	6	•	•	-5 / -6	•		
46 HEATING, PLUMBING, STRUCTURAL METAL	1	1	0	0	0	1	•	33	238 / 47	76 / 41	62 / 59	52 / 60	69 / 61	-7 / -5	3 / 37	2 / 29	2	•	2	12	11	69 / 37	7	9	35 / 10	•	1 / -3	17 / 31	17 / 5	•	-1 / -6	1 / 7 / 25		

GROWTH-VOLUME TABLE FOR FORECAST OF THE AMERICAN ECONOMY, 1963–1975 (continued)

	Investment								Construction																		Ultimate Use				
Seller → Buyer	22 ELECTRICAL MACHINERY	23 MOTOR VEHICLES	24 OTHER TRANSPORTATION EQUIP.	25 INSTRUMENTS	26 MISC. MANUFACTURING	27 TRANSPORTATION	28 COMMUNICATIONS	29 UTILITIES	1 RESIDENTIAL	2 INDUSTRIAL	3 OFFICES & WAREHOUSES	4 STORES, RESTAURANTS, GARAGES	5 SOCIAL & RELIGIOUS	6 FARM (NON-RESIDENTIAL)	7 RAILROAD	8 GAS UTILITY	9 ELECTRIC UTILITY	10 TELEPHONE	11 OIL & GAS WELLS	12 ALL OTHER PRIVATE	13 MILITARY	14 WATER & SEWAGE	15 HIGHWAY	16 PUBLIC SERVICE ENTERPRISES	17 CONSERVATION & DEVELOPMENT	18 EDUCATION	19 ALL OTHER PUBLIC	IMPORTS	EXPORTS	STATE & LOCAL GOVERNMENTS	FEDERAL GOVERNMENT	CONSUMPTION
GROWTH RATES	27.	50.	1.	37.	48.	37.	25.	48.	43.	33.	57.	51.	57.	−15.	29.	39.	44.	37.	38.	38.	−16.	31.	33.	32.	31.	6.	37.	−0.	−0.	−0.	−0.	−0.
47 STAMPINGS, SCREW MACHINE PRODUCTS	•	•	•	•	•	•	•	•	•	15	•	•	1	•	•	•	•	•	•	•	•	•	•	•	•	•	5	−12	26 / 21	42 / 41	23 / 17	62 / 22
48 HARDWARE, PLATING, VALVES, WIRE PRODUCT	0	0	•	1	•	3	•	2	61	3	6	5	8	3	0	•	•	1	•	0	•	1	•	1	1	3	•	−25 / −31	33 / 27	9 / 41	16 / 9	42 / 29
49 ENGINES AND TURBINES	3	4	1	1	1	5	•	158	61	3	6	5	8	•	7	•	11	•	•	•	•	•	•	•	•	•	•	−18 / −31	165 / 60	65 / 41	18 / 28	108 / 69
50 FARM MACHINERY AND EQUIPMENT	0	0	0	0	0	11	0	1	14	•	•	•	•	•	•	•	•	•	•	•	•	•	•	•	•	•	•	−55 / −31	123 / 60	9 / 41	6 / 13	3 / 25
51 CONSTRUCTION + MINING MACHINERY	0	0	0	0	3	8	11	•	•	2	3	1	2	•	0	•	1	0	25	•	•	2	3	0	1	1	•	101 / 30	239 / 30	9 / 41	26	•
52 MATERIAL HANDLING EQUIPMENT	7	26	8	•	6	71	9	•	36	22 / 45	78 / 69	24 / 64	26 / 69	•	•	•	•	2	•	•	7	•	•	•	•	•	•	−22 / −81	109 / 70	54 / 41	75 / −5	•
53 METAL WORKING MACHINERY + EQUIPMENT	32	22	7	12	7	•	•	1	•	•	•	•	•	•	•	•	•	•	•	•	•	•	•	•	•	•	•	−23 / −81	240 / 85	27 / 41	7 / 1	26 / 25
54 SPECIAL INDUSTRIAL MACHINERY	6	14	2	0	7	•	•	1	5	30 / 45	22 / 69	21 / 64	12 / 69	•	1	•	1	1	•	•	•	1	•	0	3	•	•	−61 / −101	251 / 70	12 / 41	1 / 1	1 / 5
55 GENERAL INDUSTRIAL MACHINERY	4	7	1	1	3	4	1	13	•	•	•	•	•	•	1	•	1	1	•	0	3	1	•	1	7	•	•	−21 / −81	126 / 20	41 / 41	4 / 9	•
56 MACHINE SHOPS + MISC MACHINERY	•	•	•	•	•	•	•	•	•	•	•	•	•	•	•	•	•	•	•	•	•	•	•	•	•	•	•	−7	6	35 / 41	21 / −3	15 / 25
57 OFFICE AND COMPUTING MACHINES	10	6	3	4	5	10	9	7	•	•	•	•	•	•	•	•	1	•	•	•	•	•	•	•	•	•	•	−52 / −81	259 / 109	34 / 41	37 / −1	14 / 25
58 SERVICE INDUSTRY MACHINES	2	3	1	0	0	24	0	1	•	•	•	•	•	•	•	•	•	1	•	•	1	•	2	0	1	•	•	−5 / −101	109 / 70	11 / 41	19 / 29	98 / 25
59 ELECTRIC APPARATUS AND MOTORS	7	15	3	1	2	3	45	128	16	7 / 45	66 / 75	5 / 64	15 / 76	•	0	0	3	1	•	0	1	2	•	0	1	•	−5	−74 / −119	60 / 40	43 / 41	43 / 37	31
60 HOUSEHOLD APPLIANCES	•	•	•	•	•	•	•	•	25 / 61	•	•	•	36	•	•	•	•	•	•	•	•	•	•	•	•	•	•	−91	43 / 42	1 / 42	33 / −5	648 / 25
61 ELECTRIC LIGHTING AND WIRING EQUIP	0	0	0	0	0	50	1	•	94 / 62	32 / 45	91 / 75	22 / 64	29 / 76	•	•	•	•	•	•	1	•	•	5	•	1	21 / 24	1	−18 / −72	29 / 42	9 / 41	6 / −6	116 / 32
62 COMMUNICATION EQUIPMENT	2	1	2	0	0	7	131	•	•	•	1	•	•	•	0	0	0	22	•	•	5	•	•	5	•	24	1	−49 / −72	56 / 47	11 / 41	253 / 249	241 / 41
63 ELECTRONIC COMPONENTS	3	1	0	•	0	0	3	•	•	•	•	•	•	•	•	•	•	•	•	•	•	•	•	•	•	1	•	−80 / −72	71 / 47	41 / 41	48 / 42	60 / 40
64 BATTERIES, X-RAY + ENGINE ELEC EQUIP	0	0	0	0	12	7	0	•	•	•	•	•	•	•	•	•	•	•	•	•	•	•	•	•	•	•	•	−13 / −31	101 / 82	25 / 41	49 / 3	147 / 31

Input-output / growth-rate data matrix (Sectors 65–90 and Employment)

SECTOR NUMBER	22	23	24	25	26	27	28	29	1	2	3	4	5	6	7	8	9	10	11	12	13	14	15	16	17	18	19	-0	-0	-0	-0	0
GROWTH RATES	27.	50.	1.	37.	48.	37.	25.	48.	43.	33.	57.	51.	57.	-15.	29.	39.	44.	37.	38.	38.	-16.	31.	33.	32.	31.	6.	37.	0.	0.	0.	0.	0.
65 MOTOR VEHICLES	1	0	0	0	1	19	5	2	.	.	.	.	.	.	.	.	.	.	.	.	.	.	.	.	.	.	.	-33 / 52	28 / 41	17	.	586 / 40
66 AIRCRAFT AND PARTS	0	C	.	1	0	51	0	3	.	.	.	.	.	.	.	.	.	.	.	.	.	.	.	.	.	.	-33 / 101	176 / 82	. / 29	.	577 / -24	4 / 69
67 SHIPS, TRAINS, TRAILERS + CYCLES	.	.	1	.	.	245	.	.	.	.	.	.	.	.	.	.	.	.	.	.	.	.	.	.	.	.	-86 / 119	. / 29	14 / 41	.	136 / -18	292 / 54
68 INSTRUMENTS AND CLOCKS	2	1	0	1	0	1	0	4	6	2	5	1	4	.	0	2	.	.	4	.	0	.	.	.	.	.	-101 / 101	348	19 / 41	.	77 / 2	84 / 48
69 OPTICAL+ PHOTOGRAPHIC EQUIPMENT	0	2	3	.	0	1	.	.	.	.	.	.	.	.	.	2	.	.	.	.	C	.	.	.	.	.	-80 / -73	163 / 100	9 / 41	.	39 / -8	373 / 57
70 MISC MANUFACTURED PRODUCTS	0	1	0	0	0	0	0	3	5	2	0	3	5	.	0	.	.	.	.	.	C	.	.	.	.	.	-65 / 41	19 / 21	38 / 41	.	5 / 12	523 / 47
71 TRANSPORTATION	0	C	C	0	0	1	1	21	21	2	3	2	3	0	0	1	0	2	0	1	2	2	11	0	1	2	57	114 / 70	17 / 41	.	31 / -1	256 / 31
72 COMMUNICATION	.	.	.	.	45	.	.	.	4	.	1	0	1	.	0	0	0	0	0	0	0	0	1	0	C	C	.	10 / 82	22 / 41	.	13 / 17	469 / 53
73 RADIO, TV BROADCASTING	.	.	.	.	.	.	.	.	.	.	.	.	.	.	.	.	.	.	.	.	.	.	.	.	.	.	.	10 / 82	.	.	.	.
74 ELECTRIC UTILITY	.	.	.	.	.	.	.	.	5	1	1	0	1	.	0	0	0	0	0	0	0	0	1	0	C	C	-3 / 52	3 / 41	26 / 41	.	5 / 6	556 / 64
75 GAS UTILITY	.	.	.	.	.	.	.	.	.	.	.	.	.	.	.	.	.	.	.	.	.	.	.	.	.	.	.	14 / 41	25 / 41	.	26 / 6	578 / 58
76 WATER UTILITY	.	.	.	.	.	.	.	.	.	.	.	.	.	.	.	.	.	.	.	.	.	.	.	.	.	C	.	74 / 41	11 / 8	.	515 / 44	
77 WHOLESALE AND RETAIL TRADE	0	1	0	0	2	1	2	15	2	2	2	3	.	0	0	0	0	1	0	0	0	1	3	0	0	2	9 / 57	20 / 58	4 / 41	.	4 / -4	695 / 37
78 FINANCE AND INSURANCE	.	.	.	.	.	7	1	.	7	1	1	1	1	.	0	0	0	1	0	0	0	0	2	0	0	0	2 / 57	1 / 58	9 / 41	.	631 / 55	
79 REAL ESTATE AND RENTAL	.	.	.	.	.	1	3	0	1	3	0	0	0	0	0	0	0	0	0	0	0	0	0	0	C	0	.	2 / 41	5 / 25	.	25 / 25	689 / 47
80 HOTELS, PERSONAL + REPAIR SERVICES	.	.	.	.	.	.	.	.	.	.	.	.	.	.	.	.	.	.	.	.	.	.	.	.	.	4	.	10 / 41	17 / 17	.	17 / 17	788 / 43
81 BUSINESS SERVICES	.	.	.	.	.	46	5	8	46	5	8	5	8	.	0	2	.	3	1	3	.	11	.	1	2	4	.	8 / 58	27 / 58	.	16 / 16	80 / 45
82 RESEARCH AND DEVELOPMENT	.	.	.	.	.	.	.	.	.	.	.	.	.	.	.	.	.	.	.	.	.	.	.	.	.	.	.	763	.	.	-6	.
83 AUTOMOBILE REPAIR SERVICES	.	.	.	.	.	15	2	2	15	2	2	1	2	.	0	0	0	1	1	0	0	1	3	-0	1	1	.	13 / 41	13 / 41	.	560 / 37	
84 AMUSEMENTS AND RECREATION	.	.	.	.	.	.	.	.	.	.	.	.	.	.	.	.	.	.	.	.	.	.	.	.	.	.	.	36 / 41	-15 / 41	.	3 / 41	759 / 29
85 MEDICAL AND EDUCATIONAL INSTITUTIONS	.	.	.	.	.	1	0	0	1	0	0	0	0	0	0	0	0	0	0	0	0	0	0	0	0	0	0	0 / 41	14 / 41	.	39 / 35	912 / 51
86 FED GOVMT ENTERPRISES	.	.	.	.	.	8	2	1	8	2	1	0	0	.	0	0	0	0	0	0	0	0	0	0	.	.	8 / 57	21 / 41	8 / 41	.	13 / 22	179 / 146
87 STATE AND LOCAL GOVMT ENTERPRISES	.	.	.	.	.	.	.	.	.	.	.	.	.	.	.	.	.	.	.	.	.	.	.	.	.	.	0	0 / 41	0 / 41	.	32 / 45	109 / 160
88 IMPORTS	.	.	.	.	.	18	2	3	18	2	3	2	3	.	0	1	0	3	1	1	1	1	4	0	1	1	.	208 / 41	. / 41	.	169 / 41	424 / 56
89 BUSINESS TRAVEL AND ENTERTAINMNT	.	.	.	.	.	.	.	.	.	.	.	.	.	.	.	.	.	.	.	.	.	.	.	.	.	.	-21 / -40	.	.	.	.
90 OFFICE SUPPLIES	.	.	.	.	.	.	.	.	.	.	.	.	.	.	.	.	.	.	.	.	.	.	.	.	.	.	.	117 / 41	41 / 16	.	.	.
EMPLOYMENT	00	00	00	00	00	00	00	00	00	00	00	00	00	00	00	00	00	00	00	00	00	00	00	00	00	00	00	00	00	00	00	00